T0369686

Excavating the Memory Palace

Excavating the
MEMORY PALACE

ARTS OF VISUALIZATION FROM
THE AGORA TO THE COMPUTER

Seth Long

The University of Chicago Press   CHICAGO AND LONDON

The University of Chicago Press, Chicago 60637
The University of Chicago Press, Ltd., London
© 2020 by The University of Chicago
Published 2020

29 28 27 26 25 24 23 22 21 20   1 2 3 4 5

ISBN-13: 978-0-226-69514-3 (cloth)
ISBN-13: 978-0-226-69528-0 (paper)
ISBN-13: 978-0-226-69531-0 (e-book)
DOI: https://doi.org/10.7208/chicago/9780226695310.001.0001

Library of Congress Cataloging-in-Publication Data

Names: Long, Seth, author.
Title: Excavating the memory palace : arts of visualization
from the agora to the computer / Seth Long.
Description: Chicago : University of Chicago Press, 2020. |
Includes bibliographical references and index.
Identifiers: LCCN 2020021304 | ISBN 9780226695143 (cloth) |
ISBN 9780226695280 (paperback) | ISBN 9780226695310
(ebook)
Subjects: LCSH: Mnemonics—History. | Memory.
Classification: LCC BF381 .L66 2020 | DDC 153.1/4—dc23
LC record available at https://lccn.loc.gov/2020021304

For my parents
And to Doug Mitchell, in memoriam

Time moves in one direction, memory in another.
We are that strange species that constructs artifacts
intended to counter the natural flow of forgetting.

WILLIAM GIBSON, "DEAD MAN SINGS"

"It's a poor sort of memory that only works
backwards," the Queen remarked.

LEWIS CARROLL, *THROUGH THE LOOKING-GLASS*

Contents

Memory vs. Mnemonic

A memory:

My wife asks, "What was the name of the bar we hung out in? After classes in college?"

I draw a blank. There are a lot of bars in that part of Orange County, California.

"The one next to the frozen yogurt place?" she says.

Frozen yogurt? Right. Frozen yogurt place. I remember that. Pink chairs and tables, cute Japanese frog mascot, more toppings than yogurt.

"The red walls, remember?" my wife persists. "The walls in the place were velvet red. You were getting into scotch."

Dark red walls. Scotch. Next to the yogurt shop with the pink tables.

My mind becomes less blank: "The District," I announce. I have not set foot in this bar in over a decade. I have not thought about it for almost as long.

"The District!" my wife says. "I was thinking about it," she says from across the couch, "because I heard this song on the radio the other day." She turns up the volume on her laptop—an old pop tune from the mid-2000s, saccharine and synthesized. "Remember I'd dance to it when it came on?" She's hinting that we should dance now, but I don't respond. My mind is time traveling.

Yogurt shop. Pink tables. The District, red walls, smell of scotch. Sound of a synthesizer in minor key.

I have not thought about these things in a decade, but suddenly I'm there, in the eye of the imagination. I'm not only at the District when this stupid song came out. I'm also in 2006. From the red walls to the scotch to the song and beyond, my mind conjures and connects a thousand details I'd misplaced, a thousand details I'd forgotten I'd misplaced: my German professor's name, the plot of a short story I was writing, every menu item at the Mexican place across from campus, where I had lunch with my friend's sister who lent me that book (what was it?—right, *Confederacy of Dunces*, her copy was missing half the cover). Each detail discloses five more. Where have these memories been hiding?

This is not an exercise in association. Not in the logical sense of that word, anyway ("A is to B, as C is to _____?" or "What do you think of when you hear the word *America*?"). Rather, it is sensory association of an explicitly personal nature. It is the optical idiosyncrasy of subjective experience. Would anyone else remember *A Confederacy of Dunces* by way of a yogurt shop?

The phenomenon should be a familiar one: a chance picture, a song, a smell, and all at once the details of another lifetime rush to the mind's eye, one after another, details unlocked from unconscious spaces you didn't know existed.

This is what the ancients called the art of memory.

More accurately, it is the natural process that the art of memory hacks into and harnesses for rhetorical ends. This book provides a history of the art of memory—the memory palace technique, as it is known today—and recovers its precepts for the digital age. I write *recovers* rather than *refigures* or *retheorizes*, because classical mnemonics require only minor upgrades to be relevant to the electronic age. Unique among rhetoric's five canons, memory is and was concerned not with language alone but also with graphic depiction and systems of visualization. An emphasis on the sensory rather than linguistic dimensions of rhetorical activity makes the fourth canon already compatible with the icons, apps, data visualizations, and other means of graphic communication ubiquitous in the digital media ecology.

Recover is also an apt verb because the fourth canon's visual precepts have yet to be taken up by contemporary rhetorical theorists in a consistent way, despite the fact that the canon has long since been "rediscovered" and given a central role in the field. Upon inspection, however, rhetoric's new *memoria* retains only a fragile connection to the memoria practiced throughout history. The new fourth canon is not the same as the old— which would not be an issue if the old canon were no longer relevant to the twenty-first century. However, the ancient canon of memory remains deeply relevant to the contemporary moment; it was and is useful for more than memorizing speeches. The canon's rich history, I suggest, can be a touchstone for novel explorations of memory in our hypervisual, hypermediated culture.

To be sure, across the last thirty years of rhetorical scholarship, one can locate provocative allusions to the fourth canon's visual mnemonics. For example, Jay Bolter moves in the right direction when he says that the art of memory was designed to address "the gap between writing and memory" and that the way it does this is by writing, not with letters but with images, "visualizing one's speech and mapping it into a mental structure."[1] Likewise, Sharon Crowley has acknowledged that classical memory practices suggest a rhetoric that is not solely "literacy-based."[2] Richard Young and Patricia Sullivan have considered the connection between spatial and linguistic memory, arguing implicitly that the fourth canon evokes semiotic modes beyond language.[3] More recently, the collection *Rhetoric, Remembrance, and Visual Form* has brought together numerous scholars to explore the "intersections among visual culture and practices of memory," the "potency and fallibility of images as mediums of the past," and the "simultaneously authentic yet manipulated qualities of memory when conjured through visual modes."[4] In the collection's introduction, Bradford Vivian and Anne Teresa Demo recognize that memory and imagery were intimately linked in the classical era's mnemonic practices, contending that the same can be said for memory practices today: "Individual proficiency in the classical art of memory depended on a host of visual exercises. . . . The *ars memoriae* required orators to conjure elaborate mental images of roomy palaces or public spaces in order to memorize lengthy and complex discourses. Both personal and computational, or artistic and digital, memories find their raison d'être in the visual media upon which they rely. To remember, then as now, is to see."[5] As suggestive as this sounds, however, Vivian and Demo go on to prove my initial point that the visual precepts of the fourth canon, though recognized, are often treated as a historical curiosity no longer relevant to theory or practice. Vivian and Demo state that mnemonics were simply "a metaphorical substitute for cognitive mental operations."[6] While this is perhaps true for Aristotle's understanding of mental imagery, it is not true for the *ars memoria*, the art of memory, whose practitioners took the creation of images literally and seriously. In addition, although Vivian and Demo begin their collection with a nod to visual mnemonics, none of the collection's authors do the same. They instead explore artifacts such as public memorials, war photographs, and paintings. Collectively, they seem to use the canon of memory not as a starting point for new theories or practices—it is no longer a "performative technique," Vivian remarks elsewhere—but as a "mode of inquiry."[7] This is a good description of the way memory has been taken up in rhetorical scholarship. Memory is examined in its natural, social, or psychological sense and used as a bridge to cultural criticism, historical inquiry, and so on. It is adopted as a pretext for analyzing the many ways humans mediate the past with objects, from community cookbooks to national war memorials, so that scholars might pose the critical question "Who

wants whom to remember what, and why?" as Alon Confino puts it.[8] Few
rhetoricians have expressed interest in recovering mnemonic precepts as
such or in asking what relevance these precepts have for the present. Of
course, I am not suggesting that the current direction of rhetorical memory studies is misguided in any way. There is plenty of room in the field for
that continuing project. However, in this book, I take rhetorical memory
in a different direction (though one that ultimately finds common ground
with the larger body of rhetorical scholarship on memory).

My starting point is a suggestion made by Collin Gifford Brooke in
Lingua Fracta. "Memory," Brooke states, "is the one canon whose status
as *practice* is in need of rehabilitation."[9] This notion of mnemonic practice was central to the canon historically and must remain so if it is to be
useful today. Memory as practice—in particular, a visual practice—is a
common theme in the history of rhetoric's memory arts. Ancient, medieval, and early modern rhetoricians made a clear distinction between
"natural" memory and "artificial" memory, the latter denoting mnemonic
techniques, methods, and habits through which one's memoryscape could
be harnessed for rhetorical action. It was the job of the rhetorician to develop and teach these precepts for mnemonic practice.

As I have suggested, the most valuable insight to be gained from the
canon of memory is its emphasis on the visual. Stewart Whittemore defines rhetorical memory as a practice of data management, and as he
rightly notes, the idea of memory qua information management is an ancient one.[10] While Whittemore's book *Rhetorical Memory* emphasizes the
organizational aspects of memory, I want to emphasize the optical, sensory ones—which are related to but not synonymous with the notion of
organization. From pre-Socratic Greece until the early modern period, the
art of memory espoused the principle that words and information could
best be recalled when re-mediated into a visual form possessing emotional
resonance with the rhetor. "Perceptions received by the ears or by reflection can be most easily retained," states Cicero in *De oratore*, "if they are
also conveyed to our minds by the mediation of our eyes."[11] Converting
information into images—housed in memory palaces in the mind or on
the page—turned thinking into a form of seeing.[12] It translated the semiotics of language and thought into a more palpable semiotics of sight, dimension, and affect. Importantly, this association between memory and
the *oculus imaginationis*—the eye of the imagination—was central to the
long-standing link between memory and invention. Visualizing information made it easier to recall, browse through, and integrate when inventing new discourse or speaking extemporaneously.

Visualizing information to aid invention is an ancient practice, to be sure, but one that should resonate with anyone who has ever used a computer. Though no longer occurring in the mind, the work of transforming and accessing information with visual modes is as commonplace today as it was in the past. The terabytes of information stored on the world's servers would be useless without the graphical user interfaces developed to aid access to them. Data have multiplied, but the techniques used to manage access are the same today as they were for Cicero: *make it visual, make it spatial*. The history of rhetoric's fourth canon can thus provide a wealth of insight into the rhetorical dimensions of graphical data representation, which is omnipresent in and fundamental to the new media age. Indeed, the memory palace can be understood as one of history's first interfaces. It was a medium, recognized as such, connecting the knower with the thing known (or, to put it in digital terms, connecting the user with some form of underlying program logic, which is, of course, just another semi-visual layer connecting the user to the metal). Words and information are abstract. By incarnating them in image, they become not "real" but more accessible to the human who would use them to coordinate activity. The history of rhetoric's ars memoria can thus be read as a history of information visualization systems, from emotionally charged mental phantasms to mundane pictures in print to full-scale memory theaters—and, eventually, to file folders, icons, and network maps. Across their varied guises, the images of the ars memoria have acted as visual portals between information and the users seeking to integrate information into a new assemblage.

The history of the art of memory is also a history of memory. Although I make a distinction at the outset between natural memory and artificial mnemonics, a dynamic relationship exists between the two, as it exists in all cases between humans and their artificial, secondary knowledge. Mnemonics mirror memory. Artificial memory techniques tap into natural memory processes and thus reflect, at one remove, how our minds convert a trillion flickers of continuous sensory impression into semistable visual models we call *memories*. For ancient rhetors, the memory palace was a site of purposeful visual curation; memory itself, whatever else it may be, can also be understood in those terms. Without reproducing a naïve Lockean theory of mind as tabula rasa—contra Locke, the human system emerges prewired to attune to some things but not others—we can nevertheless assert that human brains do curate the world's interminable data streams into sensory-driven models. Expectedly, humans do consciously what their brains do automatically: they reduce complex information to lucid visual depictions.

The impulse to capture knowledge of intangible things by converting the intangible to tangible, visible maps or models is a universal one. The impulse is synonymous with the workings of memory itself. However, the human ability to conjure secondary knowledge—in the form of visual models of intangible information—is rife with ethical complications. When the intangible is made tangible or the nebulous is made visible, it can be harnessed, controlled, objectified, commodified, and used for unethical ends. Should image making or at least certain images be condemned? The dialectical forces of image creation and image destruction are as universal as the powers of remembering and forgetting. Looming behind the imagery of memory—in natural and artificial form—is the countering force of iconoclasm. From Plato to Oliver Cromwell to contemporary software critics, iconoclasts have condemned those who convert intangible data into visual, tangible knowledge. Images become idols. Idols lead to the worship of false gods. But where idols exist, prophets arise to smash them. The history of ars memoria is thus a history not only of visualization but also of its opposite: iconoclasm.

A detailed history of rhetoric's memory arts—written for rhetoricians or new media scholars as opposed to historians—is lacking in the field. This book in part is intended to fill that gap. More essentially, however, a discussion of the mnemonic tradition's digital relevance becomes possible only when grounded in a comprehensive history. This book is thus arranged in chronological order. It begins in chapter 1 with the art of memory's classical origin. I provide an overview of its earliest treatments in *Dissoi logoi*, Plato, and Aristotle before moving on to its treatment by the Roman rhetoricians Cicero and Quintilian. Chapter 1 argues that the fourth canon, from its earliest conception, exploited the psychological principle of sensory-emotional association to produce an art of info management through info visualization. The chapter explores further the art of memory's close connection with *inventio* in ancient Mediterranean rhetoric. This memory-invention link is reiterated throughout the book, supporting the argument that a digital ars memoria should similarly adopt the classical outlook that data visualization is an art of invention rather than a method for data mastery.

This book also examines, as a secondary concern, how the fourth canon's precepts have adapted to the social and technological ecologies into which they have migrated. Chapter 2 follows the art of memory in the Middle Ages as it moves from the secular, public agora to the more "interior" scribal culture of the Christian monastery. Working from the foundational scholarship of Mary Carruthers and Frances Yates, I locate the influence of classical mnemonics on medieval figures such as Alcuin of York, Hugh of Saint Victor, and Thomas Bradwardine, exploring how the visual character of the ars memoria did and did not change in its Christianized form. I also draw attention to imageless memory systems that circulated alongside the visual art of memory, allowing me to examine an important distinction between information *management* and information *visualization*—between spreadsheets and data visualizations, as we might say today. Chapter 2 explores how this difference manifested itself in medieval mnemonics and why it matters.

Chapter 3 tracks the art of memory's evolution into the early modern period, during which time the mnemonic arts witnessed a renewed interest across Europe—except in England. Assessing, confirming, and enlarging a thesis forwarded by Frances Yates, I contend that a unique confluence of iconoclasm and Ramism (an imageless memory system) contributed to the marginalization and loss of visual mnemonics in Reformation England. Several English memory treatises—including John Willis's *Mnemonica*—are read against this iconoclastic backdrop. I argue that an iconoclastic tendency robbed English rhetoric not only of memoria's imagery but also ipso facto of the ancient link between memoria and inventio.

After pitting iconoclasm and visual mnemonics against each other, I further highlight, in chapter 3, a tendency toward "digital iconoclasm" in the work of Wendy Hui Kyong Chun, Friedrich Kittler, and other new media scholars and philosophers of technology. I connect Puritan iconoclasm with the contemporary distrust of visually mediated information: then, as now, visual knowledge was criticized for its role in sustaining, circulating, and justifying unethical power structures.

Iconoclastic dogma led to the marginalization of the memory arts in England by the early 1600s. However, by the Enlightenment in the eighteenth century, the mnemonic tradition found itself marginalized in most European contexts. The tradition, surprisingly, then underwent a resurgence in the nineteenth century. Chapter 4 offers one of the first contemporary overviews of the memory palace's Enlightenment and modern-era trajectory, examining works on memory by well-known figures (such as Gottfried Leibniz) and more obscure ones (such as Marius D'Assigny). During its period of Victorian resurgence, the memory arts grew in popularity but became detached not only from rhetorical invention but also from the rhetorical arts generally. The art of memory migrated into the orbit of faculty psychology, then later into the handbooks of train-your-memory teachers, a progression that ultimately diminished the importance of mnemonics within Western traditions. The art of memory, among other mnemonic techniques, was bowdlerized into a tool for rote memorization, disconnected from any epistemological or imaginative concerns. Far removed from Cicero's exalted treatment, the art of memory met an ignominious end, which can be read as a proxy for the marginalization of rhetoric itself in an increasingly "scientific" age.

Chapter 5 arrives in the present, grappling with technological concerns introduced in previous chapters. I frame contemporary data-visualization technologies as a renewed manifestation of the visual mnemonic tradition, exploring how digital mnemonics might or might not be informed by the memory palace technique. Walking a line between the elusive goal of complete data mastery and the familiar iconoclastic censure of artificial memory in all its guises (from writing to software), I suggest that we return to the classical conception of mnemonic technique as an aid—not to flawless recall but to rhetorical invention and knowledge construction. Responding to the work of digital humanists such as Stephen Ramsay, Wendy Hui Kyong Chun, and Johanna Drucker, I examine how digital tools and techniques can function as aids to inquiry—that is, as starting points for knowledge construction rather than as idols that speak transparently for themselves. Indeed, I argue that data visualizations are valuable for their ability to picture not knowledge but the process of constructing knowledge from partial information and biased data—which is precisely what human minds do when creating memories. As a mnemonic device, data visualization can thus illuminate the workings of natural memory qua dynamic interface. In the chapter, I explore the theoretical and social implications of this artificial/natural memory binary in the digital age.

Whereas chapter 5 examines the scientific imagery associated with the term *data visualization*—networks, interactive maps, graphs, and the like—the final chapter returns to the principle of sensory-emotional association harnessed by the classical art. It investigates the life of *personal* artificial memories circulating on Facebook, Instagram, Twitter, and other apps in the social mediascape. Working from an idea first developed by Jeff Pruchnic and Kim Lacey, I read social media as a digital memory palace, created and arranged with associative images of our own design. However, unlike the *imagines* or images of the interior memory palace, mnemonic images constructed online are networked, searchable, public. The externalization and "socialization" of the memory palace raises problems and offers potentials as the (digital) art of memory migrates once more into a new technological ecology.

This book explores an abstract thing, the art of memory, in various historical eras. I undertake many close readings of primary and secondary material, but at certain points I use computational methods to gain a perspective on the concept that is either much larger or more microscopic than the individual text. In each case, texts, their features, and/or their bibliographic metadata stand in as imperfect but still-revealing proxies for discourse about the fourth canon in various periods and contexts. Some of these methods are straightforward. For example, in chapter 3, I graph the publication sites of over four hundred memory treatises, the graphs acting as evidence for larger claims regarding early modern memory practices. Other methods, however, will be unfamiliar to the humanities and thus do require an explanation, which I provide in endnotes, in-text explanations, and references.

I adopt these computational, corpus-based approaches because a link exists between them and the classical art of memory. Recall what I said about the art's visual precepts: the creation of mnemonic imagery and memory palaces converted the semiotics of language and thought into the semiotics of sight and dimension. Memory, it was believed, operates most keenly when occupied with visual forms. The images of the classical art of memory are thus similar to the data visualizations of computational analysis. Graphs, charts, networks, even word lists—these objects distill into a single image a greater totality of information than working memory alone could readily synthesize. They are memory aids, and creating them constitutes a mnemonic practice. Like the art of memory, computational methods can be used to visualize words and knowledge to aid invention. By incorporating visualizations into the book, I provide a present-day equivalent of historical memory practices, demonstrating their utility as arts of invention for the twenty-first century.

CHAPTER 1

Arts of Memory in the Agora

At the twilight of the Roman Republic, circa 55 BCE, the orator and states-man Marcus Tullius Cicero wrote his *De oratore*, a treatise on rhetoric and its moral role in political leadership. In the text, Cicero works his way through the five rhetorical canons—the first three being invention, ar-rangement, and style—arriving in the second book at memoria, the canon of memory. About the fourth canon, Cicero states, "As Simonides wisely observed, the things best pictured by our minds are those that have been conveyed and imprinted on them by one of the senses. Now the keenest of all our senses is the sense of sight. Therefore, things perceived by our hearing or during our thought processes can be most easily grasped by the mind, if they are also conveyed to our minds through the mediation of the eyes."[1] For Cicero, as for Quintilian after him and the Greek sophists be-fore him, the practice of memoria is an eminently visual one. It is the prac-tice of converting words and abstract information—"things perceived by our hearing or during our thought processes"—into visual form. The mind, Cicero states, can "grasp" visual, sensory things better than it can grasp the abstractions of linguistically mediated information. To remember, the or-ator should thus convert information into vivid imagery within the *oculus imaginationis*: the mind's eye, not just the mind, must be engaged if infor-mation is to be capably recalled, integrated, and applied. From its earliest elucidation, the art of memory operated on this basic premise.

In 1995, in the midst of the digital revolution, computer engineer James A. Wise and his colleagues published an article entitled "Visualizing the Non-Visual: Spatial Analysis and Interaction with Information from Text Documents." Graphical user interfaces had been part of the computer landscape for over a decade at this point, but Wise et al.'s article offered an early attempt to apply graphical thinking to text-based documents, which, by the mid-1990s, had begun to multiply into gigabyte territory. "The need to read and assess large amounts of text," Wise et al. state, "puts a severe

upper limit on the amount of text information that can be processed."
Working memory, in other words, is not capable of comprehending me-
ga- and gigabytes of textual information; text at these scales cannot be
"read" in the traditional sense. The solution, Wise et al. argue, is to over-
come constraints to working memory through "content abstraction and
spatialization," transforming documents "into a new visual representation
that communicates by image instead of prose." Comprehending information contained within thousands or millions of texts, Wise et al. continue,
can be facilitated by converting the raw textual data into "a spatial representation which may then be accessed and explored by visual processes
alone." Re-mediating texts into navigable images allows users to deploy
their "powers of visual perception" to explore patterns emerging across
multiple documents.[2] The best way to access and comprehend proliferat-
ing textual databases, in short, according to Wise et al., is to visualize them.

Juxtaposing these two texts—one an ancient rhetorical treatise, the
other a computer engineering article—reveals that across two millennia
both the orators of the ancient world and the scientists of the digital one
arrived at an identical conclusion about mnemonic access: visualization
is key. The most efficient way for humans to access and utilize information is to deploy semiotic modes other than the written or spoken word. A
more visual medium is required. Put another way, what these texts demonstrate is that, from the agora to the computer, the art of memory has been
an art of visualization—of converting information into imagery, vague
thought into lucid sight. The technology has changed, but the concept has
remained the same. Telling the story of how we got from the memory palace of the mind's eye to the one on our screens is the objective of this book.

"Memories. You're talking about memories."

What, precisely, is the ars memoria, the art of memory, as conceptualized
and practiced throughout history? Taking a cue from Cicero, I think the
best way to introduce it is by way of moving pictures.

In an early scene in Ridley Scott's *Blade Runner*, a woman named Rachael enters a boardroom in the Tyrell Corporation building, where she
is asked by Rick Deckard and Eldon Tyrell to take an empathy test.[3] The
test will determine if Rachael is in fact a human or a replicant—a robot,
banned on Earth, to be "retired" upon discovery. The empathy test measures "capillary dilation, the so-called blush response; fluctuation of the
pupil; involuntary dilation of the iris." Replicants fail to display these responses when hearing statements that would make humans blush, fluctu-
ate their pupils, or dilate their irises.

Rachael humors Deckard as he sets up the empathy test machine. He proceeds to ask her a gamut of sensation-inducing questions: "You have a little boy. He shows you his butterfly collection, plus the killing jar . . ."

One hundred questions later, Deckard turns off his machine. Tyrell, who has arranged the meeting, asks Rachael to leave the room. "She's a replicant," Deckard announces. He is concerned. The test has failed to make an efficient identification. Rachael exhibits human empathy more convincingly than other replicant models. Deckard asks Tyrell how it's possible.

"We've gifted them with a past," Tyrell explains, "creating a cushion or pillow for their emotions."

Memories. The key to advancing replicant evolution, Tyrell has discovered, is to implant real human memories into the replicants' neural systems. "After all, they are emotionally inexperienced, with only a few years in which to store up the experiences you and I take for granted." With built-in memories, replicants learn more quickly and replicate human behavior more accurately. It makes them more human.

Later in the film, Deckard confronts Rachael with his knowledge of her private memories, telling her they came from someone else's past.[4]

"Remember when you were six?" he says. "You and your brother snuck into an empty building through a basement window. You were gonna play doctor. He showed you his, but when it got to be your turn you chickened and ran. Remember that?" And then, "You remember the spider that lived in a bush outside your window? Orange body, green legs. Watched her build a web all summer. Then one day there was a big egg in it. The egg hatched—"

"The egg hatched," Rachael echoes, "and a hundred baby spiders came out. And they ate her." Distraught, Rachael leaves Deckard. She is shattered to learn that her memories are somebody else's, merely implanted into her own neural system.

I begin with these scenes because they provide three insights into the natural memory mechanisms the ars memoria exploits.

Memories, first and foremost, play a crucial role in developing— indeed, in determining—a sense of self in the present, regardless of their relationship to an actual past or one's place within it. Rachael is Rachael because of her memories, whether or not they are "hers." Memory involves the now, not the past—or, at least, not only the past.

Just as importantly, the scene above suggests that one's self-forming memories are visual phenomena—little snippets of private cinema ("Orange body, green legs. Watched her build a web all summer"). It also suggests that memories are idiosyncratic, bespoke, like neural fingerprints.

Everyone has a childhood memory involving spiders—it is nearly an American archetype—but if I were to ask a thousand people to recall those memories, none would perfectly resemble Rachael's. A thousand minds would conjure a thousand mental spaces, all imbued with unique sensory associations, viewed in reverse through a thousand lived trajectories. This is elementary.

If *Blade Runner* offers a model of memory in its natural sense, the novel *Hannibal* by Thomas Harris provides a model of memory in its artificial sense—memory as mnemonic. In the book, the eponymous psychiatrist retires at times to his "mind palace," either as a place to wander in respite or a place from which to retrieve information. Like Rachael's (implanted) natural memories, Dr. Lecter's memory palace is eminently visual and bespoke. However, unlike Rachael, Dr. Lecter has harnessed those features of natural memory and formed a power to move at will inside his visual, custom-made memoryscape:

> As once we visited Dr. Lecter in the Palazzo of the Capponi, so we will go with him now into the palace of his mind. . . . The foyer is the Norman Chapel in Palermo, severe and beautiful and timeless, with a single reminder of mortality in the skull graven in the floor. Unless he is in a great hurry to retrieve information from the palace, Dr. Lecter often pauses here as he does now, to admire the chapel. Beyond it, far and complex, light and dark, is the vast structure of Dr. Lecter's making. . . . We catch up to him as the swift slippers of his mind pass from the foyer into the Great Hall of the Seasons . . . ; it is airy, high-ceilinged, furnished with objects and tableaux that are vivid, striking, sometimes shocking and absurd, and often beautiful. The displays are well spaced and well lighted like those of a great museum. . . . Like Giotto, Dr. Lecter has frescoed the walls of his mind. He has decided to pick up Clarice Starling's home address while he is in the palace, but he is in no hurry for it, so he stops at the foot of a great staircase where the Riace bronzes stand. These great bronze warriors attributed to Phidias are the centerpiece of a frescoed space that could unspool all of Homer and Sophocles. . . . A thousand rooms, miles of corridors, hundreds of facts attached to each object furnishing each room.[5]

In this passage, Thomas Harris provides a vivid example of what the ancients called *artificial memory*, or the ars memoria, the art of memory. It is not a theory or model of memory so much as a conscious practice. Dr. Lecter hacks the involuntary mechanisms of memory and uses them for his own ends. Our minds naturally recreate the past through (sometimes hazy, sometimes intense) visual models, one sensation evoking others in a chain of sudden reminiscence. Lecter, however, has taken control of this immersive sensory experience. Natural memory for him becomes artificial mnemonic. To be sure, his inner visualization remains idiosyncratic—based on his Italian travels and his proclivity for all things classical and ornate—but Lecter has tamed the mind's instinctive tendency to stray through memory in an accidental, uncontrolled manner. He has rendered his memoryscape as a carefully constructed palace, a vast yet purposeful structure "of his own making." The memoryscape regulated, Lecter now moves within it in a deliberate manner—or, more aptly, in a *visually* deliberate manner, for his palace is not constructed from disembodied principles of logical association (as Aristotle divines the art) but from the imagistic phantasms of his own embodied sensorium.

Placed in contrast, the treatments of memory in *Blade Runner* and *Hannibal* evoke the natural versus artificial memory binary. Memory versus mnemonic. This is an essential starting point for any history of rhetoric's memory arts. To be sure, the latter is never far from the former, but the ancients conceptualized this difference in order to describe how the powers of memory could be exploited, as Dr. Lecter exploits them, for more conscious ends. The result was the ars memoria, which we know today as the memory palace technique.

Contrary to popular conceit, the history of this technique is not a history of a memorization trick. Rather, it is a history of information management, of the relationship between memory and human creativity, and of the West's persistent desire to grasp at abstraction with sensory models. It is, in short, a history of the quest to turn thinking into a form of seeing—to turn raw information into lucid, manipulatable knowledge, as Stewart Whittemore has put it[6]—so as to more efficiently integrate knowledge and then use it to coordinate action in fleshspace. This history bleeds into the present via the endless proliferation of data visualizations and graphical user interfaces that constitute the new millennial cyberscape. Analysts roam customized visual models of data and teenagers roam curated Instagram pages as orators once roamed their personalized memory palaces, the goal of each interface being to provide access to as much information as possible while exerting the least amount of cerebral energy. From the app icons and JPEG grids beckoning from iPhones to the polychrome network graphs evoking a godlike sensation of total knowledge, these new visual formations find their intellectual ancestry, I argue, in the mental phantasms of the ars memoria.

Tracing this lineage is this book's primary goal.

The Memory Palace Technique: A Brief Primer

A book on the history (and present) of the memory palace must at some point address an obvious objection that has bedeviled the technique for two thousand years: that like all memory tricks, this one is ineffective and frankly ridiculous. From Quintilian onward, observers have gazed at the idea of the memory palace and expressed a baffled skepticism about its efficacy. Does it really work? The common retort is that it seems harder to master the technique than simply to learn things by rote.

This skepticism fundamentally misunderstands the art of memory. First, as Mary Carruthers has argued for three decades, the art was never intended to be a technique for rote memorization (not primarily, anyway); rather, it was a mental practice, a frame of mind, whereby one set the stage for invention of new material, while writing a text or extemporizing before an audience. The art, Whittemore explains, created "new things" out of "old things" tagged in the visual space of the mind qua virtual database.[7] I will return throughout the book to this vital connection between mnemonics and inventio, which Carruthers rightly associates with creativity. However, regarding skepticism about the memory palace technique, there is yet a more fundamental response: It's not difficult.

To reiterate, one of the core precepts underlying the technique is that one's memory palace must be custom built, that it must harness and employ the idiosyncratic associations and images that constitute one's natural network of memories (as Dr. Lecter harnesses his memories of Italy and its ornate palazzi, busts, and textiles). One early memory treatise puts it this way: "practice whatever you hear" and "connect it to what you already know."[8] The technique simply requires one to take a mindful control over the instinctive process of reminiscence—of the peripatetic daydreaming or mind wandering, if you like, that neurotypical humans permit themselves every day. As an athlete takes control of natural anatomical movement and converts it into body-enhancing exercises, so does the memory artist take control of natural memory and convert it into a mind-enhancing practice.

A neurotypical human, for example, should find it easy to conjure before his or her mind's eye a flame from young adulthood: a date, a kiss, a dance. Can you see it? The more awkward the better. It should then require only a bit more effort to associate with those nostalgic flashes—those visual, aural, olfactory things—a new piece of information exigent right now, so that, after a little repetition, whenever you conjure those old flames and flings, there too is the new information. (Using images of loves lost is precisely the technique recommended in a Renaissance treatise called *The Phoenix*. A "fayre mayden" named Junipere is the flame evoked in that text.)[9] If not loves lost—if you're not a nostalgic sap—any easily conjured vision of the past will do, so long as it is laden with affect and so long as it conjures other *loci*, other spaces of memory: a funeral parlor, a childhood bedroom, the hospital where you held your first child. The Renaissance polymath Giordano Bruno understood the concept well: "they are those things that make the heart pound, having the power of something wondrous, frightening, pleasant, sad; a friend, an enemy . . . ; things hoped for or which we are suspicious of, and all things that encroach powerfully on the inner emotions. . . . It is the power of the senses and imagination, and not only the cognitive faculty, that are able to make the imprint on memory."[10] Granted, associating new information with and somehow visually re-mediating it into the sensory traces of "what you already know" is not the easiest thing to do, but it should not present itself as an impenetrable technique. The memory palace is not a memorization trick useful only to those born with preternaturally large memory banks. We are all born with large memory banks. Time and minor effort are all we need to convert the memoryscape into a controllable, graphical user interface.

Of course, to many, the idea that humans can exert active control over the shapes and purposes of memory might seem quaint or even ideologically offensive. Memory's essential selectiveness and fallibility—*especially* in its artificial or secondary forms—remain central presuppositions of critical theory and even psychological research.[11] I will touch on these concerns where appropriate, but in general, the book adopts the contrary if speculative perspective of the ancient orator, for whom memory's accuracy was less important than its ability to transform, compress, recall, and integrate information. Whether or not the sensory, affective mechanisms of memory produced universally valid models of the world ultimately was not the point; the point was that the mnemonic cue allowed rhetors to "find the right information at the right moment" and to "create new things out of old things," to quote Whittemore again.[12] As far as the rhetor was concerned, the accuracy of his memory palace—so far as it mattered to rhetorical practice—was demonstrated through the production of a successful discourse. To revise George Box's famous aphorism, all mnemonic images are wrong. Some are useful.

Memory in Contemporary Rhetorical Studies

Our visual, sensory models of the past—our memories—work their influence whether or not they possess an ontological relationship to past time and space. (Deckard to Rachael: "Implants. Those aren't your memories.")[13] The essence of memory as humans experience it is, to borrow linguistic terminology, synchronic rather than diachronic, consisting of dispersed mental apparitions conjured in the present. Memories "should be thought of as fictive devices that *the mind itself makes* for remembering."[14]

Humans have devised many ways to represent, construct, or interface with the past; each method tends to mask its own artifice in one way or another. Since the renewal of memory as a rhetorical canon in the 1990s and 2000s, scholars have rebranded rhetorical memory to denote these reconstructions of the past, the externalizations of memory, found in all world cultures. Due to this rebranding, the canon of memory no longer describes a particular "performative technique" of mental visualization developed along the Mediterranean circa 500 BCE. Instead, states Bradford Vivian, the canon has become a general "mode of inquiry."[15] It has been adopted as a pretext for analyzing the many ways humans externalize past memories and events with diverse objects, from family cookbooks[16] and songs to cemeteries and war memorials. "Who wants whom to remember what, and why?"[17] Memory is adopted in this critical, social, or psychological sense as a bridge to something other than the fourth canon—to cultural criticism, social inquiry, and so on.

In *The Book of Memory*, Mary Carruthers poses three questions that distinguish three approaches to the subject of memory: "First, what is the actual origin of information entering the brain; second, how is that information encoded, and is it in a way that physically affects our brain tissue; and third, how is its recollection best stimulated and secured, or what kind of heuristic devices are necessary for us to find it again once it has been stored?"[18] While Carruthers's first and second questions point to memory as an automatic neurological phenomenon, the third question— regarding artificial devices for recall—has been the one posed by rhetoricians throughout history: how are rhetors to best recall information when writing a speech, extemporizing, offering a prayer, sermonizing, meditating on extensive bodies of knowledge, or attempting to discover connections across that knowledge? These questions have motivated the history of the art of memory. The answer took form in various mnemonic devices, of which the memory palace technique was the most prominent. The difference between these devices and, say, a war memorial is that they facilitated general mnemonic access via info re-mediation of different sorts; they did not represent a specific person or event. To use a distinction coined by Jeff Pruchnic and Kim Lacey, artificial memory devices were "programs" that could be adapted to any "content."[19] In the information sciences, researchers have likewise distinguished between "what a user decides to store" and "the creation of the structures within which information is stored and retrieved."[20] The mnemonic arts represent the creation of the structures that facilitate recall. Equally important, most ancient mnemonic tools—the memory palace technique in particular—were *internal* forms of artificial memory, not *external* forms like the war memorial. The memory palace technique converted the raw stuff of memory into useful mnemonic objects but did not represent specific past events in physical form. Scholars today tend to focus on socially significant externalizations of specific memory content, mentioning only in passing the ancient mnemonic programs.

An article by Elizabethada Wright offers a representative anecdote of how contemporary scholars treat the fourth canon. In her essay, Wright frames rural and African American cemeteries as "memory places," but the bulk of her analysis takes its theoretical cue not from ancient practitioners or modern scholars of the memory arts but from Michel de Certeau and Michel Foucault. She makes only a brief reference to the classical art of memory and, from one paragraph to the next, moves from *Rhetorica ad Herennium*—a foundational source for the memory palace technique—to "materiality," "memorials," and "public memory." Wright does reference the work of Frances Yates, but the reference occurs in a footnote pointing the reader to *Art of Memory* to learn about "the beginnings of rhetoric and memory."[21] The rest of the essay offers a Foucauldian reading of cemeteries that could have been forwarded just as persuasively without a fleeting reference to classical mnemonics.

This intention to render the fourth canon as social history, critique, psychology, or cultural inquiry can be found in nearly all work on the subject. In his collection *Rhetorical Memory and Delivery*—foundational, to be sure, to memoria's revival—John Frederick Reynolds tantalizingly identifies "memory as mnemonic" as one of the lenses through which the field might rediscover the fourth canon.[22] However, none of the collection's authors take up that valuable lens as their primary instrument. Virginia Allen, for example, places psychology at the center of her attempt to recuperate the canon of memory: "To maintain that the problems of memory are not our concern or that they more properly belong to other disciplines is to accept the premise that rhetoric is only techne, appropriately defined by the how-to books of composition cookery. . . . A rhetorical theory that dismisses problems of the nature of mind . . . is a truncated theory."[23] Similarly, Bruce Gronbeck states that rhetoric's mnemonic tradition "lacks an intellectual problematic that can engage rhetoricians," arguing that Aristotle's psychological treatise *On Memory* "is a much more theoretically provocative and hence more suggestive work on memory" than rhetorical handbooks.[24] Kathleen Welch agrees with Gronbeck, declaring that "the most important connection that memory as a canon of rhetoric gives us is its explicit pointing to psychology."[25] Kathleen J. Ryan implies that artificial memory as described in *Ad Herennium* is responsible for the modern association of memory with rote memorization, and she argues that "instead of embracing this ancient description of memory," rhetoricians should look elsewhere to "reimagine" a rhetorical memory connected to imagination and invention.[26]

I admit it is unfair to critique scholars who wrote in the early 1990s for not diving right away into the mnemonic tradition's visual precepts, or for not recognizing its digital relevance. More recently, however, skepticism about the ars memoria continues to surface. In his discussion of digital writing, for example, Derek Van Ittersum argues that the canon of memory is valuable only "up to a point" for understanding rhetoric in the context of new media.[27] In another text, he exchanges artificial memory for a more modern analytical framework, "cultural-historical activity theory," which he and his coauthors describe as an "emergent synthesis [of] Vygotskyan psychology, Voloshinovian and Bakhtinian semiotics, Latour's actor-network theory, and situated, phenomenological work in sociology and anthropology."[28] The motive on display from Van Ittersum and the others seems to be that once the field breaks the association between the fourth canon and mnemonics, the canon may then be revived as psychology, criticism, and so on. Bradford Vivian is candid about this motivation. "The flurry of studies in rhetoric and public memory over the past scholarly generation," he states, "has revived rhetoric's close association with memory in distinctively modern fashion: not as a performative technique but as a critical or historical mode of inquiry."[29]

These anecdotes are interesting, but it is possible to represent visually the tendency among scholars to mention the memory arts in passing on the way to other topics related only tangentially to the fourth canon. (As with all visualizations in this book, figure 1.1 below allows access to more information—in this case, key-term "topics" in academic articles—than the mind could read, recall, or synthesize without the visual model.)

Using JSTOR's Data for Research website, and the dozen or so rhetoric journals accessible through the site, I gathered all articles (279 total) whose key terms included the words "memory" or "mnemonic." Key terms are defined by JSTOR as words with high term frequency–inverse document frequency (tf-idf) scores.[30] The articles ended up coming from the following journals: *Philosophy and Rhetoric, Rhetoric Society Quarterly, Rhetoric Review, Rhetorica, College Composition and Communication, College English, English Journal,* and the *Journal of Advanced Composition*. Analyzing this small corpus of 279 articles with the topic-modeling tool MAL-LET,[31] I created a ten-topic model of the articles' most prevalent thematic clusters or "topics"—defined as a collection of words that frequently co-occur together across all the articles. The ten topics generated by MAL-LET are as follows:

0   composition writing rhetoric english language cognitive university communication research teaching brain classical psychology theory
1   memory public rhetoric rhetorical political south memorial past collective history war rights civil cultural memories media politics
2   memory experience sense language time knowledge mind book words texts text important point form meaning fact
3   rhetoric rhetorical cicero invention memory aristotle classical locus delivery plato tradition loci greek theory speech
4   time poem poetry story poet man past life death present modern world lines action film mind form characters
5   writing text writers process writer reading students sentence student reader grammar language composition words system research program computer
6   memory women space rhetoric cemetery addams rhetorical holocaust century place events sappho public event history quilt images
7   students writing school class english reading read write student books people teachers book teaching high year teacher time children
8   story life past stories history family women diana american woman autobiography mother personal cultural literacy narrative college
9   food women los_alamos memories american recipes memory space cookbooks family cook file eating time african cooking world scientific

Labeling these topics is not an uncontestable procedure. In my view, topic 9 is uninterpretable and should be discarded rather than shoe-horned into intelligibility. However, the other topics, though a bit broad at times, remain within the range of interpretability. I label them as follows: "Language, Communication, and Psychology" (topic 0); "Public and Collective Memory" (topic 1); "Memory and Epistemology" (topic 2); "Classical Rhetoric and Memory" (topic 3); "Memory and Narrative" (topic 4); "Student Writing" (topic 5); "Gender and History" (topic 6); "Education" (topic 7); and "Life Stories" (topic 8).

MALLET returns a spreadsheet whose cells take the form "[ARTICLE NAME]: Topic 0, 35%; Topic 1, 22%; Topic 2, 18%," and so on, displaying which topic occurs at what percentage in each article. Figure 1.1 graphs this information. The epistemology topic occurs as the most preva-

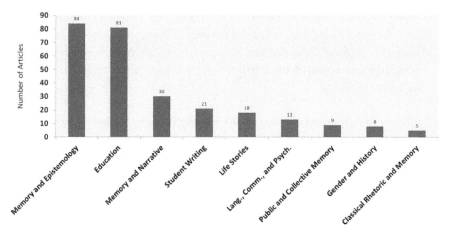

FIGURE 1.1. Most prevalent topics in 279 articles on rhetorical memory

lent topic in over eighty articles (i.e., it is the topic composing the highest percentage out of all the topics represented in these articles). "Memory and Narrative" occurs as the most prevalent topic in thirty articles. "Classical Rhetoric and Memory" comes in dead last—it is the most prevalent topic in only five articles across multiple decades of scholarship on rhetoric and memory.

What this graph suggests is that rhetoric's mnemonic tradition is not forgotten but is nevertheless marginalized as the field expands its definition of rhetorical memory to include a profusion of activities and objects. Scholars, as noted in the anecdote above, nod at the fourth canon's history before embarking on an exploration of memory in a much broader sense, one informed by a variety of other fields and subjects.

In no way am I questioning the value of a critical, social, or psychological refiguring of the fourth canon—in later chapters, I will refigure it myself, and much of the work referenced above will prove vital to that purpose. Though I am riving natural and artificial memory here at the outset, the two will reunite as the book progresses. Nevertheless, for now the separation is necessary. If the field of rhetoric dissociates itself from mnemonics, then it dissociates the fourth canon from 90 percent of its history. Such an archival divorce is problematic on its own, but more importantly, it obscures from the field the rich traditions and sources associated with memory arts throughout the centuries.

If natural and artificial memory should not be conflated, then mnemonics should not be dismissed as banal, uncritical tricks. Such a dismissal confuses two understandings of the word "artificial"—artificial as *fakery*

versus artificial as a *construction* of human effort. It is the latter connotation that makes artificial memory worth studying. Rhetorical memory is
an (art)ificial practice, requiring human input and creativity. As a consequence, the art's images and palaces are also purposely artificial. However, mnemonics are not for that reason embarrassing things best left in
the dustbin of rhetorical history. Bruno Latour reminds us that "Fabrica-
tion and artificiality are not the opposites of truth and objectivity"; rather,
the world can be known precisely because humans work in artifice, proceeding by way of constructs and concatenation.[32] In his essay "Visualization and Cognition," Latour contends that the emergence of western
Europe as a scientific and imperial power can be attributed in part to not
the printing press as such but the press's creation of what Latour calls "immutable mobiles"[33]—singular objects that used the visual aids of writing
and imagery to condense and thus "present" things that were, first, absent
(such as pictures and the geographical coordinates of distant islands),
and, much later, things not easily apprehended by the human sensory system at all (such as DNA). Thanks to the printing press, these visual aids
were *mobile*, so they traveled widely; they were also *immutable*, because
presses produced many copies of the same artifact, without scribal errors
or changes. The immutability of the object allowed many people across
many locations to study and therefore argue about the same "thing": a
particular imagistic representation of a (distant, unseen, extravisual) reality that provided a touchstone for grounded thought and debate about
that reality. Latour remarks that his famous study of scientific laboratory
work was in fact primarily a study of how scientists "transform rats and
chemicals into paper" and various "inscriptions" on it.

> Instruments, for instance, were of various types, ages, and degrees of so-
> phistication. Some were pieces of furniture, others filled large rooms, em-
> ployed many technicians and took many weeks to run. But their end result,
> no matter the field, was always a small window through which one could
> read a very few signs from a rather poor repertoire (diagrams, blots, bands,
> columns). All these inscriptions, as I called them, were combinable, super-
> imposable and could, with only a minimum of cleaning up, be integrated
> as figures in the text of the articles people were writing.[34]

The great divide between the "scientific" and "prescientific" mind, he concludes, was and remains a divide not in intellect but in skill with images
that reduce and represent an otherwise unseen reality: "The Great Divide
can be broken down into many small, unexpected and practical sets of
skills to produce images, and to read and write about them."[35] Although

Latour in his essay never draws a connection to memory as such, he does tiptoe near it through his recognition that the West's production of images fostered a rhetorical, agonistic environment within which it became necessary (and easier) to rally support for an argument in the form of a singular, verifiable image. Latour states,

> Who will win in an agonistic encounter between two authors, and between them and all the others they need to build up a statement? Answer: the one able to muster on the spot the largest number of well aligned and faithful allies. This definition of victory is common to war, politics, law, and, I shall now show, to science and technology. My contention is that writing and imaging cannot by themselves explain the changes in our scientific societies, except insofar as they help to make this agonistic situation more favorable. Thus it is not all the anthropology of writing, nor all the history of visualization that interests us in this context. Rather, we should concentrate on those aspects that help in the mustering, the presentation, the increase, the effective alignment or ensuring the fidelity of new allies. We need, in other words, to look at the way in which someone convinces someone else to take up a statement, to pass it along, to make it more of a fact. . . . This is what I call "holding the focus steady" on visualization and cognition.[36]

And to complete the mnemonic point, the reason that "writing and imaging"—writing being the first great memory aid, as Plato recognized—make it possible to muster allies is because they allow one to muster in a single object what would otherwise take enormous powers of memory to bring together. Think back to the scientists in Latour's laboratory: What would be easier to recall and "show" when arguing a scientific point? A large, inchoate data set or a single diagram, figure, graph, or chart? Latour again: "What is so important in the images and in the inscriptions scientists and engineers are busy obtaining, drawing, inspecting, calculating and discussing? It is, first of all, the unique advantage they give in the rhetorical or polemical situation. 'You doubt of what I say? I'll show you.' And, without moving more than a few inches, I unfold in front of your eyes figures, diagrams, plates, texts, silhouettes, and then and there present things that are far away and with which some sort of two-way connection has now been established."[37] In other words, it is visuals, images, and artificial representations of reality that allow us to approach, argue about, and, when the stars align, understand whatever reality exists outside the subjective viewpoint. More to the point, artificial images of reality allow us to do these wonderful, terrifying things because they relieve our memories of the need to attend to, balance, and integrate more raw data than our minds evolved to handle. Throughout history, even scientific "geniuses" have found it necessary—as it is necessary for all of us—to make recourse to artificial imagery when grasping at the real.

The constructs of the ars memoria thus provide a further example of Latour's reality-re-mediating, "artificial" inscriptions, but with this difference: when re-mediated into the creative and affective imagery of the art, knowledge no longer exists on a presupposition of direct, reified reference, as it might in the context of scientific graphs and data visualizations. Quite the opposite: knowledge qua mnemonic encourages its own deconstruction and reconstruction; knowledge becomes a thing to be broken down, moved, and assembled in new places, as one's understanding evolves or as one's circumstances demand new uses for old information. Though natural memories arise with little conscious effort—eliding their virtual nature—the objects of artificial memory, even as they act as knowledge models, also foreground their own artifice, their own constructedness. As we shall see in the rest of the chapter and throughout the book, artificial memories have a deep bond with human imagination, affect, and culture. We needn't exchange the mnemonic tradition for psychology or social inquiry to raise social and epistemological questions, for these are embedded in the history of artificial memory itself.

Greek Origins: Dissoi logoi *and Simonides*

The canon now identified as *memoria* first surfaces in the textile sediments of history in *Dissoi logoi*, a document dated to around 400 BCE. Associated with the sophists, this treatise is concerned with what it calls "two-fold arguments," binary debates about whether something is "good" or "bad," "seemly" or "disgraceful," "just" or "unjust," and so on. The author—who, if he were alive today, would enjoy trolling on Twitter—espouses the position that such debates are pointless, because what is "good" or "bad," "just" or "unjust," depends on who you are and what's at stake for you. "The victory of the Spartans which they won over the Athenians," he opines, "was good for the Spartans but bad for the Athenians and their allies."[38] The text's unflinching relativism has, rightly or wrongly, led to its association with sophism.

However, tacked on to the end of this treatise concerning the nature of binary argument is an untitled section that begins thusly: "The greatest and fairest discovery has been found to be memory; it is useful for everything, for wisdom as well as for the conduct of life." Following this brief encomium is not a reflection on natural memory but a sketch of a nascent mnemonic system. The passage is short enough to reproduce in whole:

This is the first step: if you focus your attention, your mind, making progress by this means, will perceive more. The second step is to practice whatever you hear. If you hear the same things many times and repeat them, what you have learned presents itself to your memory as a connected whole. The third step is: whenever you hear something, connect it with what you know already. For instance, suppose you need to remember the name "Chrysippos," you must connect it with chrusos (gold) and hippos (horse). Or another example: if you need to remember the name "Pyrilampes" you must connect it with pyr (fire) and lampein (to shine). These are examples for words. In the case of things, do this: if you want to remember courage, think of Ares and Achilles, or metal working, of Hephaistos, or cowardice, of Epeios.[39]

The division of this section into "steps" indicates that for its author memory denotes not natural or automatic psychology but active mnemonic heuristic. The first and second steps are banal: they are directions to pay attention and to repeat what one wants to remember. The third step, however, is more interesting: it realizes the value of the senses to artificial memory, first by recommending what Mary Carruthers calls visual homophony—"to remember the name 'Chrysippos' [...] connect it with chrusos (gold) and hippos (horse)"—then by suggesting a form of allegorical but still iconic[40] association—"if you want to remember courage, think of Ares and Achilles."

Like most pre-Socratic fragments, *Dissoi logoi*'s memory section is almost certainly incomplete. Nevertheless, in this early sophistic sliver of text we discover the foundations of a mnemonic system promoting visual and even aural association. Equally important is that though the author proposes his own associations, he nevertheless recognizes, indirectly, that one's mnemonic associations must be bespoke. Thus does he admonish the reader to connect "whatever you hear" and "what you have learned" with "what you already know" in order to develop within the memory a "connective whole." In other words, the author recommends that his techniques be adapted to the reader's own circumstance to be effective. Albeit in embryonic form, this first record of the Mediterranean art of memory already includes the most vital mnemonic features illustrated earlier: that memory is sensory, that it works via sensory rather than "logical" association, and that all sensory associations should be determined by the rhetor's own experiences, proclivities, and prior knowledge.

The embryonic memory system advanced in *Dissoi logoi* is likely connected via some lost cultural link to the one developed a generation or two earlier (circa 477 BCE) by the lyric poet Simonides of Ceos. Like the technique above, Simonides's includes mnemonic imagery. However, Simonides also conceptualizes a "place" system for storing images. The unexpectedly grisly story of how Simonides invented the art of memory is attested primarily by Roman sources, but Frances Yates notes that engravings on a Greek stele, dated to 264 BCE, verify a Grecian provenance for the tale.[41] As the story goes, Simonides was attending a banquet given by a Thessalonian nobleman. After reciting some ill-received poetry to the host and his guests, Simonides was summoned outside the banquet hall by two fortuitous visitors. Fortuitous because during Simonides's absence, the banquet hall's roof collapsed and killed everyone inside. When relatives came to collect their dead, they discovered that the corpses around the crushed table were so badly maimed that identification was impossible. Simonides, however, was able to recall before his mind's eye the place of each guest at his position around the table, thus allowing him to identify the bodies. His ability to recall the places at which each guest had sat suggested to Simonides that the spatial arrangement of mnemonic images is the key to good memory. Cicero explains: "[Simonides] concluded that those who would like to employ this part of their abilities [memory] should choose localities, then form mental images of the things they wanted to store in their memory, and place these in the localities. In this way, the order of the localities would preserve the order of the things, while the images would represent the things themselves."[42] In this canonical origin story for the memory palace technique, the ars memoria is once more described as an art of deliberate visualization. Note also that Simonides's notion of "ordering" or "arranging" mnemonic images—presuming the guests were seated more or less randomly—remains a *spatial* and *idiosyncratic* endeavor rather than a logical or even a culturally conditioned one.

What we learn from *Dissoi logoi* and the Simonides tale is that, from its earliest development, the Mediterranean art of memory was a method with which one harnessed the visual, idiosyncratic memoryscape and transformed it into a conscious mnemonic practice. It is doubtful that Simonides himself codified the practice of constructing mnemonic images and mental "localities" for the images, or that he invented the concept of visual homophony. The practice in all likelihood predates the classical period. Nevertheless, it makes sense that the agonistic Greeks would have formalized such a mnemonic art and that, in particular, the art would have been popularized within a milieu of lyric poets or itinerant teachers such as the sophists. Whether reciting poetry before nobles or making the worse case appear the better, these ancient orators trafficked in words and knowledge and therefore had need of artificial memory techniques, lest they lose their valuable currency to forgetfulness in the heat of the moment.

Platonic Mnemonic: Iconoclasm and the Memory of Forms

If *Dissoi logoi* and the Simonides tale provide a glimpse of the early establishment of mnemonic practice, Plato and Aristotle provide the first attempts at a mnemonic theory. Plato never examines the art of memory directly, but he has left an implicit trail to follow nonetheless, most prominently in *Phaedrus* and *Meno*.

In the *Phaedrus*, Plato famously describes the tool of writing as a mnemonic aid but censures writing on the grounds that it will not aid men's memories and will in fact make them forgetful. Men will conflate a knowledge of where to find information (in a book) with having acquired knowledge itself, within their own minds. Contra Plato, the ubiquity of the mnemonic arts in Greece and then Rome proves the opposite point. Men and women in antiquity were perfectly aware that information stored in writing is not particularly useful. Ancient Mediterranean society, after all, lacked anything like the content management and information access systems taken for granted today. No Google searches on smartphones. No card catalogs. Not even reference pages! Ancient written culture, with its cumbersome papyrus rolls and slender title slips, looked nothing like contemporary written culture nor even early modern print culture.[43] The Greek poet and scholar Callimachus had this to say about scrolls: "Mega biblio, mega kakon."[44] A big book is a big evil. Hence the need for a personal, inner system of visual organization and mnemonic access. If the argument that writing turns us into forgetful bores were the crux of Plato's theory of memory, it would not be worth dwelling on. However, Plato's complaint about writing in the *Phaedrus* is really two complaints. The one given the most attention—that writing makes men stupid and forgetful—is in fact the less significant of the two, for it occurs in the context of a larger debate about the pursuit of knowledge. What most concerns Plato about writing is its inferiority compared to "living, breathing" *dialectic* as a means of pursuing and obtaining knowledge.[45] This is a more interesting topic.

Plato's comparison of writing and dialectic is relevant to a study of mnemonics, because it introduces the first strands of an ideological thread running parallel to the art of memory: an iconoclastic censure of mnemonic aids as dream images, to use Plato's term, that lull humans into a false security over their knowledge, acting as deceitful imitations of the real thing. Plato's distrust of memory aids, I suggest, inaugurates a skepticism about visual models of information—about all secondary forms of knowledge—that has remained a feature of Western thought down to the present day. A tradition of iconoclastic critique travels alongside the ars memoria throughout its history. It continues today with critiques of pie charts, network graphs, and software interfaces. When Johanna Drucker states that "the rendering of statistical information into graphical form hides every aspect of the original interpretive framework on which the statistical data were constructed,"[46] she is drawing on an iconoclastic tradition that begins here with Plato's critique of the written word—a graphical memory aid so common that we tend to forget that's what it is.

Plato's first issue with writing (that it makes men forgetful) is broached by Socrates with the tale of Theuth, the ibis god. Theuth arrives in Thebes to present his many inventions before the Egyptian king Thamus. Among Theuth's many inventions are arithmetic, astronomy, draughts, and dice, but the greatest of all, according to Theuth, is the "use of letters." King Thamus looks at the ibis's inventions and offers his opinion on each, praising some while censuring others. Presenting his invention of writing, Theuth upholds it thusly: "O King, here is something that, once learned, will make the Egyptians wiser and will improve their memory; I have discovered a potion for memory and for wisdom." King Thamus, however, offers a more skeptical analysis: "Since you are the father of writing, your affection for it has made you describe its effects as the opposite of what they really are. In fact, it will introduce forgetfulness into the soul of those who learn it: they will not practice using their memory because they will put their trust in writing, which is external and depends on signs that belong to others, instead of trying to remember from the inside. . . . You provide your students with the appearance of wisdom, not with its reality."[47] With this tale, Plato explicitly defines writing as a memory aid. However, in this case, *memory aid* possesses a negative connotation. Socrates goes on to concede that external mnemonic cues are fine for people in old age who have gained knowledge but simply need a reminder about it as their minds weaken. For everyone else, the memory aid called writing will produce the conceit of wisdom without the reality. People will presume to know something simply because they know where to find it—in a scroll somewhere (or, today, on Wikipedia). A mnemonic cue for knowledge, however, is not knowledge, which properly proceeds "from the inside," on one's own, through practice. Remembering where knowledge is stored as a cue is a pale imitation of holding knowledge in one's own mind, according to Socrates.

This objection to writing qua mnemonic aid is, to repeat, valuable only insofar as it relates to Plato's other, primary objection in the *Phaedrus*: if remembering where knowledge is stored as a mnemonic cue is a pale imitation of holding knowledge itself in one's mind, then knowledge gained through reading a text (or listening to a prepared oration) is a pale imitation of knowledge generated through in-person dialectic. To clarify his position, Socrates compares a text to a painting: they both seem to say something, but if you try to question or speak to them, they remain mute. Writing signifies the same thing forever. Whatever purported knowledge lies therein, the text cannot clarify itself to a curious reader, cannot defend itself, and cannot simplify things for a simple reader or expand on them for a more intelligent one.[48] It is for those reasons an unsuitable medium for discovering knowledge, which requires not passive receptivity but critical questioning. As Claire Lauer says of conversation, "one is simultaneously privy to both product and process. The listener is compelled to proceed at the pace the speaker chooses. They follow the speaker's thinking and reflecting process, and experience knowledge as a happening."[49]

Keep in mind that, for Plato, the primary goal of life is to gain knowledge of the good, the just, the noble, the transcendental true. Any medium or practice encouraging the pursuit of such knowledge, he finds valuable; any medium or practice hindering it, he censures. Plato, through Socrates, is not denying that written texts may contain knowledge of the good and the just. The problem is that when most souls sit down to read a text (or to listen to an oration), they comprehend but dimly the knowledge existing therein. From this dim comprehension, the fool assumes he has gained wisdom, when he has done nothing of the sort; the self-aware reader recognizes that he has understood but dimly and will now demand elucidation, explanation, amplification, examples, and clarifying analogies—in short, he will demand a dialogue the text cannot provide. To be sure, many texts invite discussion and debate; but as mediums, writing and oratory encourage passivity and uncritical acceptance. Recall the entire premise of the *Phaedrus*: Lysias's speeches have been lulling young Phaedrus into uncritical approval of the purported knowledge inscribed within them.

For Plato, *dialectic* is the ideal practice, the best method to discover the just, the good, the noble, the true. It is an active and critical process. It brings seekers of knowledge into unmediated contact with the philosophers who possess it.

SOCRATES: Now tell me, can we discern another kind of discourse, a legitimate brother of this one [writing]? . . . It is a discourse that is written down, with knowledge, in the soul of the listener; it can defend itself, and it knows for whom it should speak and for whom it should remain silent.

PHAEDRUS: You mean the living, breathing discourse of the man who knows, of which the written one can be fairly called an image?

SOCRATES: Absolutely right.[50]

Socrates then says that the knowledgeable man—the man who knows what is just, noble, and good—will in fact refuse to re-mediate his knowledge into ink on papyrus. Indeed, the man who re-mediates his knowledge into the memory aid called writing deserves reproach, particularly if the text creates passive acceptance in its audience. "For to be unaware," Socrates says, "of the difference between a dream-image [writing] and the reality of what is just and unjust, good and bad, must truly be grounds for reproach, even if the crowd praises it with one voice."[51] The "reality" of the just and the unjust, the good and the bad, Plato is saying, can be apprehended only through dialectic, the "living, breathing" ritual of give and take, call and response, point and counterpoint, elucidation, explanation, and clarification through example and analogy. Only in interactive fleshspace can one draw near true knowledge. Like idols, the icons of the papyrus imitate and for that reason hinder understanding of truth.

If Plato finds fault with writing qua mnemonic aid, what would be his opinion of the ars memoria? After all, in the story of King Thamus, Plato censures writing by comparing it to the practice of remembering "from the inside, completely on [one's] own."[52] It seems at first glance that a technique of inner visualization—of converting the mind into a virtual library—would count as remembering "from the inside." Regrettably, Plato never offers a direct opinion on mnemonic imagery. The closest he comes is a brief reference in the *Hippias* dialogues to Hippias's "artful technique of memory." (Socrates seems unimpressed by the technique and even less so by the extravagant historical stories Hippias has memorized with its aid.)[53] Nevertheless, across his dialogues—most notably the *Meno*—Plato leaves enough evidence to construct a hypothetical Platonic take on visual mnemonics. Unsurprisingly, his opinion mirrors his low view of writing. The opinion cannot be reconstructed in brief, but it is worth examining because, as noted, it introduces an important counterhistory of memory that distrusts mnemonic imagery on iconoclastic grounds.

For Plato, dialectic is the soundest practice for gaining or at least approaching knowledge of the good, the just, the essential truths of the universe. In the *Meno*, however, Plato provocatively equates dialectic with *recollection*. He does so in the context of a dialogue between Socrates and Meno concerning the paradox of knowledge: How can one productively inquire into a thing—in their case, the nature of virtue—about which one knows nothing or very little? Just as one needs to know what object one is looking for in order to go looking for it, doesn't one need to already know something about virtue before inquiring into it (in which case there is little need to inquire at all)? To solve this riddle, Socrates likens the pursuit of moral knowledge to the pursuit of mathematical knowledge. He discourses with an enslaved boy, who has never been taught geometry yet learns to solve a geometry problem with help from Socrates through the step-by-step dialectical process of question and answer, trial and error, and attempt, failure, and reattempt.[54] The procedure should be a familiar one. Dialectical training is how most American children learn their figures. I was not taught a theory of mathematical proofs when learning to add. I was given addition tables and various problems to work through on my own, the teacher responded to and corrected my work, she then moved on to more difficult addition tables, and so on. Eventually, without ever being taught to add higher numbers, I nevertheless "knew" that $258 + 312 = 570$. Or, at any rate, I knew how to figure it out "from the inside." I had hit on the *concept* of adding that would assist me no matter what particular numbers need adding. This sort of "aha!" moment is what Socrates seems to have in mind when he demonstrates that an enslaved boy who knows no geometry can yet come to apprehend geometrical knowledge "within himself,"[55] in his own mind, through dialectic. And if an enslaved boy can learn geometry through dialectical reasoning, then he should be able to use this method to attain other sorts of knowledge, including moral knowledge, such as the nature of virtue, what is noble in life, what is good or bad, and so on.

Working from his demonstration with the enslaved boy, Socrates answers the initial epistemological riddle. It remains true that one cannot search productively for a thing one does not already know, for one would wander pointlessly; and so, if a boy without geometry training can solve a geometry problem through dialectical reasoning, knowledge of geometry must have existed already somewhere in his mind. His "aha!" moment was a moment not of learning but of rediscovery. All knowledge capable of being apprehended, Socrates concludes, must in fact already be ensconced in our minds. And thus dialectic must be a process whereby men do not learn so much as recollect what they already know—slowly at first, seeing truth dimly, but moving closer and closer to it as recollection blossoms into full-blown memory of transcendental knowledge (such as my memory of addition, which I apparently "recollected" in elementary school).

However, if knowledge ensconced in the mind was not gained in the present life, from whence did it come? Socrates answers: it must have been gained in the life before this one. The soul, Socrates concludes, must be immortal. "If the truth about reality is always in our soul," he says, "the soul would be immortal so that you should always confidently try to seek out and recollect what you do not know at present."[56] This final move toward theism needn't be dwelled on to appreciate the larger point: dialectic is presented in the *Meno* as a process of *remembering* knowledge hidden in the mind. For Plato, states Janet Coleman, "all knowledge is latent in the mind and is never forgotten. . . . The fixed, logical structure of truth is there to be recovered from our memories."[57] And dialectic is the recovery process. Dialectic emerges in the *Meno* as something like a Platonic practice of memory.

What sort of knowledge does dialectic-cum-recollection unlock from the crevices of memory? Is Plato alluding here to that affective, visual memoryscape that Dr. Lecter wanders in his mind's eye? Is Plato's theory of dialectical recollection compatible with the ars memoria? One needn't be a classicist to recall Plato's Theory of Forms. The Forms have been described and analyzed for centuries, so I will not add much here. Essentially, the knowledge recalled via dialectic is a knowledge of the immutable essence of reality, a knowledge abstracted from the flux of sensual, material existence. In the *Theaetetus*, Plato argues against the Protagorean view that perception is knowledge. Perceptions of the world, like the world itself, are always changing; how can one gain anything like true knowledge of the mutable, fading world of our sense perceptions? One cannot. For Plato, dialectic recalls from memory a knowledge of those abstract principles and structures—the prior ontologies—existing above and below the fluid appearances humans mistake for reality. Coleman again expounds: whatever purported "facts are sensibly experienced and stored in what we might call a personal, individual, subjective memory," Plato would not have considered "knowledge." Knowledge of essences transcends that subjective, image-laden memoryscape and transcends every moment propagated via sensation. Plato's "permanent, knowable reality," Coleman states, "does not alter and is immaterial."[58] That is why it can only be approached— remembered—via dialectic, a literal *speaking across* that transcends not only the subjectivity of the interlocutors but also the subjectivity of the sense world itself.

If dialectic for Plato means remembering the Forms latent in one's memory, and if these Forms transcend sense data, then Plato would have found no value in the memory palace technique or in any other visual or aural mnemonic. Plato does not deny the phenomenon of the personal, idiosyncratic visual associations defined earlier as memory. However, as Coleman goes on to note, the memoryscape, the "capacity to preserve in the memory sensible instances," involves no *understanding*.[59] It is nothing more than passive imprinting, as young Phaedrus has had Lysias's pretty words passively imprinted on his brain. Thus, a Platonic mnemonic would not entail harnessing "dream images" but would rediscover essential concepts existing prior to sensual experience, concepts best recalled to con-

sciousness when the recollective mind is removed from sensory stimu-
lation. To become conscious of the prior ontology, one must ignore its
particular sensible manifestations. Said less cryptically, to become aware
of acute triangles, one must not fixate on the pyramids. To become aware
of the principles of combustion, one must not fixate on a 1967 Stingray
Big-Block V8. Plato's Theory of Forms will in fact make more sense—and
seem entirely defensible—when considered as a theory of mathematics
or physics. The leap to a theory of morality or a theory of justice is a bit
far for most contemporary students.

Dialectical reasoning for Plato means recollecting the immutable, abstract structures of existence, knowledge of which is housed in our souls
from before birth. If this almost divine recollection occurs in the mind,
why on earth would a student pollute his mind with affective images (I
am tempted again to call them idols)? The entire point of dialectic qua
recollection is to exit the sensorium and enter the realm of pure ontology.
Creating palaces and visual associations in the mind would be a wasteful
diversion of rational vitality. The mind is contaminated enough with sense
memories; if a young philosopher desires to move toward the Forms, the
last thing she should do is pollute her mind with a deliberately crafted inventory of imagery. Plato almost certainly would have rejected Simonides's
and *Dissoi logoi*'s art of memory. As the means by which the soul remembers the Forms or *eidoi*, Frances Yates remarks, memory is the "groundwork" of Plato's entire conception of dialectic, so to him "artificial memory as used by a sophist would be anathema, a desecration of memory."[60]
A Platonic art of memory—if such a thing might be postulated—would
not be premised on visual or aural mnemonic models; rather, it would be
organized "in relation to the realities."[61] Indeed, it would be nearly synonymous with philosophy itself.

The tricks of artificial memory, Plato might say, are not designed to recall immaterial absolutes. On the contrary, mnemonic imagery, modeled
on sensible things, hinders direct immersion into the real structures of
existence, just as fixating on a particular addition problem hinders one's
ability to comprehend the abstract method that will allow one to solve
all addition problems. Such idols/images must be shattered if one is to
apprehend an unmediated view of reality's deep structure. As Friedrich
Kittler wrote, two millennia later, about programmable software, the discrete, programmable numbers that give rise to the visual interface reduce
the flux of real numbers as the price of programmable lucidity. If we truly
wish to apprehend the deep structures of reality or "to enter that body
of real numbers originally known as chaos," Kittler states, we must exchange the comfort of programmable visuality for a deep dive into the

"nois[y]" ontologies of existence.[62] His is a Platonic, iconoclastic conjecture through and through. Plato's yearning for unmediated immersion continues to echo across the centuries.

From Milk to White: The Aristotelian Mnemonic

If Plato's distrust of sensory mnemonic aids—writing included—inaugurates an iconoclastic counterhistory to the history of the ars memoria, Aristotle inaugurates a second parallel thread, one that refigures artificial memory as a logical tool. Put briefly, Aristotle retains a place for imagery in his theory of mnemonics but jettisons the idiosyncratic associations and affective qualities of the memoryscape. The result is a theory of mnemonic access that positions imagery as a necessary ingredient in what are otherwise abstract and logical associative chains, what scholars in the nineteenth century would call the "association of ideas."

In *On Memory*, Aristotle distinguishes μνήμης from ἀναμνήσεως, or memory/remembering from reminiscence/recollection, or "being reminded of." This distinction mirrors the rhetorical one between natural memory and artificial memory—that is, between an automatic psychological phenomenon and an active mnemonic practice. Regarding memory, Aristotle claims that sensory experience and theoretical knowledge are imprinted on the soul as images, just as a signet ring imprints its seal on wax. All thought or experience leaves this sort of trace (*phantasma*) of the original conception or perception as time moves forward. The "having" of these images is what Aristotle calls memory.

Memory is not perception or conception itself; rather, it is the imagistic copy or *eikon* humans have of prior perceptions or conceptions. Remembering, then, is the state whereby humans "have an image regarded as a copy of that of which it is an image."[63] According to Aristotle, "madness" is that state wherein one mistakes the image/copy for the real thing; the recognition that the image is an imprinted copy of the real thing generates normal remembrance. Further, it is a copy of the thing as it existed in the past, for remembering also includes the recognition that our images are not only copies of things but also copies of things as they existed before the present.

Neither memory/remembering nor any kind of thought can occur without these imprinted images. Unlike Plato, for whom objects of thought—namely, the Forms—can and should be abstracted away from sensory input and iconic signs, Aristotle believes that all cognition originates in perception. Thus all cognitive processes—including remembering—must bear at least a *phantasma* of an original sense perception.[64] To reiterate an analogy from the last section, Aristotle would claim that thoughts about triangles can never be wholly abstracted away from one's imagistic traces of past perceptions of the pyramids or other triangular objects "in real life." Richard Sorabji explains it this way: objects of thought "reside in physical objects, but the sensible forms within which they reside are received by our sense organs in perception, and after perception is over, the objects of thought reside in images."[65] The contrast to Plato cannot be stressed enough. For Plato, memory qua dialectic may at first make use of images as helpful metaphors, but eventually, memory transcends the need for *eikones* as one recalls the *eidoi*, the essential Forms or structures of reality. For Aristotle, perception is knowledge, and its imagistic traces are essential to thought. Aristotle also does not equate learning with remembering, as Plato does. First one learns or conceives, says Aristotle, then one can remember what one has learned or conceived. Learning is not for him the process of recalling transcendent *eidoi* planted in the immortal soul before birth.

Memory, then, for Aristotle, involves an imprinted image, whether it be of perception or conception, sensory experience or scientific knowledge (for, again, Aristotle argues that even abstract knowledge derives from sensory experience). So how does one access memories at any given time or place, following their initial imprinting? Aristotle terms this process of mnemonic recall ἀναμνήσεως—*anamnesis*, or recollection. It is to some degree similar to the art of memory: it is a conscious practice, based in part on visual association. However, missing from Aristotle's mnemonic theory are principles of affect and idiosyncrasy. Aristotelian anamnesis is a logical process; indeed, Aristotle calls it a "reasoning" and a "sort of search," and his description of it sounds very much like an algorithmic search process rather than an evocative wandering in the eye of the imagination.[66]

When we try to recollect something, states Aristotle, we "hunt for the successor" of the thing, "starting in our thoughts from the present or from something else, and from something similar, or opposite, or neighboring." He goes on: "Recollections occur quickest and best from a starting point. . . . And whatever has some order, as things in mathematics do, is easily remembered."[67] The comparison to mathematics indicates the type of logical process Aristotle has in mind for his theory/practice of recollection. It is a praxis grounded in logical or, at least, culturally conditioned associations and relationships. "People are thought sometimes to recollect from starting places," Aristotle reiterates. He follows up the point this time with an example of what he means: "e.g., from milk to white, from white to air, and from this to fluid, from which one remembers autumn."[68] I confess to not having the slightest idea how Aristotle gets from fluid to autumn, but the first two movements (from milk to white, from white to air) still make sense across the millennia. This associational chain demonstrates that Aristotle's place-to-place recollective movement has little to do with wandering the "places" within a bespoke memory palace. Aristotle is not theorizing here a movement based on personal experience (such as when I moved from a yogurt shop to *A Confederacy of Dunces* in the introduction, or how Simonides moved from one chair to another). Rather, he is operating on the same logical properties that underlie analogy questions (X is to Y as Y is to _____?). Anamnesis, in short, is the practice of following necessary relational chains.

In a subsequent section, Aristotle makes the point more clearly. He presents an abstract scheme in which a man has a series of memories, A, B, C, D, E, F, G, and H. If the man needs to recall H, Aristotle says, then he can begin at F and move through G. Or, further, if he wants to recall E, he can move backward from H through G and F; alternatively, he may begin at B and move through C and D. These associative chains are constructed in the mind based on some rational property: similarity, opposition, adjacency, or distance in time from the present (which Aristotle describes as a magnitude within one's mind). These associational logics exist a priori. Granted, Aristotle's schematic has an implied spatial quality to it, but even if one squints, one cannot discern in his letters anything like the bespoke imagery and loci of a memory palace. More importantly, Aristotle's anamnesis is predicated on the search for a specific desideratum: "after going to C, he will remember if he is searching for D or B."[69] The associative chain that begins with "from milk to white" ends in remembering "autumn, the season one is seeking." The Google search bar or the Find feature in a text document thus provides a good metaphor for Aristotelian mnemonics. The user knows the specific passage she is looking for, and she knows a given word occurred in that passage, so she queries that specific word in the search box. Then she scrolls through the results panel until she locates the specific passage she had in mind from the beginning. The remembered word leads her directly to the passage she wants; it is the C that brings her to D. Of course, unlike the Find feature, Google and other database-search tools can be used to locate not only a specific desideratum but also a "previously unknown match to information"; indeed, one of the key benefits of web search, according to information designers Pamela Ravasio and Vincent Tscherter, is that such searches recall more than a single "100 percent hit," providing the user instead with many close matches that she can browse more serendipitously.[70] I will say more on this distinction between "100 percent hit" searching and serendipitous browsing in chapters 5 and 6. Aristotle's *On Memory* has little to say about it. For Aristotle, mnemonic recall means a singular search for a specific thing through a chain of necessary associations. He does not discuss the idiosyncratic, affective, visual associations of the memoryscape, nor does he suggest using those bespoke associations for the purposes of inventio, creative inspiration, or serendipitous browsing (to reiterate the digital metaphor).

Nearly two thousand years later, but well before the advent of personal computing, the Victorian mnemonist Alphonse Loisette published a system very much like Aristotle's, with even more principles of relation that one could use to connect mnemonic steps to locate a particular item in one's memory bank. Loisette calls these relations the "Laws of Memory":

Inclusion: (Earth, Poles.) (Ship, Rudder.) (Forest, Trees.)
Exclusion: (Hot, Cold.) (Old, Young.) (Health, Sickness.)
Concurrence: (Lightning, Thunder.) (Socrates, Hemlock.) (Wedding, Slippers, Cake.).[71]

He provides many such examples. The idea is to associate or connect new information with these preexisting associative pairs. Once done, a person could simply follow Loisette's "logical" chains, recalling the associated information along the way. Chapter 4 explores nineteenth-century memory culture in more detail. For now, it is enough to note that this culture is an elaborate development of Aristotle's theory of recollection. It is devoid of affect; its associations are ultimately logical, not idiosyncratic or visual (even if Aristotle assumes that *eikones* play a default role in the process of logical association); and, most importantly, it is predicated on a "search" for some particular item in memory and has nothing to say about utilizing the visual memoryscape as an aid to creativity. To be fair, Aristotle's account of recollection is so abstract that it is not entirely clear if he intends his readers to adapt it to their own mnemonic associations; however, in my view, his alphabet schematic and the example of moving from "milk to white" indicate that Aristotle has in mind not the peculiar connections constituting individual memory but rather a universal set of associative logics that should form the basis of recollection.

To be fairer still, these universal associative sets (milk to white; hot to cold; lightning to thunder; Socrates to hemlock) do make use of imagery and are similar to the thematic associations offered in the *Dissoi logoi* ("if you want to remember courage, think of Ares and Achilles"). Aristotelian recollection—like nineteenth-century memory culture—is closer in conception to the memory palace technique than Plato's theory of dialectical recall of ontological structures. It is also much closer in spirit to the ars memoria than the Ramist technique of methodical arrangement, which I explore in chapter 3. Nevertheless, it is a mistake to conflate Aristotle's anamnesis with the memory palace technique. The former is a process of logical association that enables a "hunt" or "search" for particular pieces of information; the latter is a conscious harnessing of the chaotic, idiosyncratic, emotionally charged memoryscape, so as to convert it into an info palace one can wander at will, for creative purposes.

Loci et Imagines in Rome

The conflation of order with necessary, logical order and the conflation of association with necessary, logical association lie at the heart of much confused writing on the memory palace technique. (Paolo Rossi and Walter Ong are guilty of these conflations; even Mary Carruthers, who otherwise provides some of the most lucid descriptions of the ars memoria's emotional and personal characteristics, veers occasionally into a rational rendering of the technique.) The fullest conceptual model of the memory palace technique emerges among the Latins, and it is clear in their texts that although the memory palace makes use of orders and associations, these are (a) sensory in nature, (b) constructed by the user's own proclivities, and (c) more useful for creative inventio than for rote recall.

Rhetorica ad Herennium, Cicero's *De oratore*, and Quintilian's *Institutio oratoria* are the three Latin texts offering the most complete picture of the Mediterranean practice of memoria. The most detailed source is *Ad Herennium*, written circa 90 BCE. The distinction between natural and artificial memory, emphasized earlier in this chapter, is articulated unequivocally in this early text: "There are, then, two kinds of memory: one natural, and the other the product of art [*una naturalis, altera artificiosa*]. The natural memory is that memory which is embedded in our minds, born simultaneously with thought. The artificial memory is that memory which is strengthened by a kind of training and system of discipline."[72] The anonymous author explains that artificial memory is a method of improving the abilities bestowed by nature, similar to the artificial methods used by athletes to improve their natural bodies. The practice of artificial memory therefore "strengthens" the natural memory, according to *Ad Herennium*, "by a system of discipline."[73] Like most ancient authors, the author of *Ad Herennium* recognizes that one must already be endowed with a natural ability—in this instance, a good memory—if artificial enhancements are to prove advantageous; however, the author believes it is worth propagating the art of memory "to aid the less well-endowed" as much as possible.

As described in *Ad Herennium*, the art of memory uses the two ingredients noted in the Greek sources: places and images (*ex locis et imaginibus*). The locus is the background to the image. It should be a place drawn from private memory and thus easily remembered, such as a familiar house, courtyard, or intercolumnar space (the latter two would have been familiar to our Roman author). On these backgrounds, one places images that are visual re-mediations of whatever information one wants stored in the places. The author also uses the words *formae* and *simulacra* to describe the images. The loci are like wax tablets of the mind, he states; the imagines are like letters engraved upon the tablets.

The precepts for constructing loci are as follows:[74]

(1) Ideally, they should be taken from the rhetor's personal memories, or, if the rhetor feels he hasn't seen enough of the world to construct interesting backgrounds from real life, he should use his imagination. Either way, taken from the memory of real or imaginary experience, the backgrounds should comply with a few basic restrictions.

(2) The background should be modeled on a place that is deserted rather than heavily populated, for "the crowding and passing to and fro of people weaken the impress of the images, while solitude keeps their outline sharp."

(3) Backgrounds should be visually differentiated from one another, for "if a person has [for example] adopted many intercolumnar spaces, their resemblance to one another" will confuse the rhetor as he wanders his memory palace.

(4) They ought to be moderately sized rather than very large or very small, both of which "render the images vague."

(5) They should be neither very bright nor very dim, so that "the shadows may not obscure the images nor the lustre make them glitter."

(6) They should be spaced evenly, for the "inner eye of thought is less powerful when you have moved the object of sight too near or too far away."

(7) Lastly, if the memory palace contains a great number of loci, it may be beneficial to mark them by fives, as, for example, by placing a golden hand on the fifth place, a friend named Decimus on the tenth, and so on. The author here exploits the principles of visual association (hand = five) and of phonetic association or visual homophony (Decimus = a name, or ten), both principles suggested in *Dissoi logoi*.

Clearly, the loci of the memory palace are not constructed according to rational properties but take shape through visual, spatial, and otherwise sensory principles. In addition, movement from place to place is determined not by relational logic but by the rhetorical exigency informing the memory palace's construction: the idea is to be able to follow the physical backgrounds so that one can "deliver orally whatever has been committed to the *loci*."[75] Although many writers have conflated them, Herennian loci are not equivalent to Aristotle's *topoi* in *On Memory* ("e.g., from milk to white, from white to air"). Loci in the memory palace are visual, spatial, and aural phenomena; Aristotelian topoi are rational, abstract, and only incidentally sensory. Reading *Herennium*'s memory section, one cannot conclude that the text intends its readers to formulate logical associative chains or to "search" for specific desiderata. Rather, the author intends his readers to draw from personal memory—as Dr. Lecter draws from his Italian travels—to imagine a literal, physical series of spaces upon which the rhetor can position mnemonic simulacra of whatever she needs to re-member.

The simulacra, the imagines, the mnemonic imagery placed upon the loci should be equally personal and imaginative. *Ad Herennium*'s rules for constructing mnemonic imagery are as follows:[76]

(1) Mnemonic images can re-mediate both general information, content, or subject matter (*res*) and individual words (*verba*). However, our author warns against using imagery for rote, word-by-word memorization. He only mentions the possibility, not "to enable us to get verse by rote, but rather as an exercise whereby to strengthen that other kind of memory, the memory of *res*, which is of more practical use." Mnemonic imagery, in short, is best used for recalling general information or content. As emphasized earlier, the ars memoria is a technique for mnemonic access, not a trick of rote memorization.

(2) Imagines can be constructed on principles of either visual association or phonetic similarity (which, again, Carruthers calls visual homophony). For example, to remember the charges against a defendant on trial for murder by poison, the author suggests creating an image of a murder scene, each legal charge visualized within the scene (including a man lying on his deathbed, "holding in his hand a cup" to remember the poison). In addition to this straightforward visualization of legal charges, the author also suggests imagining ram's testicles to remember the purported witnesses to the event (*testiculi* suggests *testes*, or witnesses; ram's testicles were also used to make purses, so perhaps the author is implying that the witnesses were bribed, a good defense for a lawyer).

(3) Imagines should be made striking and emotionally stirring. The author recommends constructing imagery that is exceptionally beautiful, ugly, comic, colorful, or perhaps violent—by, for example, smearing blood on the subjects in the images. The author notes that "incidents from childhood" will often supply the most effective emotional imagery.

(4) Lastly, and related to the previous point, the images must be be-

spoke, their precise forms dictated by the rhetor's experiences and procliv-ities. Speaking against a Greek textbook tradition—now lost—of listing many images corresponding to certain words, the author of *Ad Heren-nium* asks rhetorically why a teacher would "rob anybody of his initiative [and] deliver to him everything searched out and ready?" After all, what is striking and affective to one person may not be so to another; one per-son's visual associations may not work as associations at all for someone else. "Everybody, therefore," the author concludes, "should in equipping himself with images suit his own convenience." He warns that the exam-ple images provided in his treatise are just that—examples, designed to display the general principles of mnemonic imagery but not to be used by the reader, for whom the work of constructing imagery should be an intensely personal one. As with loci, the imagines in *Ad Herennium* are not constructed from abstract principles of logic or necessary associa-tion. They are sensory, affective, vivid, and conjured from the subjective imagination and one's own past. "We feel that we have moved into an ex-traordinary world," Frances Yates remarks, "as we run over his places . . . , imagining on the places such very peculiar images."[77] Well . . . peculiar to her. And that's the point.

In *De oratore*, Cicero provides a truncated description of the mem-ory palace technique found in *Ad Herennium*. Nevertheless, he remains adamant about the visual foundations of the ars memoria. As he states, "things . . . can be most easily grasped by the mind, if they are also con-veyed to our minds through the mediation of the eyes."[78] Cicero's story about Simonides—who remembered the mutilated guests by picturing where they had sat around a table—likewise indicates that his concept of mnemonic "arrangement" is visual or spatial and not predicated on abstract relational properties. Nothing in Cicero's story suggests that the guests were seated according to some prior associative rule, as though Si-monides moved in his mind's eye from one guest's loci to the next as Ar-istotle moved between the topoi of milk and white or between the letters B and C.

Writing a few generations after Cicero and *Ad Herennium*, Quintilian is curiously skeptical of the memory palace technique. In his *Institutio or-atoria*, he recommends a comparatively banal mnemonic practice.[79] But his skepticism is curious, in my view, because he seems to grasp the un-derlying mechanism of the memory palace so well. Quintilian is in awe of the power of natural memory. He states in wonder "that so many old facts, revived after so long, present themselves to us once again, not only when we call them up, but sometimes spontaneously, and not only when we are awake but when we are quietly resting." He finds it "extraordinary" how the mind can let slip the recent past yet still vividly recall "events from our boyhood." And it is marvelous, he exclaims, how some things "hide themselves away" in memory before suddenly presenting themselves "quite by chance."[80] In the first paragraphs of his memory section, Quintilian describes the memoryscape the same way I described it earlier: as a visual, idiosyncratic interface connecting us to all the experiences and information stored in our minds. And like the other Latin commentators, Quintilian describes memory as a faculty unconcerned with rote memorization or logical associative chains. Given the extemporaneous demands of legal and political debate, Quintilian states, the orator must be able to access anything at any moment, and he must be able to recall things "as is most advantageous" to the particular rhetorical context. Memory, for Quintilian, is intimately linked to invention: "While we are saying one thing, we have to be looking to what we are to say next, and so, as thought is always going on ahead, it is always thinking something further away, and whatever it finds it commits to the care of Memory."[81] However, despite his theory of natural memory, written in terms so amenable to the memory palace technique, when Quintilian transitions to a discussion of artificial mnemonics, he seems to forget everything he has just written about memory. He begins to expound as though the art were a dry technique for rote, word-by-word memorization, despite Cicero's and *Ad Herennium*'s clear statements to the contrary.

Quintilian first examines the precepts regarding loci, and these, at least, he seems to understand perfectly well. Mnemonic places should be constructed, he states, from one's own experiences and memories of places: "when we return to a certain place, we not only recognize it but what we did there, persons are recalled, and sometimes even unspoken thoughts come back to mind."[82] By attaching new imagery to these familiar spaces of memory, Quintilian recognizes, we turn memory into a mnemonic art. He describes seamlessly the process of harnessing one's visual, spatial memory in order to store material for later recall. So far, so good.

However, when it comes to imagines, Quintilian loses the plot entirely. The spirit of the memory palace detaches itself from him, and he begins complaining about the impossibility of converting every word in a speech into an image. What about functional words? How does one convert conjunctions into images? What about lengthy speeches? Won't the proliferation of images required for extended orations hinder rather than aid the speech's recall? Won't it hinder a graceful, natural delivery? "How can we produce a continuous flow of words if we have to refer to a distinct Symbol for every word?"[83] Quintilian, for some unknown reason, is suddenly writing under the assumption that the art is designed for word-by-word memorization of a speech already composed. That the art is designed to aid recall of anything for any inventive purpose seems all at once alien to him. Given how Quintilian describes natural memory—and given how well he describes the visual and idiosyncratic principles underlying loci—his misunderstanding about mnemonic images is odd.

Just as odd is Quintilian's own bowdlerized mnemonic technique. Instead of re-mediating words and information into imagery, stored in the palace of one's imagination, he recommends forming "images" of the literal tablet or page on which one has written. Better still, he remarks, would be to divide one's speech into short, easily memorized sections and to form images of each section in one's head. Instead of re-mediating words into images, in other words, Quintilian recommends taking a mental snapshot of the page, creating an "image" of words segmented neatly on the scroll or tablet. (Anyone who has memorized lines in a play will immediately recognize this commonsense memorization technique.) The only hint of the Herennian technique that surfaces in Quintilian's system is a recommendation to mark particular section divisions with a literalist symbol of whatever the section is about—for example, an anchor for a passage about nautical matters or a javelin if it is about a battle. (Quintilian calls such symbols *notae*.) Otherwise, the memory palace has been gutted. Indeed, Quintilian himself admits his art bears only "some resemblance" to Cicero's, *Ad Herennium*'s, and *Dissoi logoi*'s art of mnemonic imagery. Gone in his system are the vivid, affective *imagines*. Quintilian has developed instead a system that divides prewritten words into memorizable chunks on the page. This system of textual imagery, as I discuss in subsequent chapters, exerted significant influence on the ensuing Middle Ages as well as on Anglo-Protestant mnemonics in the early modern period.

Memoria et Inventio

As theorized by the Romans—as theorized even in his own bowdlerized way by Quintilian—the art of memory is unlike Aristotle's recollective "search" process and much less like Plato's dialectical memory of immutable *eidoi*. Even with Quintilian's mental snapshots of the written page, Latin mnemonics do not use logic, dialectic, or abstract relational principles to locate specific information or essential truths. Rather, the art of memory is a practice intended to benefit composition, extemporaneous oratory, and inventio in all its guises. It is a practice whereby the rhetor wanders his mind at will, recalling and gathering information in a more creative fashion, as different rhetorical situations demand different information to be recalled. Especially in the context of extemporaneous debate, one never knows beforehand what information one will need to find or, once found, as Quintilian reminds us, what order the information should be addressed in. To be sure, the art of memory could be utilized for rote memorization of already-composed speeches or to locate specific desiderata. However, the primary benefit of the memory palace—a benefit that emerges organically from its visual, spatial form—is that it encourages creative info integration. It encourages serendipitous browsing. Not bound by necessary logics, the rhetor can wander at will, alighting first upon this word, quote, fact, piece of information, now upon that, bringing them all together into a new associative assemblage that might not have suggested itself through a search via rational or algorithmic associations. For that reason does *Ad Herennium* praise memory as a *thesaurum inventorum*—a treasure house of invention. And as Quintilian proclaims, "it is the power of memory alone that brings before us all the store of precedents, laws, rulings, sayings, and facts which the orator must possess in abundance . . . and hold ready for immediate use."[84]

The fact that the art of memory, as an active practice, could bring before the orator an entire store of information and make it "ready for immediate use" indicates, again, that the search bar is the wrong metaphor for the memory palace technique (even as it remains a good metaphor for Aristotle's theory of anamnesis). A search bar metaphor implies that the orator knows precisely what she is looking for and requires as many examples of it as possible. To be sure, the orator may in fact know precisely what she needs, and her memory palace will help her find it. However, the memory palace can also aid the orator who is *not* sure what she needs. Unlike the search bar, the artificially trained memoryscape invites its user to roam widely—drifting first to this piece of information, then to that piece, then back again, looking for creative connections that might prove advantageous within some rhetorical situation. Even if you don't know what you're looking for in the memory palace, you're bound to find something useful for present circumstances. Perhaps a hyperlink metaphor is more appropriate for the ars memoria. The memory palace facilitates what Collin Gifford Brooke calls *proairetic* invention, the (much-maligned) practice of tripping from link to link, from page to page, never lingering for long but forming a tentative web of knowledge assembled from bits of information persisting in short-term memory.[85] Brooke describes the practice as a digital one, but in its ideal configuration, the memory palace likewise aided this sort of quick movement between loci, enabling a rapid assemblage of information into something useful for a given rhetorical endeavor.

The visual, inventive spirit of the Latin treatises allows us to conclude that the *loci et imagines* of the memory palace encouraged rhetors to turn mnemonic recall into an art of bricolage. Re-mediating thought into image made it easier for rhetors to bring together a plethora of materials for invention, either while composing or during the heat of agonistic interaction. For the ancient wanderer of the memory palace, state Mary Carruthers and Jan Ziolkowski, "stored memories are the materials of cognition, and the act of knowing begins . . . with the activities of finding and collecting their 'images' from within one's mind." They continue: "Recollection is not passive, but rather an activity involving human will and thought; . . . [it] was essentially a task of composition literally bringing together matters found in the various places where they are stored to be reassembled in a new place. . . . Memory-making was regarded as active, . . . a craft with techniques and tools."[86] Importantly, however, this craft of memory does not result in a definitive visual model in the mind, a palace built from rationally and thus immutably associated images. Rather, like letters on wax tablets, mnemonic images are mutable and ever changing—"for the images, like letters, are effaced when we make no use of them," states the author of *Ad Herennium*.[87] It was ultimately the principle of visualization that linked memoria and inventio in the classical world. In contrast to Aristotle's rational anamnesis or Plato's dialectical recall of *eidoi*, the memory palace's inventive and affective imagines made knowledge fluid and adaptable; imagines encouraged the integration, composition, and assemblage of knowledge and new patternings of that knowledge. The memory palace was a place to be made, remade, then remade again, as one rearranged, deleted, or added images within it. It was not a place to locate exact information or to follow abstract chains of reasoning. It was a place, rather, to create.

CHAPTER 2

Arts of Memory in the Monastery

Formalized by the poets and sophists of pre-Socratic Greece, the ars memoria was later adopted across the Mediterranean by individuals whose professions demanded quick and robust recall of information. Whether reciting poetry, speaking extempore, making the worse case appear the better, or arguing before the law courts or the senate, ancient orators trafficked in words and knowledge and therefore had need of artificial memory devices, lest they lose their currency to forgetfulness.

With the end of the Pax Romana, however, came an end to the social and political order that had secured public spaces in which (certain classes of) people might speak, listen, and debate. "In the barbarised world," Frances Yates states, "the voices of the orators were silenced."[1] Feudal law and politics, to be sure, remained law and politics.[2] The Middle Ages were not bereft of legal pleading, politicking, or discursive strategy. To claim otherwise would be an oversimplification. However, it is accurate to say that until the expansions of canon and civil law in the late 1100s and 1200s, judicial environments in the Middle Ages did not invite the elaborate, extemporaneous oratory or debate typically associated with rhetorical practice. Nor, then, would medieval contexts have suggested the use of mnemonics as obviously as the Greek or Roman agora had. For example, one practice in medieval law was compurgation. A person accused of wrongdoing could establish nonliability by taking an oath of blamelessness and then gathering a dozen or so persons to swear they believe the oath. Another tenet of medieval law was trial by combat—that is, dueling. Because God would not allow an innocent man to suffer nor a guilty one to prosper, a duel was considered a legitimate way to settle a judicial battle.[3] Then there were the "barbarian codes"—the leges barbarorum—that governed life in medieval Europe: the Byzantine Farmer's Law, the Visigothic Code, and the Laws of London, among others. These were a mixture of older tribal law, Catholic teaching, and only a bit of Roman influence; they left little room for ethos, pathos, logos, or oratorical strategy to act as means of persuasion before a gathering of peers. To be sure, if convincing neighbors to swear by an oath of innocence or challenging an adversary to a duel, one would have profited to some degree from rhetorical skill. But the importance and application of rhetorical arts were less obvious in the feudal world than they had been in the agonistic spaces of Rome and Greece. Indeed, insofar as the primary focus of this chapter is the religious realm rather than the judicial or political one, it is fair to say that medieval mnemonics served not an oratorical but a textual culture. No longer arguing in the courts or declaring in the senate, medieval rhetors found themselves existing within quieter spaces, where reading and biblical contemplation were the advised practices. For the secular rhetor, his text was the means to an oratorical end, a template for a declamation that would involve serious extemporaneous effort. For monks, nuns, and clerics, in contrast, the Bible was both means and end, the most important interlocutor with whom one might engage. This explains why monastic mnemonics took their conceptual cue not from the mental image but, as I show in this chapter, from the written page.

The social ecologies of the classical world gave way to the new ecologies of the Middle Ages, and the ars memoria—along with invention, style, arrangement, and delivery—exited the agora and entered the monasteries. "Every discipline of rhetoric," remarks Nan Johnson, "is a creature of historical circumstances." Rhetorical practices transform in tandem with the societies in which they are embedded; they respond to the "changing needs of societies and cultures, accommodating not only an ever-changing theoretical disposition but also an ever-rearranging coalition of 'traditional' and innovative arts."[4] The transformation undergone by the fourth canon during its medieval migration offers a clear example of Johnson's point. In general, speaking before assemblies and diving into the battle of oratorical debate were no longer required tasks in the monasteries. Nor were monks concerned with the wide-ranging secular knowledge—legal, political, historical, poetic—that had occupied their pagan forebears. What use, then, did monks and clerics find for classical mnemonics? What were the *res et verba* the pious Middle Ages wished to bring before the mind's eye? Yates answers, "Surely they were the things belonging to salvation or damnation, the articles of the faith, the roads to heaven through virtue and to hell through vices. These were the things which it sculptured in places on its churches and cathedrals, painted in its windows and frescoes. And these were the things which it wished chiefly to remember by the art of memory."[5] The art of memory, in other words, was Christianized, put at the service of a more spiritual and less secular life. "Die Mnemotechnik," states Helga Hajdu in her early study of the art of memory, "ist nicht mehr die Kunst des 'Rhetors' und wagt sich nicht mehr an das Unterfangen, Hilfe für das Auspeichern eines . . . lexicalischen Vielwissens zu bieten."[6] The art of memory was no longer the art of "rhetors" but the art of the Christian faithful; the information recalled by mnemonics was no longer of the political or legal sort but was information necessary to vouchsafe one's soul. Heralding Yates and Hajdu, a twelfth-century preaching manual explains that these were indeed the things a cleric must keep in mind when writing or delivering sermons:

> Sometimes as much is accomplished with a discussion of the nature of the vices as with a discussion of the nature of the virtues. . . . The roots, therefore, of every sin ought to be carefully examined, so when the nature of sin is clearly recognized, its opposite, the nature of virtue, will be known with equal clarity. . . . And the more zealously the life which is virtue is pursued, the more carefully the death which is sin will be avoided. No preaching is more efficacious than that which would help man to know himself.[7]

Naturally, the source of knowledge about the vices and the virtues, about damnation and salvation, was a single, divine text. Medieval mnemonic practice thus took its cue not from Cicero's or *Ad Herennium*'s mnemonic imagery but from Quintilian's method of text segmentation. The art of memory had been designed to serve an oratorical culture, but in the monasteries, letter writing, homiletics, and, above all, scriptural meditation replaced public speaking and debate as the dominant modes of inquiry and discourse. Text replaced oratory as the central *medium* of information exchange. As the precepts of classical rhetoric were adapted to these textual arts, the art of memory was similarly "textualized." The memory palace became a place to store words qua words and text qua text. *Verba* supplanted imagines in the memory palace, text replaced re-mediation of text, and the art of mnemonic visualization dwindled in importance. (To introduce a digital metaphor, it is as though the monastics swapped visualizations for spreadsheets.)

This evolution was not a singular event. Nor did it involve only the memory palace technique. Quintilian's text-based treatment of the ars memoria demonstrates that the memory palace was already embedded in a process of social evolution in the classical period. As befits the Darwinian metaphor, the memory palace did not undergo swift alteration in a vacuum but competed and mingled for centuries with other mnemonic systems in a complex ecology of theory and practice. Some of these systems predated the medieval period; others were almost certainly influenced by the technique developed in *Dissoi logoi* and *Ad Herennium*. The diachronic timeline must remain uncertain, but it is an error to conflate the memory palace technique with, for example, mnemonic alphabets or combinatorial arts (as Yates has tended to do). These systems are cousins, not twins. To understand the Christianized or, more accurately, "scripturalized" memory palace, it is necessary to situate the technique within this larger array of artificial memory systems. To mix the Darwinian metaphor, the art of memory existed in the Middle Ages within a constellation of other memory arts. The story of the memory palace's christening is also a story about its contact with these rival mnemonic techniques, to which we must turn to understand the medieval narrative.

The Medieval Mnemonic Landscape

ACROSTICS

One such technique was the acrostic.[8] Products of a literate society, acrostics are compositions in which certain letters—usually the first letter—in each line of an arrangement spell out a word or a message or delineate the alphabet. For example, the first letter in each line of Lewis Carroll's poem "A Boat, Beneath a Sunny Sky" spells out ALICE PLEASANCE LIDDLE, the real-life namesake of Carroll's popular character. Acrostics long predate the Greeks and the Romans. They are found in the Hebrew Tanakh,[9] in Chinese "ring poems,"[10] and in Akkadian sources from ancient Mesopotamia.[11] While not all acrostics have a mnemonic purpose, their underlying principle is that the sounds or marks of individual letters can act as a sort of indexing system, which obviously lends itself to mnemonic use. There is no evidence that Semitic acrostics were designed as conscious memory aids; however, acrostics in Europe have long been a popular device associated with artificial memory. One of the earliest examples of an explicitly mnemonic acrostic is found in William of Sherwood's *Introductiones in Logicam*, written in the 1200s. This treatise contains a well-known acrostic used as a pedagogical tool throughout the late Middle Ages:

Barbara, Celarent, Darii, Ferioque prioris
Cesare, Camestres, Festino, Baroco secundae
Tertia grande sonans recitat Darapti, Felapton
Disamis, Datisi, Bocardo, Ferison, Quartae
Sunt Bamalip, Calames, Dimatis, Fesapo, Fresison.[12]

It's not so much a verse as a list of words and names. In each word, the vowels correspond to and thus summon an Aristotelian syllogism with its major premise, minor premise, and conclusion—*a* standing for the universal affirmative, *e* for the universal negative, *i* for the particular affirmative, and *o* for the particular negative. B*o*c*a*rd*o*, for example, would recall *o* (particular negative) in the major premise, *a* (universal affirmative) in the minor premise, and *o* again in the conclusion:

> Some preacher is not competent;
> Every preacher is a man;
> Therefore, some man is not competent.

Not every possible combination would produce a valid syllogism, but medieval teachers apparently saw value in having their students memorize all the combinations anyway. A much later example of a mnemonic acrostic is found in a 1683 text entitled *The Divine Art of Memory, or The Sum of the Holy Scriptures*. In this text, author John Shaw uses an acrostic system to order alphabetically all the verses in each book of the Bible, the goal being to aid memory of individual verses and chapters (figure 2.1).

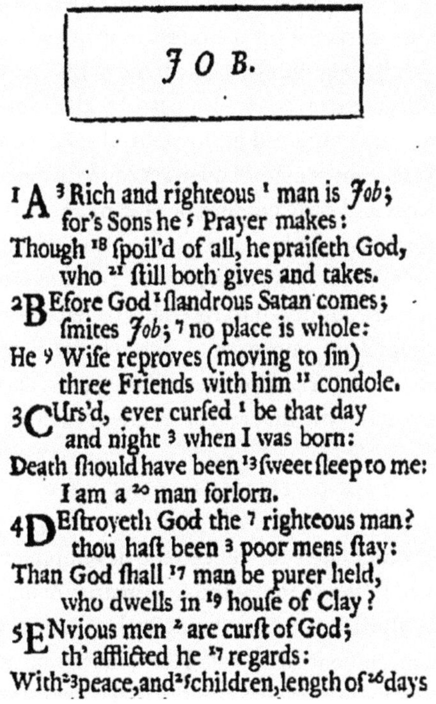

JOB.

1 A [3] Rich and righteous [1] man is *Job*;
for's Sons he [5] Prayer makes:
Though [18] ſpoil'd of all, he praiſeth God,
who [21] ſtill both gives and takes.
2 BEfore God [1] ſlandrous Satan comes;
ſmites *Job*; [7] no place is whole:
He [9] Wife reproves (moving to ſin)
three Friends with him [11] condole.
3 CUrs'd, ever curſed [1] be that day
and night [3] when I was born:
Death ſhould have been [13] ſweet ſleep to me:
I am a [20] man forlorn.
4 DEſtroyeth God the [7] righteous man?
thou haſt been [3] poor mens ſtay:
Than God ſhall [17] man be purer held,
who dwells in [19] houſe of Clay?
5 ENvious men [2] are curſt of God;
th' afflicted he [17] regards:
With [23] peace, and [25] children, length of [26] days

FIGURE 2.1. Alphabetic acrostic in John Shaw's *The Divine Art of Memory*

MNEMONIC ALPHABETS

The utilization of letters on their own, apart from any line of verse, emerged in the Middle Ages as a popular artificial memory technique. Alphabetic mnemonics operate on the same indexing principle as acrostics, each letter functioning as a graphic locus with which one associates information. The minor difference is that while acrostics operate on a principle of graphic correspondence, mnemonic alphabets rely on the principle of linear order. Once learned, an alphabet is a ready-made "place" system that requires no recourse to the invention of verse; it can index information without the incidental similarities between information and letter that acrostics rely on. In *The Book of Memory*, Mary Carruthers compiles copious evidence to demonstrate that alphabets were widely used in the Middle Ages to order material for recollection. "Tables of Greek, Hebrew, Coptic, runic, and even wholly imaginary alphabets," she states, "are found side by side in a number of monastic manuscripts."[13] Each grapheme taken from the various writing systems was used as a mnemonic form to which information was indexed, alphabets serving as alternatives to the loci of the memory palace and the simple notae recommended by Quintilian. One of the most famous medieval practitioners of artificial memory, Peter of Ravenna, boasts at the beginning of his memory treatise that he "placed" twenty thousand legal extracts, one thousand texts from Ovid, two hundred from Cicero, three hundred philosophical sayings, and seven thousand biblical passages onto nineteen letters of the Roman alphabet.[14] In the late Middle Ages and early modern period, memory treatises began to "visualize" alphabets in a manner more amenable to the imagistic precepts in *Ad Herennium*. In these treatises, alphabets are converted into pictures that resemble (or were supposed to resemble) a letter—for example, the end of a pitchfork for *M* or a horn for *C*. Thomas Bradwardine developed the earliest idea of a "pictorial alphabet" in the 1300s, and Jacobus Publicius in the 1400s printed the first real example of such an alphabet.[15]

THE COMBINATORIAL ART

Alphabetic mnemonics likely influenced the development of the *ars combinatoria*, advanced in the 1200s by the Majorcan polymath Ramon Llull. Like a mnemonic alphabet, the combinatorial art indexes information to letters for easy management and recall. However, as one might guess from its name, the ars combinatoria also uses the letters for information integration. The letters enter into a process of permutation whereby information indexed to the letters can be arranged and rearranged in a series of combinations. (This is a highly advanced version of the "combinations" of *a, e, i,* and *o* in William of Sherwood's acrostic verse.) In the final treatment of Llull's system, the combinations are literal: Llull situates the letters into a tiered, combinatorial wheel, allowing its user to move the letters and thus their indexed information into a vast array of permutations or info amalgamations. Llull's and other combinatorial arts will be examined in detail in chapter 4, where I survey the mnemonic tradition's modernization. The history of the ars combinatoria mirrors the ars memoria's transformation in the hands of faculty psychologists and professional mnemonists; both trajectories reveal the "automation" of mnemonic access that occurred after the Renaissance. However, this trajectory does not involve the medieval period, so it would be preemptive to analyze it at this point, beyond recognizing that combinatorial systems emerged in the late Middle Ages, via Ramon Llull, and were influenced by earlier mnemonic alphabets.

BODY MNEMONICS

What might be termed *body mnemonics* also circulated in the Middle Ages, although, like acrostics, similar systems can be found in earlier eras and in cultures beyond Europe (for example, in classical Chinese medical treatises).[16] These systems recommend converting the body itself into a mnemonic place system. One of the earliest European examples is the Guidonian hand, whose invention predates but was associated with Guido of Arezzo, an Italian music theorist writing circa 1000. This is how it works: in order to learn notes up and down the octaves, the student associates individual notes with the natural lines and joints of the inner hand—the music student could then look at her hand to recall the notes, or, conversely, the music teacher could point to different places on a student's hand and the student could sing them.[17] Looking beyond the Guidonian hand, Lina Bolzoni notes that using body mnemonics to impart knowledge of bodily sin was an extant medieval practice.[18] And, of course, the body by necessity played a central role in religious iconography and ritual. Making the sign of the cross on one's chest, for example, was and remains a tool for remembering Bible verses and other religious material. However, it was not until the early modern period that the body became more frequently and explicitly figured as a mnemonic place system. For instance, in Cosma Roselli's *Thesaurus artificiosae memoriae*, the body is numbered from head to toe, with each numbered body part serving as a "place" whereupon one situates information (in Roselli's case, information about nature) (see figure 3.8 in the next chapter). In other Renaissance body mnemonics, the body is figured extravagantly as a microcosm of the universe itself and thus as a mnemonic form capable of recalling a whole universe of knowledge.[19]

RHYMES

Mnemonic rhymes were a more popular device in the Middle Ages. For whatever neurological reason, rhymes are readily impressed on the memory, so it is no surprise that rhymes circulated widely in the monasteries. Monks used rhyming verse, for example, to memorize monastery library catalogs. Around 782, Alcuin of York used this verse to describe the books in the monastery library at Saint Martin's of Tours:

> There shalt thou find the volumes that contain
> All of the ancient fathers who remain;
> There all the Latin writers make their home
> With those that glorious Greece transferred to Rome;
> The Hebrews draw from their celestial stream,
> And Africa is bright with learning's beam.
> Here shines what Jerome, Ambrose, Hilary thought
> Or Athanasius and Augustine wrought.
> Orosius, Leo, Gregory the Great,
> Near Basil and Fulgentius coruscate . . .[20]

And so on for a dozen more lines. Rhymes were particularly popular during the later Middle Ages. Rhyming verses were used by young lawyers, for example, to remember canon law; Alexander de Villedieu (d. 1240) in his *Doctrinale* provides four thousand rhymed hexameters detailing the rules of Latin grammar;[21] even the acrostic line mentioned previously—William of Sherwood's "Barbara celarent darii ferio"—offers a rhyme across four of its lines (secundae, Quartae; Felapton, Fresison).

NOTAE AND TEXT SEGMENTATION

I explained in chapter 1 that Quintilian's reasonable advice for memorizing an oration—though it misses the creative point of the art of memory—is to divide the whole text into smaller, easily memorized parts. Quintilian grants that one way to remember the location within the whole of a "particularly difficult" segment is to mark it with a shorthand symbol or notae—for example, an anchor for a passage on navigation or a javelin for one on battle. When Quintilian describes notae to mark segmented passages for remembrance, he seems to be talking about simple, literalist iconography. Quintilian's notae are nothing like the affective imagery or the immersive loci of the memory palace technique. Words and information in his system are not re-mediated into images, and images are not situated within the three-dimensional spaces of personal memory. Notae, for Quintilian, function more like stenographic shorthand. Indeed, he circuitously[22] compares his notae to the shorthand systems employed in ancient Rome: the *sigla* system, which used single letters to represent words, and the famous Tironian notes, which utilized an elaborate inventory of primary and appended strokes to abbreviate functional words, syllables, and so on.[23] Quintilian's notae are like shorthand picture-symbols, to be used, if necessary, as representations of certain text segments.

Quintilian likewise makes a roundabout connection between his pictorial notae and the shorthand symbols used by the memory artist Metrodorus of Scepsis, a contemporary of Cicero. As Quintilian describes, Metrodorus had developed a personal mnemonic art using the zodiac as loci into which he placed information to be remembered.[24] Quintilian implies, however, that Metrodorus positioned in his loci not mnemonic imagery but shorthand writing—the Tironian notes. Scrawling stenographic notae within each of the 360 degrees of the zodiac in his mind's eye, Metrodorus of Scepsis performed many substantial memory feats, for which he was famous. He receives nods from Quintilian, Cicero, and Pliny the Elder, among others. Like Quintilian's own bowdlerized technique, Metrodorus's shorthand-on-the-zodiac system finds its origin in the ars memoria but is not synonymous with it. It is, in Yates's memorable description, a "bastard descendant of the classical art."[25] Today, Metrodorus's system seems comically elaborate. However, if we exercise our imaginations and place ourselves into a medieval mind-set, we can appreciate that a memory system based on symbols in the zodiac "sounds rather awe-inspiring and might give rise to rumors of magical powers of memory"—as it did give rise to them.[26]

In the Middle Ages, notae evolved in a benign direction into stenographic symbols and abbreviations. Compressing language into a more compact form, these shorthand systems were understood as memory aids, and collections of these marks "were taught as *notatoria* to ancient and medieval notaries and lawyers; students were taught the complex system of Latin abbreviations that we encounter in all medieval manuscripts."[27] However, thanks to the shorthand associated with Metrodorus's zodiac, notae were also linked with a more occult memory art—a conflation that eventually contributed to the vilification of visual mnemonics. While shorthand flourished as a text-based memory aid, notae in the Scepsian sense were to be associated in the Middle Ages and early modern period with the devilish *ars notoria,* or notorious art. We will return to this intricate evolution at the end of this chapter and explore its consequences in chapter 3.

Notae, acrostics, body mnemonics, mnemonic alphabets, and memorable rhymes—these devices circulated at various times and in various places during the Middle Ages, composing an extended family of artificial memory systems. (Others could be added—for example, the wide array of musical mnemonics or the tradition of folk remedies for improved memory.) Although they should be recognized as separate techniques, all mnemonics operate according to the basic rules of human psychology and thus share obvious resemblances; many facilitate information access via information compression, functioning like indexing systems or as "code and filing schemes," to use Carruthers's description.[28] All of them work, at a minimum, by associating information with or re-mediating information into a more compact form. It is also worth pointing out that any given memory treatise in history may recommend more than one technique or combine techniques to make an original contribution. For example, a fourteenth-century treatise by Robert of Basevorn entitled *The Form of Preaching* combines imagery and acrostics in its example of how to remember homilies. And Peter of Ravenna's *The Phoenix* discusses his use of both mnemonic alphabets and affective imagery—in particular, "fayre maydens" remembered from "whan I was yonge" who "excyte greatly my mynde." A maiden named "Junipere," Peter admits, presents to him a particularly useful mnemonic image.[29] Insofar as these and all memory techniques emerged alongside or were influenced by older traditions of artificial memory, each may be said to form one branch in the family of human mnemonics.

Memory of the Word

However, of all the mnemonic devices circulating throughout the medieval world, the most widely practiced was Quintilian's *text segmentation* method. Recall once more Quintilian's advice for memorizing an oration: divide the whole into smaller parts. The subdivisions should not be too lengthy, Quintilian counsels, nor should they be too short, "otherwise they will be too many in number."[30] It is here one finds the earliest description of a commonsense technique familiar to anyone who has memorized lines in a play: segmenting a text into small, easily memorized chunks. Quintilian implies that dividing passages literally on the page and then recreating the divisions in mental page space is the best way to go about it. As noted, he allows for notae, literalist shorthand icons, to mark certain "difficult" segments for later recall (an anchor, a javelin). Otherwise, Quintilian's system is devoid of imagery.

Throughout the Middle Ages, similar systems continued to eschew *imagines* in favor of mental snapshots of the divided page, though medieval scholars tended to utilize numbers rather than iconic symbols to mark their segments. For example, both Saint Augustine (d. 430) and Saint Jerome (d. 420) refer to Psalms numbering in a way that suggests it was a taught mnemonic device;[31] early Christians, it seems, were segmenting the scriptures into chapter and verse as a mnemonic practice long before that became a widespread citation practice. Another good example of a text segmentation system is found in a treatise by Hugh of Saint Victor (d. 1141). In Hugh's system, the student is to form in his mind a sort of mental grid numbered from 1 to 150, each numbered space corresponding to one of the Psalms. The student is then to attach the incipit of each psalm to its proper number, the incipit being the right amount of text that can be seen in a mental glance. Thusly does the student create a mental trellis, so to speak, enabling him to recall which psalm is which and in what numerical order each appears in the Bible. Then, in a separate mnemonic space, the student is to overlay a larger grid structure onto each psalm, further subdividing each into its own numbered segments—a verse-by-verse trellis to accompany the chapter-by-chapter one. The idea is to divide Psalms "into a fixed number of sections," because what the mind cannot recall in a single expanse it can recall in brief, segmented, numbered units. Once the psalms have been judiciously secured in these nested mental grids, the student will be able to recall them at will, "retain[ing] the whole series one verse at a time," as Hugh states, "first by dividing and marking off the book by [whole] psalms and then each psalm by verses."[32]

These text segmentation systems and other writing-based memory devices circulated more widely in the Middle Ages than did the memory palace technique. To be sure, mnemonic segmentation was not wholly unlike the memory palace, at least as segmentation came to be practiced in the monasteries. As we shall see, both techniques recognized the importance of emotional resonance for sharpening the things to be recalled from memory, both were concerned with *memoria rerum* (recalling the gist of things or general content) rather than rote memorization, and practitioners of both techniques recognized that facilitating creative *inventio* was the real purpose of any mnemonic device. Nevertheless, text segmentation differed from the memory palace technique in one important respect. As chapter 1 detailed, the art of memory transformed information into images. It situated mnemonic imagery within an equally visual, three-dimensional mental space. The art of memory was an art of visualization—an art of graphic info re-mediation. Medieval text segmentation, in contrast, was two-dimensional. It divided information, split it up, perhaps allocated it into grid-like structures, but did not convert it into imagistic form. The "imagery" of the segmentation method (like the "imagery" of mnemonic alphabets or acrostics) remained an image of text qua text and of words qua words.

Textual mnemonics, however, were more than suitable for Christian Europe, whose memory practices targeted a very specific text on which was inscribed everything the faithful could want to know: "the articles of the faith, the roads to heaven through virtue and to hell through vices."[33] The Bible, the written words of God, and perhaps the scattered writings of the church fathers or a particular set of monastic rules—these were what the pious scholars of the Middle Ages wanted to impress on their memory. The exigencies of information management, recall, and integration arose no longer in the context of oratorical debate and performance but in the context of reading, listening to, and meditating on *text*. Whereas classical rhetors found their papyrus rolls *mega kakon*, or at least mildly cumbersome, Christians cherished the word of God and saw no reason to re-mediate its lexical form when managing and applying its divine information. Whereas classical rhetors needed to recall information from a vast number of texts across many genres, as well as nontextual information in the form of shifting political and legal pressures, monastics primarily wanted to recall the biblical canon. To be sure, some monastics in the late Middle Ages, as I have clarified, required mnemonic access to a more complex body of canon or civil law. However, during most of the medieval period and for most monks, nuns, and priests, the scriptures alone provided the information they impressed on their minds. About the medieval practice of composing homilies and prayers, Mary Carruthers states the following: "Monastic rhetoric . . . conceives of composition in terms of making a 'way' among 'places' or 'seats' or as climbing the 'steps' of a ladder. These 'places' most commonly take the form of short texts from the Bible, or of stories also taken from that source."[34] And these "places" of a religious composition, Carruthers explains, emerge from the "places" of one's constructed memory of the text from which they derived. What the medieval rhetor situates in his mnemonic loci, therefore, are passages from scripture—written words. Medieval rhetors were given the same advice for memoria that Quintilian gave Roman rhetors: to form a mental image of the page on which the words were inscribed.[35]

Most rhetorical precepts were similarly adapted to scripture in the Middle Ages.[36] The Carolingian abbot Rabanus Maurus remarks that although rhetoric in the ancient world denoted "skill in speaking well concerning secular matters in civil cases," the art should not be avoided by clerics wishing to "treat the divine law adequately and skillfully. . . . The fact is that he is doing something worth while if he studies [rhetoric] diligently so that he may be fitted to preach the word of God."[37] Rhetoric concerned now with "treating the divine law" and "preaching the word of God," the word was precisely what the medieval rhetor needed to situate into his mnemonic system. Words replaced *imagines* in the medieval memory-scape. The composition and delivery of a sermon or prayer became intimately bound to—if not synonymous with—a person's active memory of the Bible. "Preaching," remarks the twelfth-century theologian Alain de Lille (Alan of the Isles), "grow[s] from the spring of the sacred text." It must include expertise "in both Testaments" and should only occasionally draw from other sources.[38] Likewise Thomas of Citeaux, a Cistercian mystic, states, "The preacher must have mastered the words with which to propose doctrine," but these words should be assembled primarily from the preacher's "knowledge of sacred scripture."[39] The Benedictine monk Guibert de Nogent puts it even more forcefully: "Let us speak, therefore, if we have acquired any knowledge of the sacred pages, as inspired by God, that is, as recognizing God is the foundation of all we say. After all, if there is any obligation incumbent upon the instructor of souls, it is that he ought to speak only of God."[40] And where did the preacher find the knowledge by which he might speak authoritatively of God? Only in the sacred text of holy scripture. He must therefore at all times have been impressing on his memory the divine writ.

This goal of scriptural mastery—of a robust memory of the Bible—informed all homiletic and rhetorical training and indeed all learning in the Middle Ages. In his description of the seven liberal arts, Honorius of Autun, another twelfth-century theologian, pictures them—grammar, rhetoric, arithmetic, music, astronomy, and so on—as "cities" through which an exiled soul travels on the way to its final stop, the "fatherland," which is the Bible itself: "Having followed the liberal arts, we reach our homeland, true wisdom, which shines forth from the pages of Holy Scripture. . . . After passing through all these arts, as through so many cities, we come at last to the Sacred Scriptures, our true fatherland, where wisdom rules in all its aspects."[41] In a similar way, Alain de Lille likens the soul's movement from conversion toward a full Christian life as a ladder rising from earth to heaven. After three confessionary rungs on the ladder of life, the remaining rungs are grounded entirely in scripture—the study of scripture, the interpretation of scripture, the presentation of scripture to others, and, finally, the preaching of scripture. The Bible, in short, played a central role in the intellectual lives of monastics, clerics, and even the laity. It was to be studied and emulated, studied and emulated, and then studied again. Medieval Europe was a world resplendent with *scriptural mnemonic vision* and the quiet spaces of meditative reading, preaching, and listening. It is therefore no wonder that the monastics adopted not the imagistic precepts of the classical ars memoria but text-based or broadly "verbal" mnemonic devices: rhymes and songs, mnemonic alphabets, and, of course, text segmentation. These enabled monks and nuns to fill their minds with the words of the Bible, the image of the codex page.

When medieval authors use the word "visual" to refer to mnemonic practice, Carruthers states, "it is the act of reading words that they have in mind."[42] When it came to mnemonic practice, they believed, as a rule, that it was "better to remember the things themselves (the actual words of a text) than to adopt [the] cumbersome, confusing method" taught by Cicero or *Ad Herennium*.[43] The "essential work of *memoria*," Carruthers continues, became the act of reading and of reading the scriptures in particular.[44] In his *Conferences*, for example, the fourth-century ascetic John Cassian does not recognize "any substantive distinction between images and words" when it comes to artificial memory. Cassian's chosen analogy for a disciplined memory is a child's memory of her alphabet copied out onto wax tablets. Similarly, Geoffrey of Vinsauf states that the best way to make material memorable to students is not to rely on Cicero's "theory of exotic images" but to utilize a text segment-by-segment method more or less identical to Quintilian's. (Like Quintilian, Geoffrey of Vinsauf assumes that the goal of mnemonics is to facilitate rote memorization rather than to aid creativity.) Geoffrey even disparages the memory palace technique, claiming that Cicero was likely its "sole devotee" and that he taught no one but himself.[45] Other medieval scholars suggest that, rather than mental phantasms or three-dimensional palaces in the mind's eye, the most sensible bases for mnemonic associations are lexical tropes and figures—antithesis, chiasmus, antemetabole, and so on.[46] Even the Cistercians' oft-observed iconoclasm was grounded not so much in antipathy toward imagery but rather in a belief that the text of scripture—not paintings or sculptures—should provide the "imagery" that inhabits one's mind.[47] The cloisters and monasteries, it is clear, did not receive the memory palace inviolate, in full Herennian form, but rather adopted a Quintilianesque "textual" or "scripturalized" version of the technique. Medieval men and women cleared imagery from their memory palaces and clad them in scripture instead (albeit in a scripture that resonated in emotional, sensory ways—more on that later). No longer immersed in the imagistic specters of the three-dimensional memoryscape, medieval religious implemented an art by which they instead "[saw] their *read-*

ing via cognitive-memorial images."[48] They replaced loci et imagines with mental snapshots of a subdivided page. This monastic preference for text memory characterized medieval mnemonics until quite late, circa the 1200s, when writers such as Albertus Magnus, Thomas Aquinas, and John of Garland returned a receptive eye to the memory palace technique. Until then, however, and even subsequently—evidence for the centrality of text memory continued to surface in the late Middle Ages—the codex page and the words inscribed upon it remained the ideal mnemonic cues in the monastic mind.

Hugh of Saint Victor provides a good example of the medieval penchant for textual as opposed to visual mnemonics. I have already mentioned Hugh's grid technique, with which the student is to sort Psalms into a series of nested grids, first by chapter, then by verse. The system appears in Hugh's *De tribus maximis circumstantiis gestorum*, which Carruthers translates as "The Three Best Memory Aids for Learning History." In relation to this book's primary theme, what is intriguing about Hugh's treatise is that despite its brilliant attempt to lay out Psalms into a protospreadsheet of the mind, its author seems otherwise oblivious to what, in my view, would have been the obvious mnemonic cues saturating the codex page. Writing in the 1200s, Hugh likely would have been working with the brightly illuminated manuscripts for which the late Middle Ages are famous. However, nowhere in his treatise does he suggest that the rich, gilded illustrations might themselves be useful for forming a memory of the Psalter. He recommends, amusingly, that the student instead pay attention to the Psalter's *font*:

> Have you ever noticed how a boy has greater difficulty impressing upon his memory what he has read if he often changes his copy [of a text] between readings? Why should this be unless it is because, when the image-receiving power of the heart is directed outward through the senses into so many shapes from diverse books, no specific image can remain within [the inner senses] by means of which a memory-image may be fixed? ... Therefore it is a great value for fixing a memory-image that when we read books, we strive to impress on our memory through the power of forming our mental images not only the number and order of verses or ideas, but at the same time the color, shape, position, and placement of the letters.[49]

Hugh attempts here a brief theorization of mnemonic imagery, but it remains in the end a writing-centric treatment. For Hugh, visualizing page space does not include forming mental pictures of the actual *imagery* found in illuminated manuscripts. The color, shape, and position of the *letters* remain his mnemonic focus. The emphasis on text memory in this passage typifies medieval mnemonics.

An important caveat must be noted. Even though scholars in the Middle Ages downranked imagery, they did not follow Quintilian in two important respects. First, in the Middle Ages, text segmentation remained an art of creative *inventio*, not rote memorization. Carruthers quotes Saint Augustine, who, contra Quintilian, explains that the rhetor should not attempt to memorize every word in every passage from Genesis to Revelation. Recalling the scriptures by rote is not a salutary end unto itself. Rather, the purpose of recalling scripture is to facilitate robust homiletic composition and deep meditative prayer: in other words, the spirit and not the letter of the words is what matters to the medieval rhetor. Augustine recommends remembering scripture by dividing it into brief summaries or thematic plots, which the rhetor can wander through or, better yet, pause within in order to meditate on, explicate, or expand on particularly worthy, urgent, or difficult sections of scripture. The idea is to flip here and there, through the Bible in one's mind, in order to find interesting connections, illuminate one passage with another, or appreciate more richly the intricate links within God's revealed word, about which one could then ponder or preach. Memory of scripture facilitates religious *inventio*, as the art of memory had facilitated secular *inventio*.

Second, medieval authors on text memory recognize the importance of the mnemonic cue's emotional resonance, as had Cicero and *Ad Herennium* (and as Quintilian had recognized about loci, if not imagines). Medieval treatments of *memoria* reveal the deeply felt connections that developed between scripture and its readers or listeners. Medieval authors believed that passages from the Bible, like the spaces of our memory, are electric with affect and longing and are thus perfect mnemonic cues. A single verse of scripture, John Cassian states in his *Conferences*, can in fact be an emotionally rich mnemonic formula for centering the mind on spiritual things while praying. Of Psalms 69:2, Cassian says:

> It carries within it all the feelings of which human nature is capable. It can be adapted to every condition and can be usefully deployed against every temptation. It carries within it a cry of help to God in the face of every danger. It expresses the humility of a pious confession. . . . In my soul are countless distractions. I am in fever as my heart moves this way and that. I have no strength to hold in check the scatterings of my thoughts. I cannot utter my prayer without interruption, without being visited by empty images and by the memory of words and doings. And so if I am to deserve liberation from this bleakness of spirit from which my groans and

sighs have been unable to save me, I shall be obliged to cry out "Come to my help, O God; Lord, hurry to my rescue."[50]

In his praise of scripture's power to center the mind and memory on God, Cassian sounds very much like Giordano Bruno when he exalts the capacity of mnemonic images to "make the heart pound, having the power of something wondrous, frightening, pleasant, sad."[51] The difference, however, to reiterate, is that for Cassian, Augustine, and other Christian rhetors, the mnemonic cue is *memoria scriptorum*—written memory, memory of words. The words are laden with affect and awe, to be sure, but they are not re-mediated into a more sensory shape. Transmuting textual information into imagery was not strictly necessary for the medieval memory artist; nor was associating information with the phantasms of the personal memoryscape. The word of God could remain lexical in the mind without losing any of its mnemonic power.

Text Segmentation: Cultural and Technological Influences

Above and beyond the obvious point that the Middle Ages adopted textual mnemonics because Europe collectively adopted a textual religion, what other factors contributed to the sea change in mnemonic practice that unfolded throughout the period? In my view, the philosophical core of this change is that monastics came to view linguistic/contemplative memory and visual/sensory memory as "cognitively the same thing, made in the same way," to quote Carruthers again.[52] Monastics saw no difference between text and image—between an actual image/icon and an "image" of the text of scripture—because both were obligatory proxies for spiritual truths whose primary function was to enable the finite human mind to contemplate those truths. The medium or mode of the mnemonic cue mattered far less to the monastics than did its cognitive utility—that is, its power to facilitate meditation, prayer, homiletics, and so on. For those purposes, a text was as good as a picture, data as good as a data visualization.

The monastics were not iconoclasts, for they saw value in mnemonic forms that generated human-readable comprehensibility; nor were they Ciceronian iconophiles, for they did not think imagery had more utility than words in generating that comprehensibility. They were, instead, icono-pragmatists. To explain what I mean, consider the following passage from John Cassian's *Conferences*, referenced above, in which a young novice in a monastic order fears he has lost his ability to keep God before his mind's eye when praying. God being the ultimate truth in need of some form by which humans might contemplate him, keep him before their minds, and move toward him in a process of prayerful sanctification, the novice greatly desires a "method for finding and holding God in [his] thoughts": "we desire to have shown to us some formula for the memory which will enable us to think of God and to hold incessantly to that thought so that, as we keep it in view, we may have something to return to immediately whenever we find that we have somehow slipped away from it."[53] The novice is seeking here a model prayer, or a model *for* prayer, that will keep his mind from wandering and allow him to perfect his spiritual meditations. Just as someone who wants to "achieve rhetorical eloquence or philosophic knowledge" must first learn the alphabet, the novice states, so, too, must the young monk learn the basic formulas for prayer before attaining any glimpses of divinity. Cassian responds (as noted earlier) by saying the novice is wise to compare the mental form by which "God may be taken hold of" to a child's memory of the alphabet, the letters being forms that, once impressed on the memory, allow a person to compose all sorts of wonderful things: "Models are put before [the children], carefully drawn in wax. By continually studying them, by practicing every day to reproduce them, they learn at last to write. The same happens with contemplation. You need a model and you keep it constantly before your eyes. . . . You learn either to turn it in a salutary way over and over in your spirit or else, as you use it and meditate upon it, you lift yourself upward to the most sublime sights." What is this "model," this mnemonic form, that Cassian believes will move the novice toward "the most sublime sights"? It is the words of scripture—Psalms 69:2, to be precise. "To keep the thought of God always in your mind," Cassian states, "you must cling totally to this formula for piety: 'Come to my help, O God; Lord, hurry to my rescue.'"[54] Recalling a brief passage of scripture, Cassian implies, is just as efficient at centering the mind on divinity as conjuring vivid spiritual images would be. Better, in fact, to stick with the text, Cassian may have realized, because it avoids the snare of idolatry lurking in pictorial representations of the godhead. But either way, text or image, the mnemonic cue seems to have been understood by Cassian and others as a mere concession to the necessities of human cognition. There was no "truth" in the cue itself—just as no truth exists in the correspondence between signifier and signified (between alphabet and meaning), which nevertheless must be learned, as Cassian and his novice recognize, if one wants to attain rhetorical excellence. Monastics thus perceived no important distinction between visual or textual cues when bringing divine material before the mind's eye. Word or image, these are mere signs. The extrasymbolic truth is what mattered, not the form it took in one's memory. Saint Augustine provides another example of this disinterested pragmatism regarding the mnemonic medium. Discussing the numerous representations of Christ that one encounters in different cultures, Augustine claims to see no distinction between these diverse re-mediations of the person of Jesus of Nazareth. Everyone imagines Christ differently, Augustine states. The "imagining" matters not at all (per the discussion here, it could be a painting or a written description); what matters is that the image enables one to consider and understand the implications of Christ's human existence and example.[55]

A more prosaic reason why text segmentation emerged as the favored mnemonic device in the Middle Ages is that the art of memory was already in decline in the last centuries of the Roman Empire. We saw this as early as the first century CE. Quintilian did not altogether approve of the art of memory, even though he possessed a good understanding of its underlying psychological mechanism. Julius Victor, in the fourth century, similarly offers a less than glowing endorsement: "For the obtaining of memory," Julius remarks, "many people bring in observations about places and images which do not seem to me to be of any use."[56] Also writing in the fourth century, Fortunatianus mentions but does not elaborate on the memory palace technique in his *Ars rhetorica*—all he says is that one may "assign" in the mind both "places" and "some kind of sign in the likeness of what has been written or thought." He then contrasts his lackluster memory palace with the "superior" method of dividing the text on the page, Quintilian style, and memorizing it segment by segment, "for order preserves memory most powerfully."[57] Two recently translated Greek rhetorical treatises, dating from the second and third centuries CE, make no mention of artificial memory at all but focus heavily on controversies relating to invention and declamation (a branch of oratory that uses fictitious legal or historical settings), suggesting that memory no longer stood at the center of Greek rhetorical theory as it had done in the classical era.[58] Thomas Conley's overview of Byzantine rhetoric likewise suggests that the canons of invention and style were more important than memory to later Greek rhetors, who took inspiration not from Roman treatises but from Hermogenes, the father of stasis theory.[59] Then there is Martianus Capella, a rhetorician writing at the end of the Roman Empire, sometime during the early fifth century. In his outline for a liberal arts education, he discusses the five canons of rhetoric and provides a brief but complete discussion of the art of memory's precepts for loci et imagines. These precepts, however, "require much practice and effort," Capella states, which is why "it has been discovered" that people should simply "write down for [them]selves" what they want to remember easily.[60] Capella then repeats

Quintilian's advice to divide written material into smaller sections and to mark particular passages with notae if necessary. That writing things down had been "discovered" as a more useful mnemonic device than the art of memory (Yates's translation states that "it is customarily advised" to write things down)[61] demonstrates that the memory palace had already fallen into disrepair by the end of the Roman Empire. Shorthand systems—both the sigla system and the Tironian notae—flourished in the memory palace's stead, increasing their inventory of symbols from several hundred to several thousand during the late imperial age. It is as though the classical mnemonic tradition, before entering the monasteries, had already begun to adapt itself to a budding system of writing that was to become the medieval manuscript tradition, fitting its techniques and metaphors to the written page.

The technology of the codex itself may also account for the dominance of text segmentation in the Middle Ages. Christians were early adopters of codices, preferring books to papyrus rolls. This adoption is not surprising given the centrality of the written *logos* to the spread of Christianity. Compared to the roll, the codex facilitates continuous reading, cross-reference, and transcription, all of which would have been vital to a community whose existence depended on the collection, circulation, and study of the sayings, stories, and letters of a single prophet and his disciples.[62] Though the codex was not a Christian invention, David Diringer states, "it was most promptly employed by the Christian community, and it was the growth of this community which brought it into prominence."[63] And along with this new technology came new practices for organizing the page. Codices, more so than scrolls, lend themselves to the sort of quadrangular division of page space that enables one to think about memory in terms of grid-like subdivision, segmentation, and indexing.[64] The margins of the codex page were determined by holes pricked with an awl, and by guide lines drawn from hole to hole with a stylus and a ruler. Guide lines were also ruled for the individual lines of writing; these were imprinted with a stylus, leaving furrows in the papyrus or parchment for the writer to follow. The writing itself was ordinarily arranged into two columns, though early codices are sometimes found with three or four columns. Paragraphs in codices began to be more consistently divided by a horizontal stroke or a single wedge line inserted at the beginning of each new paragraph. Word division also began to occur more frequently in the medieval codex, allowing punctuation—embryonic in the Greek and Roman eras—to continue to develop as well: the interrogative mark and the inverted semicolon (something between the semicolon and the comma) seem to have been invented during the 700s, for example. Finally, and most interestingly in terms of mnemonic representation, prearranged spaces were always left blank, leaving grid-like spaces for titles, headlines, and illuminations to be added by rubricators and illuminators after the text itself had been copied.[65] "The basic page design," Rowan Watson succinctly contends, "took place at the writing stage."[66] By the 1100s, manuscript production emphasized all sorts of in-text instruction, templates for illustration, planned grid structures, and margin designs.[67] In short, the codex page itself likely encouraged scribes and monks to see page space (and thus their memory of it) through the lenses of segmentation and division. Given the importance of codices and codex design to monastic culture, it makes sense that the practice of segmenting and dividing text in the mind's eye would find a home in the monasteries.

In addition to the grid designs that emerged along with the technology of the book, the devotional aspect of scribal labor perhaps also influenced the monastic preference for mnemonic text segmentation over mnemonic imagery. The tedious, detailed work of scribes developed into a form of devotional duty in the monasteries. Codices were highly valued, and producing them came to be considered a virtuous practice. Describing the moral implications of a scribe's labor, a twelfth-century preacher demonstrates the link not only between book production and virtue but also between the technology of the book and the preferred mnemonic technique of the Middle Ages:

> Let us consider then how we may become scribes of the Lord. The parchment on which we write for him is a pure conscience, whereon all our good works are noted by the pen of memory, and make us acceptable to God. The knife wherewith it is scraped is the fear of God, which removes from our conscience by repentance all the roughness and unevenness of sin and vice. . . . The ruler by which the line is drawn that we may write straight, is the will of God. . . . The tool that is drawn along the ruler to make the line, is our devotion to our holy task. . . . The ink with which we write is humility itself. . . . The diverse colours wherewith the book is illuminated, not unworthily represent the multiple grace of heavenly Wisdom.[68]

The passage reveals that the seemingly mundane practice of designing the codex page was brimming with purpose and righteous metaphor. The reference to a "pen of memory"—an echo of the wax tablets analogy—further demonstrates that memory was central to the pious purposes of codex design and connected emblematically with manuscript production. Given a moral commitment to the book and given memory's association with that commitment, it is no surprise that monastic culture favored text-based mnemonic techniques. The text, especially the text of the Bible, was sacred. It needn't be re-mediated into a visual form to retain its vivid, affective character. Mnemonic segmentation was thus intimately suited—literally and metaphorically—to the ruled, quadrangular, yet spiritual space of the codex.

It is impossible to consider the medieval codex, of course, without considering illumination. Does not the art of illumination—the filling of manuscripts with all manner of birds, beasts, people, and wild imagery—recall the imagines of the art of memory? To be sure, evidence suggests that illumination served a mnemonic purpose in certain contexts—for example, in bestiaries and *ysopets*.[69] However, as a culturally significant *ars*, illumination had many purposes: to aid the spiritual life of illiterate people, to beautify the object of devotion (illumination makes use of precious gold, after all), to express faith through an extralinguistic form, and to please God. Indeed, the art of beautifying text long predates formal mnemonic technique; it can be traced back as far as the twentieth century BCE, "when the Egyptians were decorating their funeral rolls in the most gorgeous colors."[70] So although illumination's vivid qualities may have served incidentally to help the reader recall a particular location, phrase, or moral lesson in a book, there is no reason to assume that illumination's primary or even ancillary goal was mnemonic access. Furthermore, during the Middle Ages, as a general rule constraints were placed on individual artistry when it came to illumination. Jonathan J. G. Alexander explains that both scribes and illuminators were under the authority not only of abbots but also of the wealthy patrons who typically ordered the manufacture of manuscripts. Especially when expensive materials such as gold or lapis lazuli were involved, a book's creators were not given free rein to invent their own designs and images. Of course, there was a tension between artistic constraint and license, and there are many examples, particularly in the later Middle Ages, of scribes and illuminators exercising creative agency over their manuscripts. However, "there can never be a carte blanche," Alexander states, "for the artists to do anything they liked." Constraints were enforced by context, legibility, and by the "artistic repertoire available at any particular historical junction."[71] To an extent, these constraints are at odds with mnemonic imagery in the classical sense, which was to be entirely bespoke and constructed according to one's emotional inclinations and past experiences. It is an open question whether or not the precepts of the ars memoria circulated very widely in the Middle Ages, but wherever they were known, the injunction to form personal and affective images in the mind would not have suggested a direct equivalence to the illumination of manuscripts—an art circumscribed by the demands of patrons and by the limits of acceptable semiotic expression inherent in any creative zeitgeist.

Beyond the influence of writing technology and scribal practice, another reason for the decreased interest in the classical ars memoria during the Middle Ages was the method of preaching favored by late Roman and medieval Christians. Precepts for a plain and unembellished style and a simple organization emerged as central components of the medieval homiletic tradition, and these precepts may not have indicated to clerics the need for an intricate technique of mnemonic access. Homiletic plainness, James J. Murphy suggests, emerged as a deliberate antagonistic choice on the part of preachers, a statement against pagan rhetorical culture, which, following the Second Sophistic, remained synonymous with figuration and embellishment. For a representative example of unadorned homiletics, Murphy points to John Chrysostom's first Homily on the Statutes: the method of preaching exemplified by Chrysostom, he states, is simply "a close oral examination of Scripture," of the sort familiar to anyone who has attended a contemporary Bible study.[72] Medieval preaching manuals are similarly replete with exhortations to compose unadorned, rhetorically restrained sermons whose chief purpose is biblical explication. Guibert de Nogent, for example, warns against lengthy, complex sermons that drag in "unrelated topics" and thus anger the listeners;[73] "if he must speak of anything else [other than scripture]," Guibert says, "then let him treat it as it relates to God."[74] "Nor does almighty God need our grammar to draw men," states the Benedictine cardinal Peter Damian, circa the middle 1100s, "since he sent not philosophers and orators, but simple men."[75] And in his *Treatise on Preaching*, Humbert of Romans argues that "a sermon should be simple, and devoid of all the empty ornaments of rhetoric." Humbert goes on to quote Augustine's advice not to "multiply the solemn Divine words."[76]

This simple homiletic method, Murphy remarks, "made the text [i.e., the Bible] the organizer of the discourse." By following the "places" of scripture with minimal amplification and in a modest style, the preacher was likely "relieved . . . of most memory and arrangement problems."[77] To be sure, crafting a sermon, a prayer, or any composition in a monastic context still required creative effort. The rhetor's movement in his mind from scriptural "place" to scriptural "place"—his ascending of the "steps" of a scriptural ladder—necessitated a keen and active use of text-based memory. Guibert, for example, says that a sermon risks being dull to parishioners whenever "the [preacher's] memory fails, the delivery is halting, and the mind is sluggish."[78] Murphy's point, however, is that whatever bricolage occurred in a priest's mind while sermonizing or praying was ultimately guided by a single, unchanging text. His process of inventio needn't consider the imminent challenges and exigencies met by classical rhetors. In the Middle Ages, it was no longer necessary to develop a robust mnemonic access point to "the complete history of the past and a store of precedents [as well as] statute law and our national law,"[79] which the pagan orator had to develop within his mind's eye and hold ready "for immediate use."[80] For the classical orator, nothing less than a virtual database, a treasure house of invention, would suffice to meet the demands of secular oratory and extemporaneous debate. For the Christian rhetor, in contrast, all that needed to be said, explicated, or meditated on came from a comparatively limited number of sources—primarily from scripture, perhaps a handful of commentaries by the church fathers, and the ancient church orders (which consisted largely of biblical injunctions). Creative bricolage was still required, and mnemonic text segmentation was valuable for assembling pieces of scripture into a connective whole while praying or composing. Nevertheless, until the late developments of canon and civil law, the Christian rhetor was relieved of the anxiety of recalling vast amounts of information that had beset his classical predecessors. It is not until the late Middle Ages[81] that we begin to see, for example, William of Ockham's Ciceronian advice to construct a total memory of "books of sacred theology, and of both kinds of law, canon and civil, of moral philosophy, and [of] the histories of the Romans, and especially of the emperors, and of the greatest pontiffs, and of other peoples."[82]

For most of the medieval era, then, with less information placing fewer demands on mnemonic access, with priests reining in the rhetorical excess of the pagan orators, with the word-centric spaces of monastery and altar replacing the agonistic spaces of senate and law court, it is understandable that an intricate mnemonic system like the ars memoria—converting the mind into a visual, hyperlinked interface—may not have been scanned as a necessary or even salutary device. Delivering structurally and stylistically simple homilies, drawing on scripture alone, medieval rhetors apparently saw no reason to construct and furnish elaborate memory palaces in their minds. It is therefore unsurprising that, after Quintilian, no new developments in visual mnemonics were forwarded until very late in the Middle Ages, when rhetorical complexities began to reemerge in the contexts of canon and civil law.

To be precise, the memory palace technique first reemerged as a conscious tool in John of Garland's *Parisiana poetria*, a compendium of grammar and poetics written in 1240. Amusingly, John of Garland—the first person in a thousand years to comment at length on the ars memoria—garbles the technique by attempting to fuse it with text segmentation and other writing-centric mnemonics. After Garland, no less-authoritative figures than Albertus Magnus and Thomas Aquinas were among those who revived interest in the art of memory. Aquinas's development of what might be called a mnemonic ethics was particularly instrumental in restoring the memory palace to its classical prominence. Following that ethical treatment of ars memoria, visual mnemonics rematerialized in earnest. For example, Francesc Eiximenis's (d. 1409) *On Two Kinds of Order That Aid Understanding and Memory* discusses how to order material according to visual, three-dimensional precepts; Thomas Bradwardine's (d. 1349) *On Acquiring a Trained Memory* contains outright bizarre mnemonic imagery, often grounded in the technique of visual homophony suggested in *Dissoi logoi*; and the anonymous *A Method for Recollecting the Gospels*, published in 1470, provides vivid pictorial representations of Matthew, Mark, Luke, and John, with numbers accorded to various spaces on each picture, whereupon are inscribed different Gospel passages.[83] Many of these treatises revive not only mnemonic imagery and spatial order but also the vital precept that mnemonic imagery/space should be informed by the individual's private experiences. "It is very useful if your places are real rather than only imagined or made up," Bradwardine states, "for real places one can frequently inspect" and thereby refine their mnemonic form.[84] It is also no coincidence, Frances Yates remarks, that the centuries following the art's recuperation witnessed a flourishing of spatially ordered imagery in literature and in art—a trend exemplified powerfully by *The Divine Comedy*'s layered arrangement of heaven, hell, and purgatory. Dante's poem, Yates suggests, is perhaps the epitome of a Christianized memory palace, a collection of imagines arranged in their supernatural loci signifying the religious rebirth of the pagan art of memory.[85]

A discussion of late medieval theories of visual mnemonics and the ethics of mnemonic practice is beyond the scope of this chapter. Suffice it to say that once eminent scholars granted authority to the ars memoria and its Ciceronian/Herennian sources, the medieval world returned its attention to the memory palace technique as a true ars with important purposes. This new foundation laid, the art of memory was restored to its former status as a legitimate system with which to re-mediate, access, and invent knowledge.

The "Natural" Memory Palace of the Middle Ages

The art of memory was designed by and for a secular and oratorical culture, not a monastic and bookish one. However, ample evidence suggests that despite the memory palace's dissolution in rhetorical contexts during the early and central Middle Ages, the idea of a visual, imaginative memory remained in circulation during this time. The cultural stability of the idea is no great mystery—it is how memory works in our subjective experience. Given the biblical milieu in which they existed, monastics simply found no reason to harness the visual memoryscape in a conscious mnemonic practice. The memory palace in the Middle Ages remained a *natural* phenomenon.

John of Salisbury (c. 1100s) nicely captures the medieval conception of the memory/imagery/creativity nexus: "As it perceives things, our soul stores up images within itself, and in the process of retaining and often recalling them [to mind], builds up for itself a sort of treasure of the memory. And as it mentally revolves the images of [these] things, there arises imagination, which proceeds beyond the [mere] recollection of previous perceptions, to fashion, by its own creative activity, other representations similar to these. . . . Imagination, accordingly, is the offspring of sensation. And it is nourished and fostered by memory."[86] I refer the reader to the work of Mary Carruthers, Lina Bolzoni, and Kimberly A. Rivers for an exhaustive discussion of natural memory in the Middle Ages. In this section, I provide examples of medieval authors who addressed both natural and artificial memory, highlighting the odd disconnect between their text-centric mnemonics and their imagistic theories of memory. The commonality in medieval discourse on the sensory, idiosyncratic, imaginative features of memory is that, wherever these features come under discussion, they tend to be severed from the rhetorical or mnemonic traditions. The precepts of the ars memoria seem to have circulated as a *studium*—that is, as a set of useful principles about memory's natural operations—but not as an *ars*, a technique by which natural memory might be consciously harnessed for larger purposes.[87]

Alcuin of York provides a good example. Alcuin's *Rhetoric*, written at the behest of Charlemagne in the late 700s, is devoid of precepts for the canon of memory. Nothing about it is known, he states, except "exercise in memorizing, practice in writing, and the avoidance of drunkenness."[88] Save the reference to text memory—"practice in writing"—rhetoric's mnemonic tradition is nonexistent for Alcuin. In other writings, however, he comments on the mind's ability to process what it receives through the senses, as if "messengers" were running into and out of the mind, filing away "figures" of what the senses have encountered and storing them away in the treasury of the memory—this is why, according to Alcuin, "the human mind makes up images" concerning anything it wants to think about.[89] Alcuin himself is reported to have had a robust memory and to have practiced the ancient link between memory and invention by weaving together collects and psalms into his meditational prayers.[90] Comparing his *Rhetoric* and his nonrhetorical writings, Alcuin emerges as a good example of a medieval scholar who wrote about the visual memoryscape even though he (and his culture) had forgotten its rhetorical link. The ars memoria had lost its status as an ars, even as Alcuin continued to recognize its underlying mechanisms.

The same can be said for Hugh of Saint Victor. Recall that his "Three Best Memory Aids" teaches a segmentation system par excellence with its scheme for subdividing Psalms into smaller and smaller units, each stored within a numbered mental grid. The mnemonic "imagery" on display in his system, like most medieval mnemonic systems, is text-centric. Hugh even recommends forming mnemonic pictures, not of the imagery one might have found on illuminated codex pages but of the color, shape, and position of a page's *letters*. And yet, in another text called *De arca Noe mystica*—"A Little Book about Constructing Noah's Ark," as Carruthers translates it—Hugh takes his reader on a spatially ordered and visually imaginative tour of Noah's ark, which then becomes the model for an allegorical interpretation of the vessel. According to Carruthers, this method of "architectural exegesis" was popular during Hugh of Saint Victor's time. The ark, the Tabernacle, Solomon's temple, and the heavenly Jerusalem are all used in other texts to guide readers through a physical and then a spiritual understanding of the structures. Reading through Hugh's ark, one cannot help thinking that he guides us through a memory palace, through mnemonic loci of the sort recommended by the classical orators, with the words and knowledge of the ancient pagan world replaced by those of the medieval Christian world: "These are in the inscriptions of the rooms: on the right side of the first room 'FAITH' is written, on the right side of the second room, 'HOPE,' and on the third room, 'CHARITY.'"[91] Hugh nowhere mentions the classical art of memory, nor does he recommend architectural exegesis as a general mnemonic technique. The text's introduction nevertheless implies that Hugh's literary ark was designed to aid the reader's memory of the didactic material it embodied. "I depict it as an object," he proclaims, "so that you learn outwardly what you ought to do inwardly, and so that, once you imprint the form of this example in your heart, you will be glad that the house of God has been built inside of you."[92] The ark as a series of places and images, the forms of which are to be imprinted on the heart—the language is Christian, but the technique would have been familiar to a pagan orator. Although Hugh is silent on the origins of architectural exegesis, and although he does not cite Cicero or *Ad Herennium*, something like the art of memory surfaces in his tour through the ark.[93] As with Alcuin, Hugh of Saint Victor teaches a writing-based mnemonic device even though, elsewhere, he recognizes the worth of visual and spatial cues for memory.

In the previous section, I argued that visual mnemonics were unnecessary for preachers trained to fill their minds with the scriptures alone. However, homiletic manuals do at times invoke the usefulness of the personal memoryscape, exhorting pastors to incorporate into their sermons their own struggles with, triumphs over, and lessons learned from past sinful activity. Although Guibert de Nogent recommends keeping a sermon (and thus the pastor's mnemonic effort) focused solely on God as revealed in sacred scripture—free of "unrelated topics"—he nonetheless recognizes that to touch "the interior life of men," the preacher must draw on occasion from his own "battling with weakness," his own "giving into" and subsequent "overcoming" of sin. The pastor's recreation of these past experiences for his parishioners, as a man who has been to war might reminisce about his wartime experiences, can be of immense value for the salvation of others:

> The events of [a man's] life, both good and bad, are indelibly imprinted on his memory; because of them he is able to act wisely for his own salvation and that of others. Any man, even one who has never been part of a battle, can talk at great length about war; but what a difference there is between this and the man who can reminisce about war, who has fought or been besieged, who has gone to war and suffered! It is the same in spiritual matters when we hear people speak with overpowering eloquence about what they have read in books or heard from others; how greatly they differ from the man who speaks with real authority of his own spiritual struggles, whose experience is like a mark to underline what he has said.[94]

Guibert goes on to state that by summoning his past experiences, the preacher can move parishioners to view their own struggles with sin as a process of working out their salvation. A converted soul would thus convert his memories of sinful activity into a memory of the long, hard road toward sanctification, thereby sanctifying those same sinful memories.[95] Alas, for the unconverted, what awaits them after death is an eternal memory of their sins as sins, the torment of which medieval scholars associate with hell. After death, states Honorius of Autun, "the vision of God will delight the blessed forever; [but] the memory of the crimes they have committed will torture the wicked without ceasing. . . . They will endure many different visions of vice, which will run about before their eyes like savage beasts."[96]

Although both Honorius and Guibert remain text-centric in their rhetorical precepts, they clearly understand memory as a visual, affective phenomenon. The visual memoryscape—the vivid memory of sin and one's overcoming of sin (or not)—is for them simply a natural fact rather than the foundation of active mnemonic practice.

In a similar vein, Carruthers has noted the relationship between private memory and medieval meditational practices. For monks and nuns, she states, the effort to attain a glorious vision of heaven or a soul-straightening vision of hell was to be aided by one's personal sensory memories. The monastics, she claims, transformed their memories of "real" things into meditative visions of paradise or perdition.[97] For example, Boncompagno da Signa, a Bolognese rhetoric professor, states that although heaven and hell have their own forms, about which he dare not think, he nevertheless cannot help fashioning an image of hell from his experience watching Mount Etna erupt.[98] (To provide a contemporary example of this meditational practice, in the film *Shadowlands*, Anthony Hopkins's C. S. Lewis imagines heaven as a painting of a rural English valley hung on the wall of his childhood bedroom.)

Alcuin's "thinking in images," Hugh of Saint Victor's ark, idiosyncratic visions of heaven and hell, summoning one's memories of sin in order to cleanse them—something like the memory palace technique was implicated in these medieval practices. I would simply argue that they were *religious* practices first and foremost, mnemonic ones only incidentally. Their goal was not information recall or rhetorical invention but forward movement on the path to salvation, a richer knowledge of God and his will. Memory's role in this spiritual progression remained a natural one. (It could also be pointed out that, according to Guibert de Nogent, the contents of the pastor's sinful memories are not to remain visual or harnessed for mnemonic purposes; rather, they are to be converted, in reverse, from mental phantasms into words in a sermon.)[99] Nevertheless, these examples demonstrate that imagery, creativity, and memory were not severed in the medieval imagination. Humans subjectively experience memory as a three-dimensional space replete with emotionally charged simulacra, and not even the scripture-focused monastics could expunge such imagery from their discourse on memory. Like Quintilian, however, scholars in the Middle Ages neglected the Herennian idea that this image-laden space could be utilized as an intentional mnemonic tool for rhetorical activity. Until a theoretical and ethical foundation for visual mnemonics was built in the late Middle Ages, the treatises would continue to be silent on them.

The Mnemonic Medium: Spreadsheet versus Visualization

Nearly all scholars of the memory arts—Paolo Rossi, Frances Yates, Lina Bolzoni—ignore or mention only in passing the shift from imagery to text that occurred in medieval mnemonic systems. The change from a visual re-mediation of words to words themselves appears particularly trivial to Mary Carruthers, for whose scholarship the medium of mnemonic access is, to be fair, not relevant. I am thus not faulting Carruthers's invaluable work when I highlight her conflation of two ancient metaphors for memory: that of writing on wax tablets and that of signet rings impressed on wax.

Cicero and Quintilian deploy the writing metaphor. Plato and Aristotle, however, compare memory to a signet ring's impression: "as we might stamp the impression of a seal ring" is Plato's wording in *Theaetetus*,[100] and in *On the Soul*, Aristotle describes the power of sense to receive into itself the forms of things without their matter, "somewhat in the way wax receives the impression of the signet ring without receiving the iron or gold."[101]

Although Carruthers collapses these allegories, there is, in my view, a significant difference between the signet ring metaphor and the Roman metaphor of writing on a wax tablet. A search through the British Museum or any other collection will reveal that ancient Greek signet rings more often contain pictorial images than alphabetic letters. Imagistic, too, are the Egyptian and Near Eastern signets and seals with which educated Greeks would have been familiar. Ancient signet rings boast highly elaborate designs. Shapes, faces, bodies in action—all manner of visual communicative forms adorn these objects. The glorious battle scene engraved on the Pylos Combat Agate, though predating Plato and Aristotle by a millennium, represents in extreme form the visual nature of signet rings and seals in the ancient world. They are nothing like writing on wax tablets. In my view, the difference between the two metaphors—the impression of signet rings versus the impression of letters—recapitulates the difference between the visual and the written medium. It is the difference between literature and film, between books and comic books. It is the difference between semiotic modes possessing their own grammars, their own practices, and their own rules for communicating information or, in the mnemonic context, their own rules for facilitating information access. The Greek and Roman metaphors for memory, in short, differ in nontrivial ways. Drawing on dissimilar media, each suggests a new model of what memory is and what it does and how to harness it for mnemonic recall. In my view, the original Greek metaphor is hardly a metaphor at all, indicating as it does the pictorial nature of memory images.

Both Cicero and *Ad Herennium* conceptualize artificial memory as a visual, imagistic practice, so their choice of metaphor is odd. The writing metaphor, it seems, had simply eclipsed the earlier Greek metaphor as a cultural commonplace, even though the art of memory aligns better with the signet ring comparison. However, taking her cue from *Ad Herennium*'s metaphor rather than its art, Carruthers downplays the art's imagistic precepts. She equates the medieval mnemonic technique of "seeing the text" with visual activity in general, describing the mnemonic "pictures" of *Ad Herennium* and Cicero as a different sort of "seeing," a "pictorial" rather than a "textual" visuality—though both are, for her, the same sort of thing. "Memories," she states, "could be marked by pictorial means; the ancient system described in *Rhetorica ad Herennium* was precisely that." However, "pictures are not the only sorts of objects we can see. We also see written words and numbers, punctuation marks, and blotches of color. . . . Moreover, we can manipulate [textual] information in ways that make it possible to bring together or separate it in a variety of ways, to collate, classify, compose, and sort it in order to create new ideas or deconstruct old ones."[102] Carruthers is correct that reading is in part a visual activity, just as oratory and musical composition are both aural activities. Nonetheless, creating oratory and creating music remain different practices. Basing a mnemonic system on one versus the other would change the functions, principles, techniques, and goals of the ensuing system. Similarities exist, to be sure, but in both the material and the mnemonic realms, the similarities will be less significant than the differences. The same holds true for writing and for more visual or, to use Carruthers's term, "pictorial" practices—painting, film, sculpture, and so on (indeed, significant differences exist between even these visual media). The distinction between image and text reveals itself in Carruthers's quote above, where her description of mnemonic practice is determined by her textual orientation. Does one "collate" or "classify" or "sort" when working in a visual medium? Do directors "sort" scenes on editing software as writers "sort" through words and phrases in a composition? Do painters "collate" chromatic shades as poets "collate" lines of verse? Again, similarities may emerge, but in general, "sorting" and "classifying" and "collating" operate according to dissimilar principles and praxes—they *look* different—from one medium to the next. Having worked with both film and text, I can affirm that "composition" and "creation," to use Carruthers's other terms, are likewise dissimilar activities in one mode versus the other.

Medium, in short, matters. It matters in the world, and it matters in the world of the mnemonic imagination. No longer an art of three-dimensional wandering, evocative visual association, or image construction, the art of memory becomes for Carruthers a practice of tinkering with words in the mind's eye, the way one might copy and paste sources together in a Word document, sort and re-sort information in a spreadsheet, or explore keywords and collocations with a natural language processing tool. Carruthers goes so far as to argue that memoria in the medieval sense "is in many ways the same as the institution of literature,"[103] and that a "textual picture is as good as a painted one in addressing memory work."[104] To be sure, this image/writing conflation was normatively true in the text-centric Middle Ages; however, instead of adopting the normative view, I would mark this conflation as an interesting but transitory medieval phenomenon. The medieval conception of mnemonic form is not the only conception, neither historically nor in the present. Like poetry versus painting, collating words and creating imagery in the mind's eye are different practices, activating different mnemonic states as well as facilitating different ways to theorize memory as a practice.

From the perspective of rhetorical theory, the shift in mnemonic medium that occurred during the Middle Ages—from visual memory palaces to textual segmentation—is a nontrivial one. When the memory palace becomes a library of words rather than a site of visual re-mediation, the rhetorical scholar must take note. The medium may or may not be the message, but to repeat, it is a basic tenet of rhetorical theory that medium matters, because a change in medium begets significant changes to practice, to epistemology, to what is and what is not made known, revealed, and facilitated.

Carruthers goes on to cite Cicero's *Partitiones oratoriae* to confirm her view that artificial memory, as a general psychological rule, draws on textual media. States Cicero, "Memory . . . is in a manner the twin sister of written speech [*litteratura*] and is completely similar to it, [though] in a dissimilar medium. For just as script consists of marks indicating letters and of the material on which those marks are imprinted, so the structure of memory, like a wax tablet, employs places and in these gathers together images like letters."[105] For Carruthers, the congruence of imagery and writing is the passage's essential point, validating her fusion of "the visual" with "seeing the text." However, in my view, the passage's key phrase is "in a dissimilar medium" [*dissimili genere*]—which could be translated also as a dissimilar "class" or "kind" or "field." My emphasis in later chapters on the art of memory's compatibility with digital media obliges me to accentuate the phrase. When Cicero states that his mnemonics are "like" writing on a wax tablet but in a "dissimilar medium," I interpret him to mean that mnemonic images are in fact different from words on a wax tablet—as different as a network from its underlying CSV file, a line graph from its underlying statistics, or a software interface from its underlying code. Historically speaking, the difference between textual mnemonics and the memory palace reveals itself in imagistic splendor in *Ad Herennium*'s actual mnemonic system, which is poles apart from mnemonic alphabets or Hugh of Saint Victor's text grid. The contrast, again, is nontrivial. The medium of mnemonic access determines how we "see" information, how we assemble it, how we use it—as well as what information we see, assemble, and use in the first place.

Occupied with an image of a text or a book *as such*, the mind can, as Carruthers says, "manipulate [the textual] information in ways that make it possible to bring together or separate it, . . . to collate, classify, compose, and sort it" in a variety of creative ways.[106] Reading this description, however, I can't help thinking that the infinitive verbs (whose object is *text*) depict the canon of arrangement rather than the canon of memory. Moving words from place to place, assembling multiple texts into a single text, separating text here, rejoining it elsewhere: if this is *memoria*, what sets it apart from *dispositio*, or arrangement? Classically speaking, the precepts were well defined. What distinguished the canons was that the rhetor assembled and reassembled words in one context and mental imagery in the other. When practicing *memoria*, the rhetor would not have been working with raw text but with visualizations. (Relatedly, *memoria* assists *inventio*, whereas *dispositio* presumes a text has already been created.) To restate the analogy: the difference between the memory palace technique and text segmentation is the difference between a data visualization and a spreadsheet. The manipulation of a mental spreadsheet or Word document is not quite comparable to the art of memory and is better understood, in my view, as an analogue to the art of arrangement.

Merging with my disagreement with Carruthers,[107] albeit from the other direction, Susan Delagrange and Anne Wysocki contend directly that the third canon is the locus of rhetoric's visual precepts and thus presages "rhetorical practice in a digital world," to use the subtitle of Delagrange's book.[108] "The making of knowledge through arrangement and visual analogy," Delagrange argues, "is a process of analogical manipulation that is deeply rhetorical. Each arrangement of objects creates new taxonomies—based on materials, or elements, or even size—that carry with them unique ways of seeing and understanding the world."[109] By designing new arrangements, she continues, one incarnates in visual form otherwise purely abstract tropes such as metaphor or metonymy, as each arrangement calls attention to different relations among objects of knowledge—"putting the visible into relationship with the invisible."[110] I agree with Delagrange (and Carruthers) that arrangement is a powerful form of rhetorical inquiry, whether one is working with text or physical objects. Through multiple iterations of transposition, the rhetor reveals relations and patterns that otherwise would have remained latent in the objects/words under consideration. However, everything Delagrange says about arrangement applies more aptly, in my view, to the memory palace. Recall that for classical orators, mnemonic imagery could and should be arranged in whatever way a situation required. Indeed, every arrangement of imagines within their loci was to be transitory, not set in stone. (Re)arrangement was a basic principle of the memory palace technique.[111] More relevant to the digital environment, the memory palace goes further than the canon of arrangement as a site of visual invention. Whereas the third canon's precepts allow information to be rearranged only as it exists in a static state (typically, as *words*), the fourth canon encourages rhetors to imagine additional dimensions of inquiry by reworking the sensory form of the information itself, accessing it via a different medium altogether.

Consider information represented in an Excel workbook—metadata about novels, say. Rearranging these data in different ways—by date of publication, genre, author gender, length, and so on—can indeed reveal abstract relationships among the books. However, discovering relationships within a spreadsheet has obvious restrictions. Spreadsheets are powerful tools of inquiry, to be sure, but as one reshuffles the novels qua textual data, only so many patterns, taxonomies, or relations come into view at any given time. When examining information from even a few hundred novels, to say nothing of the hundreds of thousands examined by digital humanists, what is "viewable" in Excel is limited by screen real estate and the bounds of working memory. It would be difficult to view in a single workbook the relational overlaps between, for example, categories as basic as date of publication, author gender, and genre. At some point, the process of metadata rearrangement produces memory overload. What is needed is not another rearrangement of the spreadsheet's cells but a tool that transforms the cells into a novel visual form, a tool allowing users to "see" all the texts at once in an interactive image. The spreadsheet must become the substrate of a data visualization, a new visual interface to the spreadsheet's content whose visuality and virtuality supports an intuitive comprehension of the data's many permutations.

Simply put, until textual or any other information is visualized as a graph, network, map, and so on, certain relationships and patterns will remain difficult to detect. The interface of the spreadsheet keeps information in too raw and unwieldy a form. Re-mediating the data's form and approaching them through a more visual interface expands the potential for inquiry beyond what spreadsheet arrangement could enable—just as mnemonic imagery was likely a more powerful aid to inventio than Quintilian's text segments or Hugh of Saint Victor's text grids.

Notae Redux

Although works from the early, central, and even late Middle Ages reveal that medieval culture linked mnemonics with recalling the words of the Bible—this was, in short, a culture replete with text memory—there is at least one intriguing exception to this tendency. Of course, the infusion of spiritual imagery into the life of the religious might be understood as its own glaring exception to the textual mnemonics popular in the Middle Ages. Didactic painting, sculpture, stained-glass windows, illumination, bodily ritual, and idiosyncratic mental imagery of heaven and hell all had a "memory" component, to be sure—but not, in most cases, a consciously mnemonic one. As I argued above, medieval imagery and iconography, within the mind and in the cathedrals, are better understood as religious aids to sanctification than as mnemonic tools for information access and for inventio (which are but incidental roles played by imagery in medieval discourse on memory). In contrast, a practice that circulated as a consciously mnemonic ars in the Middle Ages was the ars notoria. I end the chapter by taking a brief look at this "notorious art" because its strange amalgamation of mnemonics and the occult will color the art of memory's history as it moves forward.

Recall that notae, in the Roman and medieval worlds, denoted stenographic systems that utilized symbols and appended strokes to compress writing into a shorter and thus more easily captured form. Operating on similar info-compression principles, mnemonic alphabets and other mnemonic indexing systems were also referred to as notae by medieval authors. These shorthand systems, Carruthers states, were understood to be memory aids and were taught to notaries and lawyers throughout classical and medieval history.

To the uninitiated eye, however, shorthand writing such as the

FIGURE 2.2. The Tironian notes

Tironian notes might have looked a bit intriguing, perhaps even nu-minous (figure 2.2). To the creative soul, they would have stirred the imagination—the way Gothic runes, Egyptian hieroglyphics, and Az-tec ideographs stir the contemporary imagination. A hint of numinos-ity would have been palpable even in the mnemonic alphabets that, fol-lowing the rehabilitation of visual mnemonics in the 1100s, began to take on an increasingly vivid quality. For example, Thomas Bradwardine con-cludes his treatise on artificial memory (c. 1335) by saying that "whoever will learn the notary art will attain the highest perfection" in the craft of memory.[112] His "notary art," however, refers not to stenography but to a system of visually re-mediated letters and numbers that he has just described—for example, he converts *L* into an elbow, *E* into a picture of Eve "hiding her prominent breasts with her long hair," 1 into a unicorn, 7 into a lamb with seven horns, and 9 into a man with one of his thumbs sawed off.[113] Now imagine the ensuing "text"— intended to be "writ-ten" in the mind's eye—brimming with disembodied elbows, half-naked women, unicorns, seven-horned lambs, and men with sawed-off thumbs. Now we may appreciate why a notae system—particularly one as bizarre as Bradwardine's—might have exuded a magical ethos in the medieval imagination. Between simple stenographic marks and emotionally stun-ning figures, the idea of notae came to occupy a gray area between ordi-nary scribal practice and occult ritual.

Occult, secret, or hidden writing was in fact a fixture of medieval cul-ture. Often it served sensible ends, such as in the use of ciphers, sylla-ble rearrangement, or letter substitution to disguise political or military

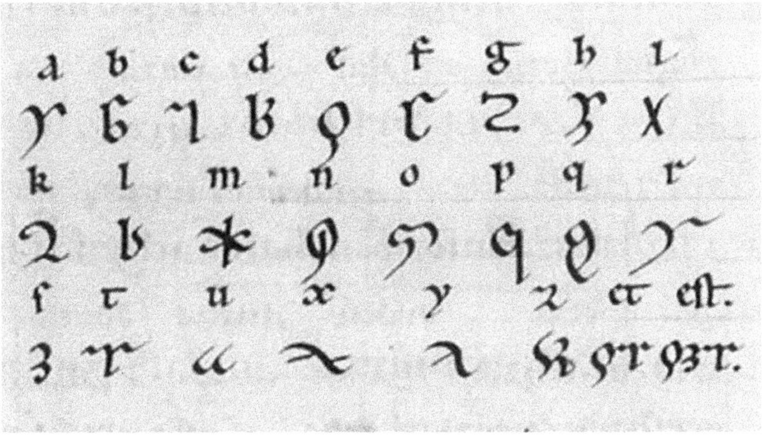

FIGURE 2.3. Hildegard von Bingen's secret alphabet

communications. Tironian notae were likewise valuable for dictating letters or transcribing the proceedings of a feudal court. Sometimes secret
writing served intimate ends: Hildegard von Bingen's invented alphabet
(figure 2.3), for example, was likely used to facilitate private communication among nuns. In other contexts, however, hidden writing was indeed
occult in the contemporary sense—designed to reveal hidden supernatural forces. John Haines notes that the key feature of occult secret writing
is that it is no longer "rational" in the sense that it can be decoded by the
initiate (as a student of Tironian shorthand could eventually read Tironian shorthand); instead, occult writing takes on an "irrational" quality.
It is no longer meant to be deciphered at all but is to be meditated on, like
the signs or seals on medieval charms and amulets.[114]

One such system of irrational writing is the ars notoria, which appears
in a treatise of the same name. Originating in the eleventh century, perhaps
earlier, the ars notoria is a bit of wordplay: it can be translated variously as
"the art of making notae [shorthand notes]" or "the art of making known,"
"the art of note taking" or "the art of making noteworthy," and "the art
of notarizing" or "the art of making notorious." The curious etymological
link between the Latin words *nota* and *notus* emerges in this medieval ars
and is perhaps the link's source and origin.

The ars notoria requires its practitioner to meditate on various notae
and to recite special prayers while doing so. The notae (figure 2.4) are fig-
urative designs, not legible shorthand symbols. The accompanying prayers
beseech God and angels—using their strange cabalistic names, such as
Assaylemath, Assay, Lemath, Azzabue—to grant the practitioner perfect

FIGURE 2.4. A *nota* of the *ars notoria*. (From *Ars Notoria*, 47.)

knowledge and memory of the seven liberal arts: the trivium of grammar, rhetoric, and logic, then moving on to the quadrivium, culminating in theology. Each art has its own nota; some arts have one figure to be meditated on, others have two or three. In general, each note increases in complexity as the art with which it is associated increases in complexity.

The word "memory" appears over forty times in the *Ars notoria*. The ritualistic prayers and accompanying notae together form a sort of magical mnemonic device. The ritual begins with a note and prayer for memory itself: "I Beseech thee, O my Lord, to Illuminate the Light of my Conscience. . . . Adorn my Soul, that hearing I may hear; and what I hear, I may retain in my Memory. O Lord, reform my heart, restore my senses, and strengthen them; qualifie my Memory with thy Gifts: Mercifully open the dulness of my Soul, . . . have patience with me, give a good Memory unto me."[115] The entire ars, however, remains an art of perfect memory via divine intercession. Thus, when praying for knowledge of grammar, the adept is to recite: "I most humbly beseech thy eternity and thy incomprehensible goodness may come to perfection in me, by the operation of thy most Holy Angels; and be confirmed in my Memory, and establish these, thy Holy works in me, Amen."[116] All the prayers are similarly loaded with pleas to God to fill the adept's memory with perfect knowledge and a godlike information mastery.

Because the *Ars notoria*—which the anonymous author claims was passed down from the biblical King Solomon—was designed to give the adept instant knowledge and memory of academic subjects, it was immensely popular among university students and monastic novices. For a while, the art seems to have been tolerated as a youthful diversion: several monastic libraries have been found to contain an *Ars notoria* manuscript. However, in the later Middle Ages, the names evoked in the text led to a skepticism about the art. As noted, strange names of angels— Azzailement, Gesegon, Lothamasim, Ozetogomaglial, Zeziphier, Josanum, Solatac, Bozefama, Defarciamar, Zemait—fill the text, and at some point, orthodox theologians began to suspect they might in fact be names of demons. On these grounds, Thomas Aquinas himself condemned the art.[117] However, whether the ars was beseeching the powers of light or darkness, the elaborate notae's similarity to the seals and signs found in explicitly occult texts—for example, *On Seals* (a thirteenth-century book detailing how to make engraved seals that harness the stellar rays emitted by celestial bodies, for various magical ends) and the *Sworn Book* (a thirteenth-century book of ritual magic offering rites for getting rich, foretelling the future, and raising the dead, among other questionable goals)—assured it would be associated with diabolical practices.[118] What's more, the cycle of the ars notoria's prayers is astrological. As the adept recites the prayers, he is to "look into" or "inspect" each note in a meditative state, but he is to do so only "at certain determinate times of the moon."[119] Offering a *Primum Mobile* explanation for the importance of the lunar sequence, the *Ars notoria* invokes the moon's interaction with a Christianized zodiac, empowered by the Holy Spirit: "because we have touched something of the course of the Moon, it is necessary that we shew what her course signifies. The Moon passeth through 12 Signs in one Moneth; and the Sun through 12 Signs in a year; and in the same term and time, the Spirit inspireth and illustrateth them; whence it is said, that the Sun and the Moon run their course."[120] This astrological connection, to the art's final detriment, is reiterated throughout the text. Christianized or not, angelic or demonic, the ars notoria's amalgamation of perfect memory, irrational notae, and the zodiac was ultimately too problematic to escape denunciation.

We have seen this amalgamation before. As described by Quintilian, Metrodorus of Scepsis developed a mnemonic system in which he converted the decans of the zodiac into mnemonic loci, scrawling within these loci the Tironian notae, the shorthand system of ancient Rome. Though for Metrodorus this method was just a personal twist on the memory palace technique, at some point between the late imperial period and the central Middle Ages, Metrodorus's stenographic notae had morphed into irrational magical notae. The Scepsian mixture of mnemonics, notae, and the zodiac had evolved into nothing less than an occult mnemonic ritual. Thus did early modern Europe also receive this seemingly demonic mixture, setting the stage for an iconoclastic censure of visual mnemonics and the wholesale removal of memory palaces from the minds of Puritan reformers.[121]

CHAPTER 3

The Memory Palace in Ruins

Formed at the nexus of public declamation and cumbersome papyrus rolls, the memory palace technique facilitated content management and information retrieval long before the world had words for content management and information retrieval. It was a hyperlinked interface before hyperlinked interfaces.

Recall the predicament of the ancient orator: he had to remember his oration (the gist of its content, if not the whole thing by rote), he had to be prepared to speak extempore if his interlocutor led the debate in directions unforeseen, he had to recollect the interlocutor's arguments so he might respond in turn, and before he had occasion to speak at all, the orator was faced with the daunting task of gathering material to remember in the first place. From composition to delivery, the ancient orator needed access to copious information—to "the whole past," Cicero says.[1] However, to access that information, the orator lacked anything like the sophisticated data-management or info-retrieval systems taken for granted today. The Greeks and Romans never even developed card catalogs. And in any event, neither the agora nor the law courts nor the senate permitted access to scrolls in the thick of a rhetorical performance. Successful inventio and declamation relied on an orator's ability to interface with knowledge on his own, so he might then assemble it together in a new rhetorical context. Lacking a smartphone, the orator had only one way to accomplish this task: to convert his mind into the access point for information retrieval and integration. In the ancient world, the key to effective information recall was thus a well-trained, visually enhanced memory— hence the famous praise of memory as a *thesaurum inventorum*. Likewise Quintilian remarks, "It is the power of memory alone that brings before us all the store of precedents, laws, rulings, sayings, and facts which the orator must possess in abundance . . . and hold ready for immediate use."[2] Notwithstanding Plato's complaints about writing, when an orator located a valuable piece of information, he likely wanted to secure it in his mind the first time, so he wouldn't need to track it down again when preparing a new oratorical work or speaking before an assembly. Given this technologically confined reality, visual mnemonics were highly regarded in classical culture.

Mnemonics continued to be valued in the Middle Ages, as we saw in the previous chapter. Though the technology and spiritual ethos of the codex influenced medieval mnemonic practice—the monastics jettisoned imagery and replaced it with text-based memory systems—and though the codex was an important advance in the history of data management, the medieval world still lacked anything like the information-recall systems that saturate the digital world. Minor misquotations of the Bible and other texts pervade medieval manuscripts, demonstrating that when the learned of the Middle Ages needed to cite a source, they frequently did so by accessing not the source but their textual memory of the source. Though an improvement on papyrus rolls, the medieval codex remained an imperfect technology for information management and retrieval. If Alcuin's rhymed catalog is any indication, the monastic library was not organized according to any set scheme. It was, to be sure, easier to inspect a book library than the scroll or tablet library of antiquity, but the former's codices remained organized in a way that impeded "efficient sorting and resorting" according to theme, author, time period, and so on.[3] Furthermore—although I did not broach these subjects in the last chapter—many religious in the early and central Middle Ages were at best semiliterate; the preaching of the Gospel sprang by necessity from verbal memory. In addition, the labor and cost required to produce a book meant that monks and clerics would not have had access to a Bible or any other text at the drop of a hat; the average abbey did not have multiple copies or editions lying around. To access information in the Middle Ages, one thus continued to rely in part on a trained memory.

Given these technological limitations in the classical and medieval eras—such as the lack of sophisticated systems for managing, retrieving and integrating information—one might assume that the innovations of print culture would lead by default to the memory arts' marginalization. What need of mnemonics when print, cheap books, encyclopedias, compact leaflets, detailed titles, conventions for chapter and section divisions, and prototype card catalogs had all become commonplace? Contrary to this reasonable assumption, the memory arts were not abandoned in early modern Europe but continued to play a role in scholarly discussion. If anything, interest in mnemonics grew in many countries.

One reason for this interest was the pursuit of classical learning that distinguished late medieval and early modern scholarship. By the 1400s and even earlier, Cicero had become an esteemed classical author, and because scholars believed he had written *Rhetorica ad Herennium*, they devoted serious attention to "Tully's" memory system (Tully being the period's favored appellation for Marcus Tullius Cicero). A more crucial motivation for the renewed interest in the memory arts, however, was that Europe found itself in the midst of an information revolution during the period's various renaissances. Long-forgotten and new texts began to circulate widely, new trade routes and imperial ventures flooded Europe with novel objects of inquiry, and natural philosophy unlocked pioneering insight into the physical world, unleashing new ways to exert agency over her. At the same time, the fifteenth and sixteenth centuries saw the founding of more universities than ever before, from Leipzig to Glasgow to Toledo. Due to this sudden abundance of knowledge and an increase in students to ponder it, a taxonomic compulsion arose within Europe's intellectual class. (In England, this impulse took shape most clearly in the "invisible college" that came together to found the Royal Society.) It was believed that to learn root truths or general principles about newly discovered and rediscovered knowledge, one needed first to organize it all. The mnemonic tradition, scholars realized, offered systems for doing just that. Scholars understood that the various memory arts—with their spacious loci and principles of info compression and info integration—could "both order and help create content," in Lina Bolzoni's words.[4] They realized that mnemonic tools could therefore be used to manage the newly expanded universe of knowledge, either in the mind, on the page, or, in the case of a sixteenth-century Italian named Giulio Camillo, in a physical memory palace built to scale.[5] In addition, Renaissance scholars recognized that organizing knowledge—from the particulate to the planetary realms, from the minerals to the angels—was but a first step. Even when ordered, the universe as such was too vast in scope for any individual to comprehend. The universe and all it contained also needed to be reduced to a fathomable human scale, re-mediated into a lucid image or model. In *Cognition in the Wild*, cognitive scientist Edwin Hutchins states that one of the key features of European and Near Eastern science was in fact the creation of artifacts that functioned as "repositories of knowledge . . . represent[ing] more than any individual can know." He points to the astrolabe as an example of a technology that reduced and "embod[ied] kinds of knowledge that would be exceedingly difficult to represent mentally."

An astrolabe is a memory for the structure of the heavens. . . . It is possible for an individual navigator to learn an internal image of the heavens so rich that he can recognize arrangements of stars, and even imagine the locations of stars that are obscured by cloud or the horizon. However, it is not possible with such mental representations to control all those spatial relationships with the sort of precision that is possible in a durable external representation. In an external representation, structure can be built up gradually . . . so that the final product may be something that no individual could represent internally. In this respect, it is a physical residuum of generations of astronomical practice. It is a sedimentation of representations of cosmic regularities.[6]

Hutchins captures in this passage the movement from internal mnemonic imagery (the "image of the heavens" contained in a navigator's head) to external mnemonic devices representing all possible images (the astrolabe or star charts) that a single navigator could not hope to produce within the eye of his limited imagination.

This mnemonic movement typifies the early modern period. The astrolabe, the compass rose, the cabinet of curiosities or *Wunderkammer*, and many other inventions reduced unwieldy information to visual coherence. An interest in visual reduction explains, in part, why the early modern period developed an interest in the ars memoria. Like its precepts regarding visual order, the art of memory's precept about visual re-mediation—transforming unwieldy data into easily retrieved images—struck the early modern world as a valuable idea for solving its information overload problem. Far from being useless to early modern scholars, the ars memoria found itself implicated in the development of the ordered systems and images of knowledge that epitomize Renaissance thought. As a result, the Renaissance memory-treatise archive is unexpectedly "abundant," as Frances Yates says, "and selection has to be made from the great mass of the memory treatises if our story is not to be overwhelmed in too much detail."[7]

This archival abundance precludes an attempt to evaluate all national or regional circumstances in a single chapter. I limit my analysis here to the art of memory's transformation in early modern England (though I use archival metadata to place the English memory treatise in context). In particular, the chapter rescues one of Yates's observations, which to date has been neither verified nor given extended treatment but is, I believe, worth considering—not only for what it tells us about English rhetoric but also for what it suggests about the complexity of the fourth canon's Renaissance evolution across Europe.[8] Put briefly, Yates's claim is as follows: in the sixteenth and seventeenth centuries, the precepts of the classical art of memory found themselves at odds with England's Protestant elite following the rise of two distinct but related forces: iconoclasm and Ramism.

Under the influence of these forces, both of which Yates links with Protestant doctrine, the fourth canon underwent a dramatic change in England. Only a few centuries after John of Garland and Thomas Bradwardine had revived the imagery of the memory palace technique—following a millennium of text-centric mnemonic systems—the mnemonic arts once again were purged of imagery. The classical art employing the *oculus imaginationis* was replaced in England with an imageless system, developed by the sixteenth-century reformer Petrus Ramus, that called on the assistance of abstract order alone.

English mnemonics not only jettisoned imagery during this period but also, as a de facto consequence, broke the classical link between memoria and inventio. In classical and medieval mnemonic practice, order was visual, facilitating serendipitous browsing and aiding creative inventio (all familiar points by now). Making and ordering imagines in the memory palace or arranging the Bible into textual grids was never an end in itself. Information in the memory palace was to be ordered and reordered, arranged and rearranged, and connected and reconnected in various ways until something new emerged—a unique oration, refutation, prayer, sermon, or spiritual insight. While early modern continental treatises continued to subordinate "order" to a visual, idiosyncratic, imaginative process of bricolage and invention, English treatises adopted ordered association as the sole element of the mnemonic tradition worth preserving. The ancient bond between memoria and inventio was thus severed—a bond retained even by the Middle Ages' text-based mnemonics. This vital link gone, interest in artificial memory declined in England, even as the memory arts flourished elsewhere as devices relevant to the early modern project of organizing and visually modeling the expanded universe of knowledge.

Since Yates's foundational work, the idea that both iconoclasm and Ramism influenced English mnemonics has been advanced by Ioan P. Culianu in his work on early modern occultism[9] and affirmed by William West in the *Encyclopedia of Rhetoric*.[10] To date, however, no one has taken advantage of bibliographic resources to verify whether memory treatises did in fact decline in England in the late sixteenth and early seventeenth centuries, a period coinciding with the influence of iconoclasm and the rising influence of English Ramism. In this chapter, I provide such bibliographic evidence, demonstrating that the publication of memory treatises abated in England following Henry VIII's reforms, up to and during the English Civil War. I expand on Yates's thesis—which remains speculative in her work—by analyzing relevant memory treatises from early modern England, establishing that the few treatises published during this period tend to downplay or expurgate imagery. The evidence suggests that the oft-noted marginalization of rhetoric's fourth canon was not solely a function of written culture or "modernist" ideologies,[11] both of which are common explanations given. (The former argument, it will be shown, is demonstrably untrue; the latter is on the right track but incomplete.)

Along the way, I draw a connection between the Reformation iconoclasts, with their anti-imagery dogma, and contemporary scholars who espouse a *digital iconoclasm*, which is equally skeptical of visual knowledge, on the grounds that it obfuscates not God but the workings of ideology and the irreducibly complex forces of history. From Plato to Cromwell to contemporary software critics, a distrust of visual interfaces always emerges alongside the impulse to mediate the intangible with tangible objects. Now, as then, ideological warfare can be understood in part as a battle between iconoclasts and iconophiles.

A Distant View of the European Memory Treatise

To begin, I turn to the hitherto neglected bibliographies of early modern memory treatises. Using 4 bibliographies,[12] I located 428 mnemonic treatises published between 1430 and 1880, 270 of which were published between 1430 and 1800. These counts include stand-alone mnemonic treatises as well as rhetorical handbooks with a substantial memory section. When one graphs these memory treatises' dates and places of publication, a striking trend emerges: Between the years 1551 and 1600 (figure 3.1), England's output of memory treatises surpasses the number published on the continent. However, between the years 1601 and 1650 (figure 3.2), with

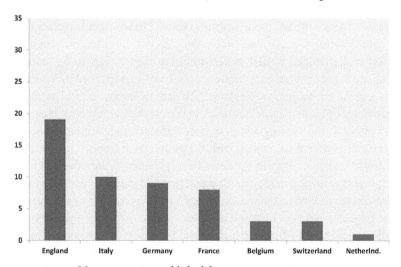

FIGURE 3.1. Memory treatises published, by country, 1551–1600

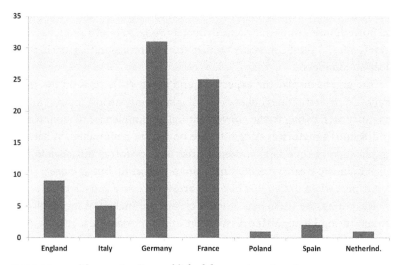

FIGURE 3.2. Memory treatises published, by country, 1601–1650

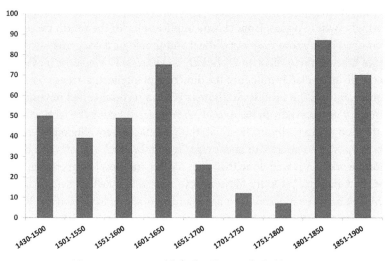

FIGURE 3.3. Memory treatises published in Europe, by half century

memory treatises flourishing in France and Germany—indeed, this period corresponds to the memory treatise's high point in early modern popularity (figure 3.3)—the number of treatises published in England decreases significantly. This trend is made particularly curious by the fact that, according to economic historians Eltjo Buringh and Jan Luiten van Zanden, the period 1601–1650 marks London's emergence as a major publication center. Prior to 1600, London produced fewer than 160,000 books per year, compared to 700,000 per year in France and Germany and 800,000

per year in Italy. After 1601, however, England caught up to the continental powerhouses, publishing approximately 700,000 books annually from
1601 to 1650.[13] Yet the memory treatise saw no corresponding rise in publication numbers.

The graphs display the expected trend if Yates's thesis is on the right
track. To reiterate, Yates believes that England early on lost interest in the
memory arts, owing to the convergent, related influences of iconoclasm
and Ramus's rhetorical system (more on that in a moment). What the
graphs show is a good fit between the rise of those forces and a halt in English memory-treatise production—not a perfect fit, but as close as one
can expect when untangling history's arrows of cause and effect.

Regarding the influence of iconoclasm, the inaugural moment can
be set during Henry VIII's dissolution of the monasteries, circa 1536 to
1541. (Granted, iconoclastic tendencies existed in England prior to the
dissolution—among the Lollards, for example—but, in my view, it is fair
to suggest that iconoclasm began exerting its greatest influence only once
it became state policy.) Although a literal smashing of the idols was devas-
tatingly swift in places, iconoclasm's implications for the fourth canon—
removed from more exigent political and theological concerns—would
have taken time to filter into scholarly awareness. Few historical events,
after all, immediately influence the direction of intellectual trends. For example, in 1553, the Protestant Thomas Wilson recommended mnemonic
imagery unreservedly in his *Arte of Rhetorique*, diverting the iconoclasts'
attention with a preliminary caveat: though images were religiously useful
in the past, he remarks, to encourage "remembrance" of saints and their
good works, "it is well done that such Idolles are [now] cleane taken out
of the Church."[14] (Oddly, Yates fails to note this excellent evidence for
the link between mnemonic imagery and iconoclasm in the English Protestant mind.) Wilson's squid ink worked, temporarily, for his treatise was
at first immensely popular, going through multiple editions until 1585—
when suddenly its reputation hit a brick wall, and no new printings were
offered again. William Fulwood's *Castel of Memorie* is another treatise that
provides a (relatively) full account of the visual, idiosyncratic precepts of
the ars memoria; after two printings in the 1560s, it, too, saw its final publication in 1573. A delay is thus to be expected when tracking the influence
of cultural forces on something like rhetorical precepts. The dry spell between 1601 and 1650 represents a generation that had come of age under
iconoclasm's political influence; and certainly it can be no coincidence
that this period, which saw slight English interest in the memory arts, also
saw a fresh round of iconoclastic destruction during the English Civil War.

The same point about delayed influence can be made regarding Ra-

mism, with its rejection of mnemonic imagery and its Aristotelian practice of memory qua abstract order. Walter Ong's bibliographic studies have
shown that the rise of English Ramism did not begin until the 1570s and
did not take off until the 1580s, when seven editions of Ramus's *Dialectica*
were published.[15] In other words, Ramus's influence cannot be much de-
tected in England until late in the sixteenth century, via the works of Gabriel Harvey, Dudley Fenner, and Abraham Fraunce. Ramus's influence
was initially limited to Calvinist and Puritan circles and did not make itself
more widely felt until the 1600s, when, in the words of Thomas Conley,
"Puritanism had gained the upper hand in English literary and political
affairs."[16] For example, the *Rhetorica* of Omer Talon—the most popular
Ramist rhetoric in the early modern period—was not published in England until 1592; it then saw printings in 1599, 1614, 1620, 1627, 1631, 1635,
and 1636. It was given a vernacular translation by Alexander Richardson
in 1629 that saw a second printing in 1657. Additionally, Ramus's *Dialectica* received only one English vernacular translation prior to 1600 (Fenner's, in 1584), but after 1626, it saw three translations across five editions.
In England, then, the Ramist treatise rose just as the memory treatise fell.
Recall again that Wilson's Ciceronian rhetoric—with its full treatment of
ars memoria—saw its final publication in 1585.

To conclude, memory treatise publications did decline in early modern England even as their printings flourished in France and Germany
(or, more accurately, in the fragmenting Holy Roman Empire). Memory
arts were so popular on the continent at the turn of the sixteenth and seventeenth centuries that in 1610 a Strasbourg printer collected the greatest
mnemonic hits, so to speak, into a single volume called *Gazophylacium
artis memoriae*. Another greatest hits volume was published in Leipzig in
1678 under the title *Variorum de arte memoriae*. To be sure, these European memory treatises are diverse in their approaches and precepts. Some
offer grandiose visions of a mental encyclopedia or a mnemonic image
of the universe of knowledge, others offer more humble systems for recalling commonplace information, some discuss mnemonics as strictly
mental practices, and others imagine "external devices" in forms rang-
ing from note cards to elaborate "rhetorical machines" or combinatorial
book wheels "capable of providing the necessary discourse for any occasion."[17] In addition, most of the European treatises discuss more than
one mnemonic tool—mnemonic alphabets, body mnemonics, acrostics,
the Herennian memory palace, pharmaceutical remedies for improved
memory—signaling preference for one system over others by its position
and length within the treatise. As a rule, however, nearly all the mnemonic
treatises published on the continent from the fifteenth through the seven-

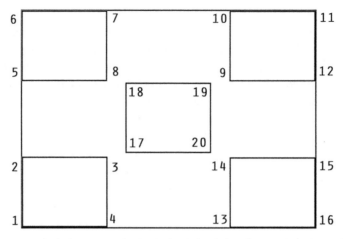

FIGURE 3.4. The basic idea of Schenkel's schematic *loci*. (Adapted from Kuwakino, "From domus sapientiae," 67.)

teenth centuries recognize the memory palace technique in one form or another. For example, Cosma Roselli's 1579 *Thesaurus artificiosae memoria* takes inspiration from Dante with a mnemonic loci system based on hell, purgatory, the earth, the heavens, and paradise, within which one situates visually re-mediated information about (respectively) damnation, secular matters, astronomy, and salvation. In *Phoenix seu de artificiosa memoria*, mentioned in the previous chapters, an Italian named Petrus Ravenna harnesses the idiosyncratic memoryscape by associating information with "fair maidens" known in his youth—a girl named Junipere in particular— whose memory continues to "excite [his] mind greatly."[18] (Tellingly, the *Phoenix* saw many publications in Europe from 1490 to 1608; its English translation by Robert Copland saw only a single printing in 1545.) The German Catholic theologian Johann Romberch, in his *Congestorium artificiosae memoriae*, recommends both real and fictitious memory spaces for situating imagery; he also recommends the use of naked bodies as images to associate information with (as does Roselli; see figure 3.8). And the mnemonic system of Lambert Schenkel—popular from 1617 onward— envisions a sort of architectural schematic comprised of compartmentalized buildings towering multiple stories, the buildings separated by streets into various districts, with each edifice housing information related to one of the seven liberal arts (figure 3.4). Schenkel's system is representative of a *geometrized* or *architecturalized* memory palace, which circulated in mnemonic treatises during and after his time: John Willis, Thomas Watson, Robert Fludd, Henry Herdson, Filippo Gesualdo, and even Cosma Roselli are among those who worked with this style of schematic loci that divided structures into smaller and smaller nooks to house information.[19] These systems neglect the classical technique's precepts for emotional imagery and bespoke loci, but they nevertheless retain the raw spatial quality of the technique. I point the interested reader to Koji Kuwakino's excellent work to learn more about this particular strand of mnemonic devices, used as elaborate—perhaps too elaborate—information management systems.[20]

On the continent, then, the art of memory survived well into the seventeenth century, even as authors continued to modify it and combine it with and rival it against other systems. At first, English mnemonic treatises did the same: Robert Copland's 1545 translation of the emotionally resonant *Phoenix* and Thomas Wilson's classical treatment of the art prove as much. However, something changed in England during the latter decades of the sixteenth century and the advent of the seventeenth. If one judges by raw publication counts (figure 3.3), 1601–1650 represents the early modern generation for which European memory arts was the most popular—a popularity that did not extend to England. There, memory treatise publications declined just as Ramist treatises, particularly those by Omer Talon, began to circulate widely. Significantly, these decades correspond to a period when Ramism and iconoclasm had been firmly established within England's ecology of ideas.

Ramism and Iconoclasm: An English Convergence

The subtle bond between these two forces—Ramism and iconoclasm—motivated Frances Yates to speculate on the effects of their unique confluence in the English context. We begin with the former. Viewed through the lens of iconoclasm, Yates argues, Ramus's "method" would have offered an attractive mnemonic alternative to Protestants uncomfortable with the visual, affective emphases of the memory palace technique.

A humanist reformer born in northern France in 1515, Petrus Ramus is known today for reducing rhetoric to two canons (style and delivery) and for enfolding the other three (invention, arrangement, and memory) into his own form of dialectical logic, an important part of which is *methodus*. The spirit behind Ramist method emerges in its well-known dichotomies and their corresponding diagrams, in which knowledge is set out on the page from the general to the specific (see figures 3.5 and 3.7). Lisa Jardine describes method as a pedagogical procedure for displaying material in a way that is clear and easily grasped by the student.[21] Method commences with a general definition of whatever subject is under consideration, then proceeds by way of binary division toward more and more specific material, providing explanations and examples along the way. Similarly, Walter Ong describes method as "the arrangement of arguments" from general to specific, "by which arrangement the whole matter can be more easily taught and apprehended."[22] For example, to treat grammar according to the precepts of method, a student would first define grammar, then divide it into its four (early modern) component parts: orthography, etymology, syntax, and prosody. Then the student would separate out the definitions of those component parts and further subdivide them into their own parts, and so on and so forth until reaching grammar's most granular subcomponents.[23] This division of material would be charted on the page in a series of branching summaries to produce something like a family tree of grammatical knowledge.[24]

The art of method—especially its binary diagrams—was understood by Ramus and his partisans as its own effective mnemonic system. In *Scholae in liberales artes*, Ramus is explicit about his disdain for the visual and palatial rules suggested by classical sources. "The art of memory," he counters, channeling Quintilian, "consists entirely in division and structure. If we seek then an art which will divide and structure things, we shall discover the art of memory."[25] Ramus here enfolds memoria into *methodus* by linking memorization of content with its "division and composition"— that is, with its organization. Jardine never uses the word *memory*, but that is clearly what she is talking about when she states that method "clarif[ies] the structure of a piece of writing so that the student can grasp its discursive organization. . . . [It] makes vivid to the student in a clearly tabulated version the complex running threads in any sophisticated piece of writing."[26] Method aids the mental grasping—the mnemonic impression—of the complex information with which one is engaged; it "relieve[s] the burden placed on memory," states Sharon Crowley, "by calling on the assistance of reason" as manifested in the logically divided diagrams.[27] This, for Ramus, is the true art of memory: the arrangement of information into a structure that enables recall by virtue of its logical order (modular organization, from general to specific) and linear order (branching dichotomies on the page).

In mnemonic terms, Ramus's method reduces the classical rule for *imagines et locis* to a simplified rule for logically ordered loci in page space. This bowdlerization echoes Aristotle's anamnesis, with its rational and sequential movements, and broadly resembles Quintilian's text-centric mnemonic advice in *Institutio oratoria*. Recall that Quintilian tells his readers to divide the words on the page into memorizable chunks, each subdivision serving as a sort of locus on the papyrus roll.[28] Quintilian's "divisions" of content, of course, were entirely functional; he offered no abstract principles according to which a student should divide material on a page, other than that each segment should be moderate in length. The monastics, too, did not conceive of their mental scripture grids as being ordered according to necessary logics; indeed, they took joy in rearrangement, finding new and insightful connections between previously unconnected books or passages. Ramus's segmented divisions, in contrast, are motivated strictly by the logical movement from general to specific. Each section becomes its own module in an integrated design, a perfectly proportioned doll in a Russian matryoshka set. Following Quintilian's mnemonic advice, different students could divide information in whatever ways seemed appropriate to them. Following Ramus's method, only one division of material would be "logically" correct (grammar → syntax → morphology); all others would be incorrect.

As evident from the depiction above, Ramist method is unconcerned with creative invention. *Methodus*—and thus mnemonic practice—is operative only once knowledge has been discovered, determined, and set in stone through other means of investigation.[29] Method simply arranges this knowledge on the page in an authoritative, easily taught, and easily memorized display. Grammar's definition and constituent parts, for example, are determined by grammarians. Once the grammarians have pronounced ex cathedra on grammar, the student of method can follow their prescriptions and organize the received material into a rationally ordered structure. Arrangement/memory of knowledge follows invention of knowledge.[30] (How does one *order* information before it has been found out? Ramus might ask.) Memory in his system is placed at the service of knowledge, to be sure, but it plays no part in its creation, its bricolage. A Ramist diagram would not encourage a student to consider, for example, what rhetoric might have to do with astronomy, or grammar with theology.

Compared to the classical ars memoria, Ramus's mnemonic art is drained of all visual and inventive precepts. It has retained the notion of "space as a vehicle of intelligibility," to use Ong's description, in the form of a technologized system of loci (the branching dichotomies).[31] But Ramus has rejected the memory palace's affective imagines, images whose order, unlike the dichotomies, could be reordered according to the orator's needs. Like Quintilian, whom he cites, Ramus removes images and refigures loci as fixed points in page space rather than in three-dimensional associative spaces drawn from lived or imaginary experience. What remains is Ramus's dichotomous system of textual order, of "division" of material, which Ramus calls method. "[Ramus's] conception of method," states Paolo Rossi, "as the *systematic and ordered disposition of notions* absorbs many of the 'rules' of mnemotechnics."[32] Ong puts it this way: "Ramus can adopt memory into dialectic because his entire topically conceived logic is itself a system of local memory."[33] However, with all due respect to these foundational Ramus scholars, Ramus's logic is *not* a system of memory as understood in antiquity nor even in the Middle Ages. It is an abridged system quite unlike the classical one. Discontinued are the vital precepts about images, their facilitation of invention, and their unfixed, idiosyncratic arrangement within a three-dimensional memoryscape.

The consequence of this change can be demonstrated visually by juxtaposing Ramist dichotomies with images taken from continental treatises inspired by the classical art (figures 3.5 to 3.8). The ars memoria is made "systematic" by Ramist method. In the classically inspired figures, words and information are transmuted into visual form. So visualized, the information becomes striking, affecting, grotesque, and embodied. The sensory, imaginative, and three-dimensional character of the classical art is on full display. There is little interest here in accurate or logical representation, for the purpose of mnemonic visualization is not accuracy but rhetorical utility: the practitioner manages information in this way because it facilitates creative use. The "truth" of the mnemonic cue is beside the point. The Ramist treatise, in contrast, transforms information not into creative imagery but into diagrams whose purpose is to organize received data in an accurate way.

To be sure, order and arrangement were always principles underlying the classical art. Simonides remembered the names of the dead dinner guests by reconstructing their places around a table. The principles of order inherent in any mnemonic tool motived Renaissance scholars, with their taxonomic bent, to adopt the memory arts for structuring the expanded universe of knowledge. Nevertheless, "order" in the memory palace was (a) visual/spatial rather than logical, and (b) one precept in an otherwise imaginative system whose images and arrangements were both mutable and determined by idiosyncratic proclivities. Few memory treatises prior to the Renaissance fail to acknowledge that the individual knows best how to excite her memory, how to construct her images, and how to organize them in a way that meets whatever exigencies she faces. Images were housed in memory palaces in a certain arrangement, but the arrangement was not fixed according to a strict logic: according to *Ad Herennium*, the entire purpose of familiar loci was to facilitate the arrangement, rearrangement, deletion, addition, and restyling of mnemonic images, as suited one's creative needs. The student of method, in contrast, could not reimagine the systematic Ramist display; he had to impress its received knowledge in his mind because it was received knowledge. Ra-

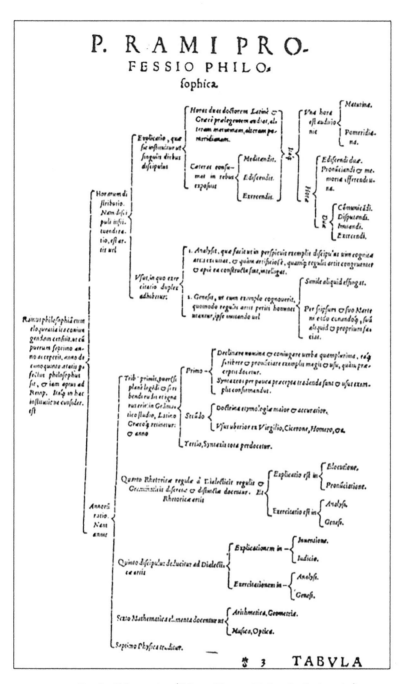

FIGURE 3.5. Ramist dichotomies. (Johann Thomas Freige, *Professio regia*.)

FIGURE 3.6. From *Rationarium Evangelistarium*, a reprint of *Ars Memoranda*. (For bibliographic information on this strange memory image, see Bouchot, *The Book*, 13.)

mism thus abandons the idea that memoria involves not only order but also sense, affect, and imagination.

The rejection of imagery that is on display in the Ramist figures lies at the heart of Ramism's severance of memoria and inventio. In classical practice, the technique of inner visualization was what linked the first and fourth canons. The insight behind visual mnemonics, Jay Bolter states, was that the way to address the "gap" between information and memory is "to write with images"—that is, to visualize what one needs to remember in an imaginative, personally affective form that brings *desiderata* immediately to mind.[34] Visual re-mediation and idiosyncratic association within the mind exploited that sensuous progression by which a picture or smell or song reignites past memory and calls before the mind's eye a thousand precise details. By harnessing this psychic process and coupling it with new information (via creative visual re-mediation), the mind becomes an interactive interface through which all sorts of information may be accessed, on the spot, for purposes of rhetorical invention. To reiterate, not only *access* but also *invention* are facilitated by this process because mnemonic spaces and imagery, by virtue of their creative forms and bespoke associations, foreground their own simulated nature. Imagines invite redesign, and, by extension, they invite the rhetor to imagine new ways to

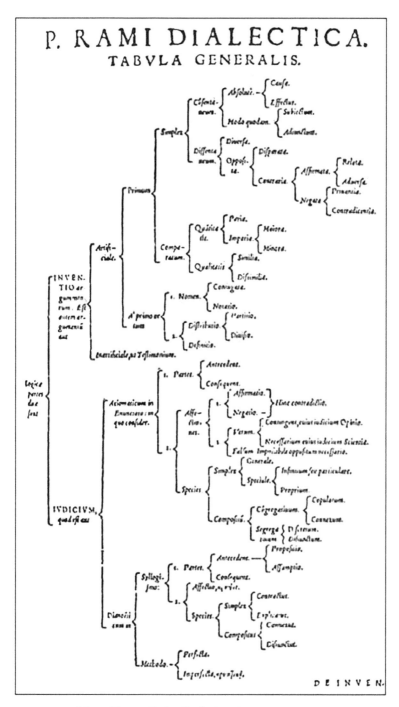

FIGURE 3.7. Johann Thomas Freige, *Professio regia*

Thefauri memoriæ artificiofæ

FIGURE 3.8. Cosmas Rosselius, *Thesuari memoriae artificiosae*

disassemble and reassemble the knowledge with which the images are associated, to consider new contacts between different pieces of information, and to contemplate how information might be artfully added to (or taken away from) the existing edifice—all of which ideally lead to novel insight in a given context. When put into imaginative form, knowledge resists reification; imagines and their spatial backdrops make knowledge adaptable, enabling the assemblage of information and new arrangements of that information.

In contrast to all this, Ramism qua mnemonic is a two-dimensional practice of dividing information logically on the page; it is a device for rote memorization and does not concern itself with mnemonic recall to facilitate knowledge construction. If anything, the Ramist diagram reifies information and its links. Indeed, that is the entire purpose of Ramist diagrams: to incarnate *the* one way to order information logically, from the general to the specific. The hierarchies of Ramist dichotomies resist their own reworking. To modify the Ramist edifice is to deform its knowledge and invalidate its necessary progression.

Thus, when Ramus jettisons images, the imaginative use of one's memoryscape goes out too. Yates remarks, "The stimulus for memory is now not the emotionally exciting mental image; it is the abstract order of dialectical analysis."[35] Following the reforms of Ramus, Talon, and others, memory becomes synonymous with order—loci become imageless, two-dimensional points on a page, whose connections are immutable. The canon of memory, in short, becomes allied with the canon of arrangement, leaving the invention of knowledge to other arts. Though he does not discuss mnemonics, Thomas Sloane argues that classical invention—a process that takes not only logic but also "sense [and] imagination" into consideration—is irreparably neutered by Ramus's iconoclastic system.[36] The Ramist understanding of memory was so strong in certain quarters that Francis Bacon, writing many decades after Ramus, could equate artificial memory entirely with rational order: "The memory-aids perform the following function: they help one to draw up a particular history whose parts are disposed in a particular order from the immense multitude of particular facts and from the mass of general natural history. The order of the particular history makes it easier for the intellect to work on the materials and execute its proper functions."[37] As with any cultural change, of course, England's adoption of Ramism and neglect of the ars memoria cannot be explained by a single factor. Multiple motivations, considerations, worldviews, and practices were involved. Method was also implicated, for example, in the pursuits of early modern natural philosophers (see Bacon above). It was not only the Ramists, in other words, who emphasized rational method over imagistic creativity in intellectual pursuits.[38] According to Yates, however, one of the more important cultural forces motivating the adoption of Ramism to the exclusion of mnemonic imagery was the iconoclasm that arose within certain Anglo-Protestant circles in the sixteenth century.

Though scholars have noted Ramus's enthusiastic reception by many European reformers[39]—particularly after Ramus's martyrdom at the Saint Bartholomew's Day massacre—Yates goes further to suggest that English Protestants in particular adopted Ramism due to their doctrines on image making. Yates's insight is that the memory palace technique is an extraordinarily graphic, sensual art. Given the technique's emphasis on emotionally exciting images, it makes sense that certain Protestants would seek to remove such fantasies from rhetorical practice, whether on the basis of a conscious iconoclastic ideology or an unconscious distaste for corporeal art and religion. Just as the Protestant smashes the idols "without" in the churches, Yates argues, the Protestant rhetorician smashes the idols "within" by removing from his mind the "wicked" and "idolatrous" images of the ars memoria.[40] Following this dissolution of the memory palace, Ramus's imageless method would have offered an attractive mnemonic alternative.

There was of course a banal wickedness inherent in some mnemonic imagery: Peter of Ravenna's fair maidens, Thomas Bradwardine's nude Eve and sawed-off thumbs, the testicles and bloody bodies in *Ad Herennium*. And perhaps the Herennian advice to exploit one's past and proclivities to rile up the passions of the memoryscape smacked of insalubrious narcissism. However, since the Middle Ages, a deeper wickedness had flickered in and out of the margins of the mnemonic tradition: the occult notae of the ars notoria. Described in the previous chapter, the "notorious" art was a strange amalgamation of the zodiac, geometric symbols or notae, and prayers to the secret names of angels (or demons). It was designed to grant its practitioner a perfect mastery of the seven liberal arts. Although the ars notoria had circulated for centuries—sometimes tolerated, other times condemned—in the late 1500s an excommunicated friar named Giordano Bruno returned cultural attention to occult mnemonic imagery just as iconoclasm began its ideological ascent in the Anglosphere. As if the imagery of the classical and late medieval ars memoria weren't questionable enough, Bruno's seemingly occult work ensured that the memory palace technique and all visual mnemonics would be met with iconoclastic censure in Protestant England.

Bruno's arts have received ample critical attention, so my treatment here will be brief. In his mnemonic works, Bruno draws on imagery, the ars combinatoria, and, of course, the irrational geometric notae, which Bruno calls "seals."[41] In *De umbris idearum*, Bruno describes a system for creating his version of a memory palace by positioning onto a tiered combinatorial wheel various places (or "subjects," in his terminology), images (or "adjects"), and attributes of or activities for the images.[42] The wheels themselves contain letters and symbols, but each letter or symbol stands for a mental image of some sort: A for image x, B for y, C for z, and so on. Combining these symbols in Bruno's wheel would produce an image containing actor, action, and context:

A Lycaon	A feasting	A in his chains
B Apollo	B with the Pythoness	B wearing his belt
C Argus	C herding the cows	C beheaded

Although featuring a finite set of people, activities, and backdrops, the tiered, rotating wheel could combine them all in endless amalgamations and thus suggest a whole pantheon of loci et imagines to populate the memory palace. (Bruno likens his system to the letters of the alphabet, which can represent with a finite symbolic set an infinite number of expressions.) But Bruno's images are not letters. As manifested in the examples above, they are unabashedly pagan, violent, and often profane things. They include a wolf eating a corpse, a suspended woman, Isis, Osiris, Minerva, Cyclops, Zoroaster, created idols, people partaking in prostitution, and a panoply of zodiacal imagery—for example, a naked man in his prime in the face of Taurus, and in the face of Scorpio, a woman bound hand-and-foot being beaten. Bruno also situates into his wheel images of the planetary gods, as described by Egyptian and Persian philosophers. Other imagery is taken directly from Cornelius Agrippa's book on ritual magic, *De Occulta Philosophia*.

This fantastical imagery was not designed to appeal to the Puritan scholar. It does, however, conform to the classical ideals—it is immersive, affective, grotesque. Bruno's system is also attuned to the Herennian idea that the memory palace must be a bespoke construction; Bruno tells his readers that the precise nature of the suggested images and backdrops should be "created and ordered . . . according to your judgment."[43] "The images are the things of imagination and thought; they are those things to make the heart pound, having the power of something wondrous, frightening, pleasant, sad; a friend, an enemy . . . ; things hoped for or which we are suspicious of; and all things that encroach powerfully on the inner emotions—bring these to bear."[44] Furthermore, like the memory palace technique and like all combinatorial wheels, Bruno's wheel of images is designed to facilitate creativity: "This art does not simply confer an art of memory," Bruno remarks, "but also opens many faculties of invention."[45] The images and their permutations are to represent/transform words and information, allowing one to reduce them ("to clothe subjects," as Bruno says)[46] into a more imaginative form that better facilitates mnemonic impression, recall, and use.

In another treatise, *Thirty Seals*, Bruno exchanges combinatorial imagery for geometric seals, similar to the notae of the ars notoria. Some of his seals include letters arranged spatially into, for example, the shape of a tree or a staircase. These seals are to be used as mnemonic loci into which images are situated or, alternatively, as memory images themselves to remediate complex ideas. Scott Gosnell likens the seals to "data structures" because they provide the user with various assemblies on which to display information.[47] Of course, to reiterate, Bruno's method of info management and display is informed not by disembodied "logic" but by a principle of visual transformation that, according to him, better enables recall and invention. Nonetheless, using the language of data science to describe Bruno's seals and his whole art is justified because, for all their strange and zodiacal imagery, the Brunian treatises provide scant evidence that they proffered "magical" systems. As far as Bruno was concerned, he was doing with images what other Renaissance scholars were doing with numbers and diagrams: constructing a system by which the vast chain of existence, from the particles to the planets, might be reduced to a model fathomable to the finite human mind. Bruno, states Paolo Rossi, developed his fanciful system not as an "indulgence" but as a legitimate alternative to the deductive procedures of logic and method that impelled Ramism, the encyclopedic tradition, and natural philosophy. Bruno considered himself a man of science but simply proposed in his works "a gradual approach to the rational faculties" via the imagination and memory. "He preferred fleeting images," Rossi states, "to the rigid concatenation of causes."[48] His art of memory was not developed against the early modern project of constructing ordered systems of knowledge so that humans might know and thereby master nature; it was implicated in it. Bruno counted himself among those scholars who sought to reduce knowledge to a system, structure, image, or model—the metaphor is fluid—to aid knowledge "inquiry," knowledge "invention," and knowledge "retention," to use Bruno's own words.[49]

As I remarked at the beginning of this chapter, early modern scholars had begun to realize that the world and, indeed, the universe were vaster places, full of a vaster array of things to be known, than scholars in earlier centuries had dared conceive. This expanding encyclopedia of knowledge heralded challenges to the insular assurance of Christian dogma. With their musings on and models of the natural world, viewed anew by the light of experiment and observation, some intellectuals inched nearer than others to the precipice of heresy. Some men, like Athanasius Kircher and Lambert Schenkel, escaped scrutiny by producing religiously imagistic,[50] austere, diagrammatic, or even pseudomathematical models (which is not a slight; as we know, math and geometry would turn out to be the winning "systems" through which the universe could be reduced to knowable, operable models). Bruno, on the other hand, drew heavily from the memory palace technique, zodiacal memory systems, and the graphic notae of the ars notoria. His choice of imagery—pagan, violent, licentious— guaranteed that his art would not only be rejected as natural philosophy but also condemned as heresy, tarnishing all mnemonic imagery by association in iconoclastic England.

To illustrate the iconoclastic grounds on which English Protestants rejected mnemonic imagery like Bruno's, Yates points to an influential Puritan theologian named William Perkins. In 1584, in a text entitled *Antidicsonus*, Perkins takes the offensive against an intensely image-laden memory treatise, *De umbra rationis*, penned by one Alexander Dicson, a

Scottish Catholic disciple of Giordano Bruno. As expected of a Brunian, Dicson's treatise is replete with zodiacal imagery and those strange seals reminiscent of the ars notoria. One can imagine how a Puritan might react to such symbology, imported by an Italian Catholic of all people. In his response to Dicson, Perkins declares his art of memory, so-called, morally reprehensible and full of carnal intent; it is "absurd" and "nonsense" and "utterly vain,"[51] for only a heretic would populate his mind with astrological signs. Perkins then compares Dicson's work to *The Phoenix*, whose Italian author, as we have seen, admits to using the memory of a beautiful maiden from his youth to create a striking mnemonic picture with which to associate information. "Such an art," Perkins states, conflating the Brunian and Herennian memory systems, "is clearly not for pious men, but has been made up by impious and confused people who disregard every divine law."[52] In a later text, *Prophetica*, Perkins continues to rebuke mnemonic imagery on religious grounds: "The animation of the images which is the key of memory is impious," he declares, "because it calls up absurd thoughts . . . which stimulate and light up depraved carnal affections." Perkins concludes with uncompromising iconoclastic censure, "A thing faigned in the mind by imagination is an idol."[53] Mnemonic imagery thus denounced, Perkins goes on to promote his preferred memory technique—the Ramist method: "[Dicson's] use of the celestial signs in memory is absurd, . . . for logical disposition is the sole discipline for memory, as Ramus teaches. Whatever of art may help the memory is the order and disposition of things, the fixing in the soul of what is first, what is second, what third. As to those places and images which are vulgarly spoken of, they are inept and rightly derided by any master of arts."[54] Following the cultural zeitgeist, Perkins decouples memory from visual imagination and reconnects it with "the order and disposition of things." Ramist order is what "helps the memory," the "fixing in the soul" of what is first, second, and third. Imagery be damned.

With Perkins as her representative anecdote, Yates argues that the Herennian memory palace as well as mnemonic imagery of any sort would have been deeply incompatible with the iconoclastic impulse. The Protestant who bristles at the sentiments induced by statues of the Virgin Mary will of course balk at the idea of populating one's mind with young maidens, bloody bodies, or ram's testicles. As if the imagines of the memory palace weren't carnal enough, it was quite easy, as Perkins demonstrates, to conflate mnemonic imagery per se with the blatantly heretical imagery of Giordano Bruno, whose systems and thought were roundly rejected by Anglo Protestants.

The debate between the Puritan Perkins and the Catholic Dicson (c.

1584) occurred when Bruno himself was in England, a visitor at Oxford and a houseguest of the French ambassador to Queen Elizabeth. (Bruno's presence in England likely sparked the Dicson/Perkins controversy in the first place.) While in England, Bruno wrote a number of treatises—including *Thirty Seals*—as he tried to secure an appointment at Oxford. His attempt was unsuccessful. A believer in the Copernican system, Bruno found little favor in the eyes of Oxford's Aristotelian faculty. After giving a lecture on Copernicanism to an audience of Oxford dons, Bruno was met with not a teaching post but disdain for his ideas and mockery of his Italian accent.[55] Outside the circle of self-professed Brunians, such as Alexander Dicson, Giordano Bruno was never accepted in Protestant England. Anglo disinterest in Brunian ideas is well represented by the poet and historian Samuel Daniel, who had met Bruno and later remarked that the Italian's love for hieroglyphic-esque imagery, in the form of esoteric and astrological signs, was unsound. Pronouncing such images "unperfect, by reason of the diuersitie of the natures of beastes and other things which they figured," Daniel instead praised the easily interpreted symbology and mottos of military insignia, which "disclose their intent by a more perfect order."[56]

Thus did Bruno's imaginative philosophies—which, from his perspective, served a scientific end—fall on the dry soil of an increasingly rational, Ramist, iconoclastic England. Branded a superstitious man, Bruno traveled to France for a time, then wandered from university to university—Marburg, Wittenberg, Padua—for several years but never secured a permanent appointment. He applied for a chair of mathematics at Padua but was turned down. (The chair went instead to a man named Galileo Galilei.) Nevertheless, like his apprentice Dicson in the face of William Perkins's criticism, Bruno doubled down on his ideas, becoming more and more heretical in the process, to the point where the Inquisition could no longer ignore him. In 1592, while teaching his art of memory to a Venetian nobleman, Bruno was handed over to the Inquisitors. After seven years of trials and imprisonment, Bruno was declared a heretic by Pope Clement VIII and, in 1600, burned at the stake.

This was the man whom England now associated with an art of memory based on imagery, imagination, and the invention of knowledge. Although Bruno's art of memory was not on trial at Oxford or before the Inquisition—other epistemological issues, to be sure, were involved in those debates—the rejection of his whole corpus of ideas meant that any memory art utilizing imagery was tainted with a Brunian association (and, again, there's little reason to doubt that mnemonic imagery of any sort was already tainted as far as England's iconoclasts were concerned). Although contemporary scholars have pointed out that not all English Protestants

were as wildly iconoclastic as Yates would have it,[57] even cautious historians do not allow for a Protestantism happy to encourage students to populate their minds with zodiacal, lustful, or otherwise affective imagery. Predictably, then, the memory palace technique and other visual mnemonics
began their retreat in England.

If at that point mnemonic imagery had no place in Anglo-Protestant
rhetoric, what was to replace it? Post-1600, the answer was obvious. The
old mnemonics were replaced by the imageless memory system developed
by Petrus Ramus. "The success of Ramism in . . . England," Yates remarks,
"may perhaps be partly accounted for by the fact that it provided [an] inner iconoclasm corresponding to the outer iconoclasm."[58] Indeed, as a
mnemonic system based on "imageless dialectical order," she argues, Ramism was custom made for Puritan and Calvinist iconoclasts.[59] Thus do
we find Thomas Wilson's and Robert Copland's visual mnemonic treatises
disappearing by the late 1500s, just as Ramist treatises rose to popularity.

Ramus was a French Huguenot, a group noted for its sometimes violent iconoclasm.[60] Various passages in Ramus's work suggest that he too
was "sympathetic to iconoclastic movements," so it is unsurprising that
his system offers a mnemonic art expurgated of imagery.[61] Of course, as
Yates notes, and as I would emphasize, there is no one-to-one correspondence between Ramism and Protestantism across all of Europe nor one
between Ramism and iconoclasm. For example, Ramism was also a force
in Germany, but iconoclasm less so. A "dissolution" of Catholic iconography was never state policy in Germany, as it was in England, and Martin
Luther early condemned the violent tendencies of iconoclasm, taking a
generally tolerant attitude toward religious imagery.[62] Thus one finds in
German rhetoric a fondness for Ramism but not a coinciding antipathy
toward imagery. Lutheran reformer Philipp Melanchthon provides a case
in point. Although he elects not to treat artificial memory in his rhetorical handbooks, he makes room for the emotional power of imagery in his
treatment of style. In a commentary on Cicero, Melanchthon states that
"rational and useful things" must be "clothed with circumstantial details,
in which pictures, which rush into our eyes, carry force to the eyes" and
thus have a greater rhetorical effect; he then provides a particularly violent example of intense word imagery from Virgil.[63] Another example is
the encyclopedist Johann Heinrich Alsted, a German Calvinist who in the
early 1600s published treatises on Ramus, Llull, and Giordano Bruno.[64]
To my knowledge, there is no English equivalent who found value in both
the Ramist and the Brunian systems.

This section's historical argument should thus be read as a cautiously
limited one. However, if we assume, as I think we can, that William Per-

kins is indicative of an *English* zeitgeist, then it stands to reason that in England—where Protestant leaders never condemned iconoclasm, as Luther did in Germany, and where iconoclasm had been de facto state policy—scholars found reason to not only adopt Ramism but also adopt it to the exclusion of classical mnemonics, which had problematic precepts about affective and often sensual imagery. Ramist method, devoid of imagery, was thus England's favored mnemonic technique heading into and during the 1600s.

Iconoclasm Now

It is a quirk of etymology that today "iconoclast" has a range of connotations, many positive, while the abstract "iconoclasm" cannot escape its principally religious connotation. The latter conjures images of black-clad purists like William Perkins combing the countryside for art, rosaries, stained-glass windows, and ornate crucifixes before setting fire to them all. This is an unfortunate association that keeps iconoclasm locked in the past, when it is in fact a common and contemporary force. The equalizing balance of image creation and image destruction remains as relevant today as it once was in London and in those more distant sites of iconoclastic fervor: Jerusalem, Constantinople, Mecca. For every tangible image or artifact created to mediate the intangible—God, truth, information, the real—there is an iconoclast ready to smash those mediating images, to reveal their putatively direct, complete, and transparent mediation for the constructed mystifications they are. As Jesus heretically proclaimed that the temple, made by human hands, was no longer a necessary medium between the Israelites and God, so do secular critics today seek to "show the hands of humans at work everywhere, so as to slaughter the sanctity of religion, the belief in fetishes, the worship of transcendent, heaven-sent icons, the strength of ideologies."[65]

There are similarities, I want to suggest, between iconoclasm and various strains of contemporary criticism. All share a revolutionary urge. They seek to unmask power and to demystify the world. For many philosophers of the twentieth century, the critical project par excellence was to break the identification between signs and the things they stand for—to argue, like an iconoclast, that our representations of things are not only proxies but also morally questionable ones whose designs are motivated by interests of power. "Since Antiquity," Bruno Latour states, "critics have never tired of denouncing the devious plots of humans who try to make others believe in non-existing fetishes. . . . The more the human hand can be seen as having worked on an image, the weaker is the image's claim to offer truth."[66] At least, that is how the iconoclast would describe it. The Islamic State's destruction of Palmyra or Oliver Cromwell's banning of Christmas might lead some to conclude that it is better for the world to remain mystified by icons and images.

I am not drawing a moral equivalence between Jesus, ISIL, and cultural criticism via their shared iconoclasm. I am merely suggesting that iconoclasm is a useful framework with which one can understand an array of ideological kit. Iconoclasm is ideologically promiscuous. One never knows among whom the impulse might arise, because it turns on who holds power, who does not, and who wants to demystify the means by which power circulates and sustains itself. Circa the new millennium, few would question the idea that smashing the icons of the powerful is an essential struggle. It is thus necessary to state at the outset that my critique of iconoclasm—insofar as it is a critique of critical projects themselves—is a constructive *provocation*, not an ideological fight picked in earnest; and the critics are expedient foils, not legitimate foes. I compare iconoclasm and critique because the move allows me to highlight curious similarities arising at incongruous joints in history and to explore how the blind spots of iconoclasts in the past resemble the blind spots of digital critics in the present.

For those who believe that twenty-first-century power structures need to be unmasked, claiming the iconoclastic mantle means turning a critical glare on the visual icons through which power and ideology most ubiquitously circulate: the screens and software interfaces that inundate contemporary life. Though I will expand on the concept in chapter 5, I want to present a few examples here of what I call *digital iconoclasm*. Put simply, digital iconoclasm is the spirit behind the trilogy *The Matrix*. In my view, much work in the philosophy and criticism of technology is a complex rendering of those films' basic idea: that the seductive projections on our screens obfuscate devious material machinations. Needless to say, there is more to this work than iconoclasm, and there is more to that iconoclasm than a theory-driven rendering of *The Matrix*. I will develop a deeper discussion later on. For now, my purpose is to highlight an iconoclastic tendency among digital critics, drawing a line from the historical censure of mnemonic imagery in the mind's eye to the contemporary critique of visualized information on the computer screen.

The iconoclastic tendency emerges, for example, in Wendy Hui Kyong Chun's *Programmed Visions*. Describing the analogous functions of software and ideology, Chun sounds every bit the iconoclast when she suggests that "software and ideology fit each other perfectly because both try to map the tangible effects of the intangible and to posit the intangible cause through visible cues. Both, in other words, promise a vision of the whole. . . . Through this process the invisible whole emerges as a thing, as something in its own right."[67] "What else is software," Chun asks in an earlier article, "if not the very effort . . . of making something intangible visible, while at the same time rendering the visible (such as the machine) invisible?"[68] Her critique here is *iconoclastic* through and through: the visual interface reduces the interactions of electricity and metal into a knowable but obfuscating image; it obfuscates the hardware, the real thing, the material—and thus the economic, political, historical—substrate. The collective energy of her argument is dedicated to unmasking (visual) software to reveal the (material, real, more complex) hardware underneath. This move discloses the literal economics that subsidize literal interfaces, but as Alexander Galloway notes, it also provides Chun with an allegory for all visually codified images—that is, ideological reductions—of a more nebulous, perhaps irreducibly complex world.[69] Chun highlights the obvious parallel to racial categorization as a reduction of nebulousness to naïve visual fetish. She might also have pointed to Giordano Bruno's wheel of images or Cosma Roselli's celestial spheres as yet another ideological reduction of a universe that cannot or at least should not be reduced to a (putatively) comprehensive visual form.

Chun's skepticism of visual reductions of irreducible complexity— whether on the screen or in the mind's eye—leads her to ask how necessary such visual, perceptual "maps" of the world really are. She even questions maps constructed with progressive goals in mind, such as Fredric Jameson's cognitive mappings, which submit social structures to a "spatial analysis" that enables a subject to situate herself and her daily activities within the larger social totality.[70] Jameson's maps, after all, like any data visualization, seek information mastery. ("Nothing is more beautiful than to know all," Athanasius Kircher wrote about his combinatorial mnemonic device.)[71] By replacing one image-map of the world for another, Chun suggests, perhaps even the ethical critic reinscribes the imperial drive to know and control: "to what extent is the desire to map not contrary to capitalism but rather integral to its current form, especially since it is through our mappings that we ourselves are mapped? That is, to what extent is our historically novel position not our ignorance and powerlessness, but rather our determination and our drive to know?"[72] Crafting through her iconoclasm an ethics of epistemology, Chun seems to be asking whether or not the "drive to know"—which, by default, means rendering the world's nebulous, real-time data streams visual and tangible to human perception—is in fact a net benefit to humanity. As all-too-human idols, Chun argues, maps and models of the world should be viewed skeptically, more questioned than used. "Could it be," she asks, "that rather than resort to maps, we need to immerse ourselves in net-worked flows—time-based movements that both underlie and frustrate maps?"[73] For Chun, the opposite of the idol seems to be a sort of immer-sion into the uncodifiable intricacy of lived reality, the adoption of an at-titude of contentment with knowing *what is before us* without a desire to know *everything else there is* through reductive coding and categorization. Indeed, in Chun's work I can't help hearing an echo of the Protestant Re-formers, who urged the faithful to immerse themselves in the mystery of direct, real-time communication with the Almighty, unmediated by priests or icons at codified times and in codified ways.

Another exemplar of digital iconoclasm is Friedrich Kittler's "There Is No Software." This essay could be read in its entirety as an exercise in skepticism about visual knowledge. "The so-called philosophy of the com-puter community," Kittler remarks, "tends to systematically obscure hard-ware by software, electronic signifiers by interfaces between formal and everyday languages." "Perfect graphic user interfaces," he continues, "hide a whole machine from its users."[74] Kittler's overall point in the essay is to highlight the obfuscating effects of the graphical user interface, which is not, according to him, an ethically neutral or accidental obfuscation: he reveals the strange capitalist logic that allows software—merely the vi-sual manifestation of electrical pulses on a silicon substrate—to be copy-righted. The shiny, user-friendly surface of software allows the fundamen-tal workings of physics to be harnessed for capital gain. Kittler concludes the essay by imagining a nonprogrammable, hardware-only computer that does not obfuscate its underlying physical, mathematical operations and invites the user "to enter that body of real numbers originally known as chaos."[75] (Again, notice the motif of *direct immersion*. One cannot help thinking about Plato's pursuit of direct, unmediated immersion into the prior ontologies of existence.) In Kittler's essay, as in Chun's work, the vi-sual interface is described as an ethically questionable fixation. Like Chun, Kittler wants to obviate the need for mediation between the knower and what she would comprehend, because through such visual mediation the thing itself becomes secondary knowledge: reified, false, and too easy to harness for unethical purposes.

Software's visual interface is of course powered by programmable code. Code is a hidden substrate of the interface even as it is also another visual interface—insofar as program languages are visual—between the user and the physics of the metal. Code, then, as much as the interface, is a tool of and analogy for ideological obfuscation. Indeed, returning to Chun, her critique in *Programmed Visions* is aimed largely at code, for she argues that it is programmability—the activity of reducing nebulous processes through codification—that acts as the cornerstone of power. Or as Friedrich Kittler has written elsewhere, code is the medium of long-distance control. Code itself is thus as ripe for critical unmasking as any app or graphical user interface. Mark C. Marino argues, with familiar iconoclastic rhetoric, that it is the job of the code critic to show that "code functions, typically, without being observed, perhaps even as representative of secret workings, interiority, hidden processes. This hidden language is what we can uncover, explore, access, and engage."[76] To reveal the human power at work behind not only pixels but also the code transforming machinic substrate into pixels—such is the job of the iconoclast, according to Marino, in our hypermediated, hypervisual ecologies.

For iconoclasts of the Reformation, like William Perkins, religious idols needed to be destroyed because they caused the faithful to seek carnal things, to worship objects instead of God, and because they were an important source of power for the papist hierarchy, who owned the most venerated and moneyed icons and relics. For iconoclasts of the digital age, visual interfaces are ripe for critique because they encourage their users to mistake image-models of the world for the world, mimicking and thus further inuring us to other ideological reductions, including racial codification, and because they are an important source of power for men in control, who have ample motive to create simplistic models of the world that constantly reinforce their power over what you click on and what you believe (which are, by design, often the same thing).

The urgency of digital critique should be palpable even to the most jaded netizen. Marino's, Kittler's, and Chun's digital iconoclasm is crucial. At the same time, one cannot deny the visceral *usefulness* of software's icons, data visualizations, and other imagistic models. Let the person who is without a social media account cast the first stone. As long as the icons of the iPhone and iPad capture the human gaze, a practice of digital iconography is as necessary as a critical unmasking of it. Critique is important, but we should admit the possibility of using digital interfaces without ceding them total control. Utilizing icons need not mean worshipping idols (a point the sophists understood but Plato did not). Learning to utilize something without being enthralled to it is, in my view, its own form of power and critique.

To take my argument further, we must learn a practice of digital iconography—what I will eventually call a practice of digital memory—not only because humans find it impossible to look away from new media but also because *being human* means needing and utilizing mediators. The screen is simply the latest layer. Iconoclasm in all its forms overlooks the salient rebuttal of the icono-pragmatist (not quite the iconophile) to whom Bruno Latour has given voice: "we cannot do without images, intermediaries, mediators of all shapes and forms, because this is the only way to access God, Nature, Truth and Science."[77] The icons of the screen may obfuscate and they may enable power, but we need icons nonetheless. Jesus was the great iconoclast, according to C. S. Lewis,[78] but as his fellow Inkling Owen Barfield points out in his study of idolatry, Jesus toppled the idol of the temple only to replace it with new mediators between humanity and God—namely, himself, the Eucharist, and his parables for salvation.[79] The human, it seems, cannot approach complexity without a simpler, more tangible form to guide it. Thomas Nagel argues in his comparison of bat and human perception that a human's eyes, ears, skin, and the whole nervous system already act as an interface between "self" and the universe's interminable bombardment of wave and particle.[80] As the human exists, an unmediated immersion into the universe's data streams would trigger a moment of schizophrenia followed by a heart attack. We need our embodied interface to survive. And we need re-mediations to think. We may critique media, but humans cannot escape the necessity of mediation; they are trapped in blind solipsism if they try.

Indeed, what else is memory but the brain's attempt to encode and curate the world's nebulous real-time happenings into visual-spatial models, to interface with a nearly limitless past via a reductive but therefore comprehensible image of it? Our digital interfaces code and categorize complexity because our bodies and memories do the same thing. This is fundamental. A critical mind-set is ethically and practically important, to be sure. It is necessary to bear in mind that we never *actually* grasp the world, the past, or one another in fullness and transparency any more than the classical memory palace *actually* accessed Cicero's "whole past with its storehouse of examples and precedents"[81] or any more than Bruno's wheels *actually* reduced the universe of knowledge to a manageable inventory of images. Nevertheless, one can accept this critical point while recognizing that humans also need an ethical practice of imagistic reduction, a practice of memory formation in both its natural and artificial forms.

As the ars memoria once converted the unconscious processes of memory into a conscious art of mnemonic imagery, so, too, might a digital mnemonic art turn the often unconscious consumption of the screen's visuals into a conscious art of rhetorical invention. The key, again, is to learn to manipulate digital icons without turning them into idols, to not *be invented by* someone else's image-models but render our own image-models in ways that facilitate the activities, lives, and cultures we find most salutary. I doubt even Chun wants to relinquish the human "drive to know" simply because our image-models never tell the whole truth. I would suggest that a beneficial supplement to critique is a practice of image rendering that centers the image's useful half-truth.

In chapter 5, I'll undertake a fuller articulation of the issues raised in this short section: iconoclasm, iconophilia, and their relationship to memory formation as a conscious rhetorical art and, today, a digital one.

The Memory Palace in Ruins

Ramus's method—devoid of imagery—was the preferred mnemonic framework in England from the late 1500s onward. To be sure, English memory treatises were published during this time, but they have about them a dry, unimaginative quality that stands in sharp contrast to continental memory treatises (such as Cosma Roselli's, with its celestial spheres), medieval English memory treatises (such as Thomas Bradwardine's, with its surrealist imagery), and, of course, the precepts of *Ad Herennium*. Surveying a few of these late-sixteenth-century and seventeenth-century treatises will provide further evidence that mnemonic imagery was in retreat in Anglo-Protestant rhetoric during this period of iconoclastic and Ramist reform.

William Fulwood's *Castel of Memorie*—printed in 1562, 1563, and 1573—emerges from a distinct tradition of folk remedies for improving the memory. In fact, the treatise is a translation of a medicinal text by the Italian chemist Guglielmo Gratarolo. Gratarolo was a Calvinist who fled Italy to seek refuge in Strasbourg and Basel. (Fulwood himself was likely a Protestant, for he dedicates *Castel* to Robert Dudley, a suitor to Queen Elizabeth I and, according to Susan Doran, a supporter of the Huguenots during their iconoclastic furors in the 1560s.)[82] Given its status as a pharmaceutical text, Fulwood's *Castel* focuses mostly on medicinal and herbal remedies for improving the memory: one chapter discusses "chiefe causes, whereby the Memorie is hurt, with their signes and cures"; another reports on "certaine best approued and chosen medicinable compounded remedies, and preseruatiues greatly encreasing the Memory."[83] The loci et imagines of the classical art Fulwood cites fleetingly at the end of the text: "the vii. Chapter entreateth in fewe woordes of locall or Artificiall Memorie." Where he mentions imagery, Fulwood does offer a Herennian explanation, noting that mnemonic images are most effective when drawn from unique personal experience or when emotionally charged: to "styre up the memory," he states, one should construct images of "mery, cruell, iniurious, merueilous, excellently faire, or exceedingly foule" things.[84] He also discusses visual homophony and devises a bawdy example (involving urine poured on someone's head)[85] of how to remember names. Indeed, earlier in the chapter I compared Fulwood's treatment of the ars memoria to its treatment in Thomas Wilson's *Arte of Rhetorique*. Both of these texts, I noted, met their final printings just as Ramist treatises began to circulate widely. However, Fulwood's discussion of mnemonic imagery is overall a brief one, and his chapter on the ars memoria dedicates more attention to the loci. Fulwood goes into detail, for example, about the exact number of feet that should exist between one's mnemonic places. An obsession with the nature of the loci—turning the Herennian rules into some sort of primer for architectural design—is a feature of English memory treatises in the 1600s, and it is already here in miniature in Fulwood's mid-1500s text. Loci, one presumes, were safer mnemonic tools in Fulwood's iconoclastic England than were imagines. In addition, Fulwood gives the final word in his treatise to a more logical, Aristotelian treatment of artificial memory, one that presages Ramus's impending influence: "Order consisteth in a certayne proportion and connexion," he states. "And if you take anye one thinge of those that are set in an exquisite and perfecte order, the reste will followe and forthwyth by a certayne necessarye continuation eyther of Nature or of Arte."[86]

An English memory treatise that more explicitly diminishes the role of imagery is John Willis's *Mnemonica*, published in Latin in 1618, with English translations printed in 1621, 1654, and 1661. Willis discusses imagery, to be sure, and his system is unambiguously influenced by the memory palace technique. However, Willis's mnemonic visuals are literalist and plain, lacking the affective, idiosyncratic quality of the classical ars memoria. For instance, Willis suggests that if one must remember to inquire into the price of seed at market, one should construct an image of a countryman "pouring wheate out of a sacke into a bushell"; to remember that one needs to procure mowers to cut down the meadow grass, one should construct an image of husbandmen "whetting their sithes."[87] This mundane, literalist sort of imagery fills the treatise. "Willis's primary concern," states Adam Rzepka, "is to make the mnemonic imagination . . . re-stage the world as it is."[88] There is no sense in which Willis's art is one of visual re-mediation or creative info integration. The height of his inventiveness comes in the suggestion to remember information about ants by constructing an image of an ant heap because an image of a single ant would escape one's mnemonic sight. In addition to being literalist, his mnemonic imagery also seems purposefully ascetic. Referring obliquely to Peter of Ravenna's *Phoenix*, Willis taps into his inner Puritan and chastises the practice of using women and men "in animation" in the mind's eye. "It is impious and dangerous," he states, "to cherish lustful or scurrilous images in the mind."[89]

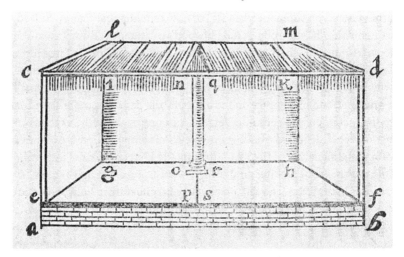

FIGURE 3.9. A "repository" in John Willis's *Mnemonica*. (As printed in von Feinaigle, *New Art of Memory*, 248.)

While Willis conjures little imagination or affect when it comes to mnemonic imagery, he devotes ample resourcefulness to the creation of his place system, his "repository," as he calls it, which is to exist in the form of a mental "theater" (figure 3.9). Willis describes his repository with all the care of a draftsman: "A Repository is an imaginary fabrick, fancied Artificially, built of hewen stone, in form of a Theater, the form whereof followeth; suppose the Edifice to be twelve yards in length within the walls, in breadth six yards, and in height seven yards, the roof thereof flat, leaded above, and pargetted underneath. . . . Let all the walls be wainscotted with presse boards, so artificially plained and glewed, that the Joynts be indiscernible."[90] And so on for whole paragraphs. Willis is more concerned here with building an orderly, mental place system than with conjuring imagery to fill it. To be sure, Willis's place system requires the reader to imagine a true three-dimensional space—very like the classical memory palace, unlike the text-space of medieval mnemonics, and very unlike Ramus's two-dimensional diagrams. Willis's *Mnemonica* thus gets the classical art half right. Missing, however, are affective imagines, and precepts regarding their mutability for purposes of inventio. Willis's conversion of the memoryscape into a solitary "theater" in fact arrests the mind's eye and immobilizes its immersive movement within the bespoke loci of memory. Instead of wandering from, say, the locus of a childhood bedroom out to the front yard where I smell newly cut grass, then down to the park and the sounds of dogs and basketball—each space disclosing the re-mediated images of whatever information I have placed there—I can never leave the confines of Willis's carefully designed theater. Even more so than the admonition against affective imagery, this confinement of the mind's eye demonstrates Willis's misunderstanding of the classical precepts.

To be fair, Willis states that his art is written to be useful to commoners, so he does not concern himself with those complex issues of law, politics, and theology that occupied other mnemonic writers and that perhaps stimulated more imaginative visualizations. In addition, Willis's insistence on one-to-one mimesis for mnemonic imagery leads him into interesting confrontations with the instability of the imagination's relationship to the world outside it. For example, I would have difficulty recreating in the mind's eye even something so mundane as cutting grass without imbuing it with subjective (and affective) associations. Nevertheless, a lingering distaste for mnemonic imagery and the Ramist link between memory and order have both left their mark on Willis's treatise: by applying care to "the greater parts" of a speech and the "Logical Arguments [with which] each part is handled," Willis states, the rhetor sets the stage for easy remembrance, because "the perfect Method of a speech . . . doth much conduce to remember the whole."[91]

Other English treatises exemplifying the retreat of imagery from the fourth canon include Henry Herdson's *The Art of Memory Made Plaine*, which saw two printings in 1651 and another in 1654, and Thomas Fuller's 1641 book *The Holy State and the Profane State*, which contains a section "On Memory." Herdson's text is a modest adaptation of Willis's precepts but with even duller imagery and an even greater obsession with the precise measurements and layouts of the repositories. Herdson discusses how to convert numbers and letters into such uninspiring mental pictures as a candle, a foot, a pipe, and similar household items (compare this to Bradwardine's half-naked Eve and a lamb with seven heads).[92] Thomas Fuller's text is entirely dismissive of the art of memory. He names its practitioners "memory-mountebanks," offering instead such advice as write things down that need remembering.[93]

However, perhaps the best example of iconoclasm's and Ramism's influence on early modern English rhetoric is Charles Butler's *Oratoriae libri duo*. Originally published in 1597 as a commentary on Ramus's and Talon's work, it was supplemented by Butler with original material and published under its new title in 1621.[94] In his chapter on memory, Butler draws on Thomas Wilson's *Arte of Rhetorique*, so ostensibly his book offers a Ciceronian treatment of the canon of memory. However, although Butler's general plan mirrors Wilson's—for example, first treating the physiology of memory, then offering examples of mnemonic feats throughout history, and next dividing the subject into its natural and artificial kinds—the sections on image making are revealingly unalike.

Let's look at Wilson's treatment as the comparison point. He begins with what are perhaps the two most important points about classical mnemonics: that the images should be adapted to the rhetor's own context and inclinations, and that the images are to be purposely affecting: "But the Images we may chaunge, as the matter shal giue iust cause, vsing such as shal serue best for the knowledge of thinges. The which Images must bee set foorth, as though they were stirring, yea, they must be sometimes made ramping, & last of al, they must be made of things notable, such as may cause earnest impression of things in our minde."[95] Wilson goes on to provide an original, detailed discussion of the practice of constructing mental imagery. For example, to remember criminal charges—adultery, manslaughter, and theft, among others—leveled against a particularly iniquitous friend, Wilson suggests a small parade of icons from myth and history: Venus for adultery, Richard III or some other "notable murtherer"[96] for manslaughter, the fire-breathing giant Cacus[97] for theft, and so on. Wilson also notes that one's loci should be equally imaginative. He suggests using beasts that stand for letters of the alphabet and then assigning images to various parts of each animal—"in the Head, the Bellie, in the Taile, in the former parte of the legges, & also in the hinder part."[98] Wilson next explores *Dissoi logoi*'s technique of visual homophony, such as remembering a man named Wingfeelde by picturing "the wing of a birde, and a greene feelde to walke in."[99] He concludes his memory section by defending visual mnemonics against authorities such as Erasmus who doubt its efficacy. Channeling Cicero's high view of the ars memoria, Wilson states that the eye "conteineth the impression of things more assuredly, then any of the other sences" and that "when a man . . . seeth a thing (as by artificiall memorie, he doth almost see thinges liuely), hee doth remember it much the beter."[100] He concludes by citing the older Greek metaphor for memory as a "Seale" or insignia in wax rather than the Roman metaphor of letters on wax—for Wilson, the art of memory is a pictorial, not an alphabetic, form of inner writing.[101]

In contrast to Wilson's lengthy depiction of image making, Charles Butler's depiction—although based on Wilson's text—is essentially nonexistent. Bowdlerizing its source, Butler's memory section offers but one short quote from *Ad Herennium* on imagines: "Images are a kind of forms and marks and patterns of the object we wish to remember; if we wish to recall a horse, a lion, or an eagle, we must set the images of these in fixed places."[102] And nothing more. Although he devotes ample space to the physiology of memory as well as to Aristotle's philosophical work on the subject, Butler offers no original contribution to the making of mnemonic images; he fails to note their re-mediational, purposely emotional qualities, and he tells his readers that if they "wish to know more about the image[s]," they should simply consult *Ad Herennium*.[103] Butler then moves on to quote—not Cicero, as Wilson does—but Quintilian, who among classical authorities is the most skeptical about the art of memory's efficacy. Echoing Quintilian's complaint, Butler says that it is probably more difficult to construct a memory palace than it is to simply remember things by rote.[104] He declares that he, at any rate, cannot see the appeal of the art. He then moves on to more comfortable Ramist ground, writing that good "order" helps the memory and that "the parts of order in knitting the oration together are division and composition."[105]

Moving from Wilson's beasts, birds, fire-breathing giants, goddesses, murderous kings, and Ciceronian quotations to Butler's Quintilianesque incredulity and dismissive directive to just read *Herennium* if you want to know how to construct images, one senses a remarkable change in English memory arts from the Elizabethan to the Ramist world. Not only does England fail to produce many memory treatises post-1600, the memory treatises that the country does produce are largely devoid of the inventive images that mark earlier English treatises and that continued to mark treatises on the continent. Like Yates, I believe that part of the explanation has to do with the unique confluence of iconoclasm and the imageless alternative found in Ramus's *methodus*. To be sure, Ramism spread widely, but only in iconoclastic England did the adoption of method coincide so closely with the removal of imagery from the ars memoria.

Wherefore Art Thou, Memoria?

Rhetoricians have long noted that, somewhere along the way, the canon of memory largely disappeared from rhetoric. A common argument is that the rise of written culture is to blame for memory's demise. However, in light of the bibliographic evidence presented in the earlier figures, this claim seems questionable. It is not until the 1700s—well into the reign of print—that we see a wholesale European decline in memory treatises. Yet even this decline is followed by an unexpected resurgence in mnemonics in the 1800s; Robert Connors claims that this is the period when written rhetoric was replacing oratory in school settings.[106] In addition, the bibliographic evidence suggests that the story of memory's decline will need to be told at a regional or national scale. Following Yates, I believe that the unique convergence of iconoclasm and Ramism explains why England lost interest in the memory arts. What explains the decline in England, however, may not explain it in Italy, Germany, or anywhere else. Placing blame on writing, print, or "modernist" ideology in general elides important distinctions and developments that must be tracked if the field wishes to understand more fully this crucial phase of rhetoric's evolution. For now, however, I set aside this early modern story for future research. Moving forward, I want to turn attention, in the next chapter, to the steep decline in mnemonic publications in Europe during the eighteenth century and their subsequent rise in the nineteenth.

CHAPTER 4

The Memory Palace Modernized

England lost interest in artificial memory in the late sixteenth and early seventeenth centuries. The whole of Europe, however, was not long behind, collectively losing interest in it after the middle of the seventeenth century (see figure 3.3). By the eighteenth century, the entire mnemonic tradition seems to have lost its status as a minor but valued branch of Europe's cultural repertoire and was altogether forgotten. Yet, unexpectedly, this Enlightenment-era decline was followed by a sudden resurgence in interest in mnemonics during the 1800s. In my view, both the decline and the resurgence compose two parts of the same story and can be grouped together into a period I call the memory arts' "modernization."

To reiterate the previous chapter's argument, England lost interest in the memory arts due to the unique confluence of Ramism and Puritan iconoclasm that occurred there from the middle 1500s through the middle 1600s. Lacking the influence of Petrus Ramus and the rejection of Giordano Bruno, however, the Anglosphere would have abandoned mnemonics in the long run anyway. The publication trends introduced in the previous chapter speak volumes about the tradition's lack of popularity in the Age of Enlightenment. The years between 1650 and 1700 saw the continued frenzy of publication activity in England, France, and Germany. England and France published nearly one hundred million books each during these decades, which also saw the growth of publication centers in Ireland, the Netherlands, Sweden, Spain, and Poland.[1] Instead of keeping pace with those raw publication trends or holding steady against them, the number of mnemonic treatises published during the latter half of the seventeenth century plummeted from its zenith in the first half of that century. This downward trend hit its nadir in the 1700s.

The few treatises published during the early 1700s were notably different from the pictorial alphabets, schematic loci, and Herennian moods pervading their late medieval and early modern (continental) predecessors. They were forerunners of what became in short order a pseudopsy-chological, technical mnemonic tradition informed by the period's empir-icist, scientific ethos. Incubated in the age of reason, this new mnemonic culture in fact surged in popularity in the 1800s. It had little to do with rhetoric's tradition of ars memoria (even less so than Ramist method, which, for all its faults, at least retained memoria's rhetorical provenance). What did the modern mnemonists produce? They produced systems in which rote memorization of facts and figures was the solitary goal, visual precepts were further bowdlerized or trivialized, and the memoryscape lost all relevance to rhetoric, affect, and the invention or even the orga-nization of knowledge. Unlike the art of delivery—which did not disap-pear from rhetorical theory so much as migrate to the niche quarter of the elocutionists—the memory palace technique found itself in the modern era wholly divorced from rhetorical activity, falling from its former Cicero-nian glory to a "train your memory" technique reduced to cultural sterility. The current chapter examines this rote, pseudopsychological mnemonic culture, then outlines another (more interesting) trajectory taken by the modernized memory arts: the ars combinatoria in its original Llullian and later "computational" conceptions.

Mnemonica Technica

In midsummer 1888, the New York Supreme Court issued a preliminary injunction against a man named George Fellows. The court ordered Fel-lows to stop printing a tract he had written entitled *Loisette Exposed*. The suit had been brought against Mr. Fellows by Professor Alphonse Loisette, the author of *Instantaneous Art of Never Forgetting*, which Loisette had ad-vertised as an original and unique system for strengthening the memory. In Loisette's own words, his system was "the first and only system that re-ally rests on nature" and "a unique and original device, or method of fix-ing in mind the things to be remembered" and "wholly unlike mnemonics in conception."[2] According to Professor Loisette, George Fellows's little tract was a complete reprint of his—Loisette's—original memory system. *Loisette Exposed* amounted to little more than "literary piracy." The New York Supreme Court initially agreed:

> Ordered, that the said defendant, George S. Fellows, . . . and all others act-ing in aid or assistance of him . . . are hereby restrained, prohibited, and enjoined, under the penalties by law prescribed, from printing, publishing, selling, or giving away . . . the plaintiff's system of teaching memory men-tioned in the complaint, published by the defendant, entitled "Loisette

Exposed." . . . This injunction is granted on the ground that the plaintiff has a right of property, as the author of his system for teaching memory.[3]

During the ensuing legal battle, however, George Fellows argued that he had every right to reprint Loisette's "original" memory system because there was nothing original about it. Loisette could no more claim ownership of his memory system than a math teacher could claim ownership of calculus. The purpose of *Loisette Exposed*, Fellows explained, was to alert the paying public to the fraudulent claims made by Alphonse Loisette. The so-called "Loisettian School of Physiological Memory, or Instantaneous Art of Never Forgetting" was nothing more than a modification of mnemonic systems dating back centuries. To make his case, Fellows and his counselors rallied encyclopedia entries attesting to the ancient provenance of artificial memory techniques. Submitting testimony on behalf of Mr. Fellows were men of such eminent office as Thomas H. McKee, assistant librarian to the US Senate, and Charles W. Johnson, chief clerk of the Senate. The suit ended with a mutual settlement between George Fellows and Professor Alphonse Loisette—or, more precisely, it ended with a settlement offered by Professor Loisette that Mr. Fellows refused to sign. The professor withdrew his suit anyway. Mr. Fellows continued to publish *Loisette Exposed* and even rewrote it for a more widely circulated volume entitled *Memory Systems New and Old*, published in 1888 by A. E. Middleton.

This is an interesting story because it tells us there was a large enough market for artificial memory systems in Gilded Age America that Professor Loisette felt his livelihood threatened by the "libelous" claims of George Fellows. A significant sum of money was involved in the suit: a lawyer operating on behalf of Loisette offered six thousand dollars, not a trivial figure at the time, to Fellows to remove *Loisette Exposed* from the market. That a man could make a living by teaching mnemonic techniques is interesting. More interesting is that several government officials were concerned enough about the history of artificial memory to become involved in the case against Loisette's claims to originality. Here, at the turn of the century, in New York City, a small drama played out over whether or not one could copyright a mnemonic system. Artificial memory was still on the intellectual radar—not in the universities as it had been during the Renaissance or in the monasteries as in the Middle Ages, but in the hands of itinerant teachers, as in the pre-Socratic era.

But these itinerant teachers were not sophists, and the modern West was not ancient Greece. The extemporaneous arts of oratory, eristic, agonistic debate, and lyric poetry and the supporting art of mnemonics were not what people wanted to pay for. In readings of Loisette's and other modern memory systems, it becomes evident that they are nothing like the sophistic or Herennian art, with its precepts for visual information remediation and affective memory spaces. Nor are they like monastic text-based mnemonics nor even the late medieval and early modern adaptations of the classical memory palace technique. They are, rather, grounded in a rationalist psychology similar to the associational principles put forward by Aristotle in *On Memory*—what scholars in the nineteenth century came to know as "association of ideas."

Memory systems like Loisette's "school of physiological memory" are the end point in our history of Western mnemonics. They are, in fact, *mnemonics* in the twenty-first-century sense of the word—denoting self-help memory-improvement strategies on one hand or, on the other, the sort of impressive displays of rote memorization indicative of genius or high IQ, such as Akira Haraguchi's memorization of pi to 111,700 digits.[4] To be sure, this contemporary mnemonic culture is a fascinating one. It has been profiled by Joshua Foer in his bestselling book *Moonwalking with Einstein*. Nevertheless, for all intents, practices, and purposes, it is not a direct descendant of the memory palace technique developed along the shores of the ancient Mediterranean. It descends, rather, from the pseudopsychological and technical memory culture that emerged during the Enlightenment and gained popularity in the Victorian era.

It might be said that this culture took embryonic form when authors of memory treatises, explicitly labeled as such, began to relegate the Herennian art to a minor role within the whole treatise. As early as 1562, as we saw in the last chapter, William Fulwood had demoted the memory palace's imagistic precepts to a brief mention in the last chapter of his *Castel of Memorie*. Fulwood's devaluation of the Herennian art and his larger interest in medicinal forms of memory enhancement were most likely responses to the iconoclastic zeitgeist of early modern England. However, by 1700, the de-emphasis of mnemonic imagery had become a common characteristic of not only English memory treatises but continental ones as well. One of the best examples of this collective demotion appears in Marius D'Assigny's *Art of Memory*, which saw three printings by 1706 and a German translation in 1720.[5] This relatively popular treatise spares only a single page for the *locis et imagines* of the classical art. The rest of D'Assigny's work, despite its title, has little to do with memory as a visual ars to facilitate invention. Its chapters point instead to natural memory now informed by protopsychological ideas: "The Temper or Disposition of the Body best and worst for Memory, with the natural Causes and Reasons of both . . . Some General and Physical Observations and Prescriptions for the remedying, strengthening, and restoring a Memory injured by the ill

Tempter of the Body, or the Predominancy of one of the four Qualities in the Brain . . . Of such Natural Things as may be assisting to, and may comfort Memory."[6] A later chapter discusses, more promisingly, "Rules to be observ'd for the Acts or Practice of Memory." Here, the reader is given eighteen precepts, most of which are banal: memorize in a quiet place or at a calm part of the day, recite things out loud, don't try to remember too much at any time, and study diligently. Certain classical and early modern precepts do find their way into this chapter—pictorial alphabets in the form of "beasts" and familiar locations, such as a hometown or a friend's house, are mentioned as mental loci with which one might associate information. However, the mentions are brief, and the classical precepts for mnemonic imagery are otherwise muddled in the chapter:

> Let every thing we desire to remember, be fairly written and distinctly, and divided into Periods with large Characters. . . . Let the first Letters or Words of every Period, in every Page, be written in distinct Colors; yellow, green, red, black . . . for by this means we shall the more readily imprint the Matter and Words in our Minds, the more remarkable the Writing appears to the Eye. Therefore Cicero tells us: That the Eyes of the Understanding (and consequently the Memory) are carried more easily to things that are seen, than to those that are heard.[7]

This is a curious passage. Cicero's explanation of mnemonic imagery has suggested to D'Assigny that one should (a) divide writing into "periods" and (b) make letters big and colorful. The author unwittingly conflates Cicero's art of memory with Quintilian's advice to memorize text by dividing it on the page. In other words, D'Assigny cites Cicero to forward Quintilian's system, even though Quintilian's system represents a rejection of Ciceronian imagery. This is a remarkable conflation. It demonstrates how confused scholars had become about the visual art of memory by the eighteenth century. Interestingly, D'Assigny's recommendation to write in "distinct Colors" echoes the medieval instruction to form images of the "color, shape, position, and placement of the letters" on a manuscript page, to quote Hugh of Saint Victor.[8] For Hugh, who would have been working with illuminated manuscripts, connecting mnemonic imagery with ornamental fonts would have made a certain amount of sense. It is an odd piece of advice, however, in the eighteenth century. Predictably, D'Assigny offers a much clearer exposition when it comes to memory in its Ramist sense: "Let there be a Method and convenient Order observ'd, and a Coherence in the Discourse we design to deliver; for it will be far more easy to mind and remember things that have a mutual dependence on one another, than such as are without Order or Method."[9] D'Assigny's *Art of Memory* represents the typical memory treatise that began to circulate in the 1700s. They are dry and unconcerned with inventio; they ignore, simplify, or fumble the memory palace technique; and, as befits the Enlightenment era, they are designed to aid the user in recalling facts and figures from math, geometry, history, and so on in a show of intelligence rather than as a precondition of inventio.

The mnemonic spirit of the age can also be revealed by the development of what is known today as the major system.[10] While classical, medieval, and early modern mnemonics re-mediated and recalled any and all information—including but not limited to numbers[11]—the major system was designed to recall numbers only, and long lists of numbers in particular. Suitably, a French mathematician and astronomer named Pierre Hérigone developed the technique in his *Cursus mathematicus* in the 1630s. (However, it must be noted that Hérigone's system is nearly identical to the Hindi Katapayadi system, which dates to seventh-century India and was utilized by South Asian astronomers and mathematicians.)[12] A decade later, in 1648, a German named Stanislaus Winkelmann published the same system as a general mnemonic device in *Relatio novissima ex Parnasso de arte reminiscentiae*.[13] The major system operates on the idea that recalling words is simpler than recalling numerical information (in direct opposition to the memory palace technique, which assumes that any information—lexical or numerical—is best recalled when presented in visual form). The practitioner is to associate each digit, 0 through 9, with a consonant or with several consonants and, when memorizing long numbers, to form words out of the ensuing consonant clusters, inserting vowels where necessary. Most systems do not map vowels onto numbers so that different number/consonant strings can be converted into different words, according to the learner's own preferences. Figure 4.1 provides an example of a "key" to a basic major system.

Once the number-consonant associations are memorized, it is supposed to be a simple task to create words or lines of verse to represent very long numbers or lists of numbers. For example, 132 corresponds in the key below to *d-m-n*, or *damn*; 32 corresponds to *m-n*, or *men*; 13,232 corresponds to *d-m-n-m-n*, or *damn men*.

Throughout the eighteenth and nineteenth centuries, many keys of this type were devised. The most popular version of the technique was concocted by Richard Grey in his *Memoria Technica*, published in 1730. This book inspired more than a century of memory treatises focused on the most efficient means of converting numbers into words, for the purpose

1	2	3	4	5	6	7	8	9	0
T	N	M	R	L	P	F	H	Q	S
D	Ng	·		B	V	Sh	K	Z
Th						W	Ch	G
							J		

FIGURE 4.1. Key to a major system. (From Middleton, *Memory Systems*, 45.)

of recalling mathematical formulae, dates of historical events, and other numerical information. *Memoria Technica* went through multiple editions and was still in publication as recently as 1880; one historian has even suggested that the history of modern mnemonics was largely a succession of improvements on Grey's eighteenth-century numbers-to-words system.[14] Nearly all mnemonic handbooks published during the nineteenth century were nothing more than major systems with new keys, each purporting to expedite more-natural word construction.[15]

Perhaps the popularity of this system is unsurprising. The major system was well suited to a self-consciously scientific age—better suited, in any event, than the fanciful memory palace technique. It was not altogether clear how one might use the classical art of memory, for example, to memorize pi to the fifteenth decimal place. Using a major system, however, the task would be a straightforward one. All the student needed to do, according to one major system, was to memorize the word *tafaloudsutuknoit*.[16]

The "modernization" of the memory arts that began in earnest in the 1700s reached its apogee in nineteenth-century memory culture. The 1800s, per figure 3.3, witnessed a surprising upswing in publication of books on artificial memory. However, to reiterate, these new mnemonic arts were no longer anchored to the rhetorical tradition (as even Ramist method had been anchored) and were not informed by the classical link between artificial memory and creativity—a link severed early in England and one that seems to have dissolved everywhere else during the mnemonic nadir of the 1700s. The influences guiding nineteenth-century memory culture were not Cicero or Thomas Bradwardine but British empiricism, faculty psychology, and eighteenth-century treatises like those by Marius D'Assigny and Richard Grey. These new mnemonics were devoted to rote memorization of facts (especially numbers and dates), devoid of affect, and confused about visual mnemonics in general and the memory palace technique in particular, but often less confused about Ramist order, which held on in the modern era as a vestigial component of mnemonic practice. Thus decoupled from rhetorical theory, discourse production, visual re-mediation, or info management of any sort, the memory arts became "mnemonics" as that term is parsed today—technical tricks for rote memorization, advertised in books and workshops as part of the self-improvement culture that emerged in the industrial world.

Ironically, as I noted, despite their detachment from rhetoric, these mnemonic systems circulated just as they had in the pre-Socratic Mediterranean—within a milieu of itinerant teachers and regional pedagogues (headmasters and such) who, like the Greek sophists, peddled their arts to whoever was willing to pay for the courses and books. There was, for example, Gregor von Feinaigle, a native of Baden, who in the early 1800s delivered lectures throughout Europe on his "New System of Mnemonics and Methodics," which were followed by the "public performance of remarkable mnemonic feats by his pupils."[17] For the lectures, Feinaigle charged a fee of five guineas. Much later, the Reverend T. Brayshaw, headmaster at Keighley Grammar School, improved on the Feinaiglean system, taught it at his school, and popularized the system in the general community. Then there was William Stokes, who lectured at the Westminster Aquarium in England in the 1860s, charging five guineas, which seems to have been the going rate for mnemonic lectures. Stokes's lessons, however, were given only on the condition that his students not divulge the secrets of his system. A Mr. Woollacott also taught mnemonics throughout England for many years before publishing his system in 1882 in a sixpenny pamphlet entitled "Phrenotypics, or the Science of Memory." Although A. E. Middleton's overview of this culture of lecturing mnemonists—from which the above examples are taken[18]—reads like a curious modern version of itinerant sophist culture, a significant difference separated the ancient Greek world from the modern European one. Whereas the sophists and rhapsodes served an oratorical culture, these new mnemonic artists worked within a mechanized and self-consciously "scientific" one—a fact reflected in their marketed techniques.

What were their techniques? We turn again to Alphonse Loisette's school of physiological memory or instantaneous art of never forgetting as a representative anecdote. Loisette's system is based on what was known in the nineteenth century as the "association of ideas"—the notion that one might move between disparate words or concepts via a logical or, at least, a culturally conditioned connotative chain. For example, to connect *coal* with *time*, one simply needs to follow a chain such as this one: *coal → fire; chimney → mantel; clock on the mantel → time*. The belief was that every word or concept should, in the normal brain, suggest other words or concepts as a matter of necessary course; such links exist a priori. Loisette enumerates many such preexisting connotative or correlative pairs and chains, which he calls the "Laws of Memory." Here are a few examples:

Inclusion: (Earth, Poles.) (Ship, Rudder.) (Forest, Trees.)
Exclusion: (Hot, Cold.) (Old, Young.) (Health, Sickness.)
Concurrence: (Lightning, Thunder.) (Socrates, Hemlock.) (Wedding, Slippers, Cake.)[19]

The memory systems developed by Loisette and other modern mnemonists simply use these associative concepts to recall information, the idea being to associate new information with the relational chains and then use them as mnemonic "steps" when searching for a particular item in one's memory bank. If one can recall what is attached to Socrates, for example, one can always recall what is attached to hemlock.

Though this technique may seem to bear a superficial resemblance to the loci of the memory palace technique, it is in fact a practical application of psychological concepts developed within various strands of Enlightenment and post-Enlightenment thought, from British empiricism to faculty psychology. The associationist idea, Sharon Crowley states, is that minds work "according to the principles of relation."[20] It can be found as early as John Locke, who states in his *Essay Concerning Human Understanding* that "the understanding, in the consideration of anything is not confined to that precise object: it can carry any idea, as it were, beyond itself, or at least look beyond it to see how it stands in conformity with any other."[21] His idea that the human mind is born with the ability to find "relations" between things further leads Locke to define knowledge itself as "the perception of the connection of and agreement, or disagreement . . . , of any of our ideas."[22] Any single idea or sense impression will, through definite relationships, recall other ideas or impressions; this is how mind and memory work, according to Locke. Writing two hundred years later, the British empiricist Alexander Bain was still reiterating Locke's basic associationist theory: "The ability to retain successive impressions without confusion, and to bring them up afterwards, distinguishes mind; it is a power familiarly known as Memory. Now, the chief way in which memory works is this: impressions occurring together become associated together, as sunrise with daylight; and, when we are made to think of one, we are reminded of the accompaniments. . . . The mental association of things contiguously placed, is a prominent fact of the mind."[23] "Definite relationships" among "contiguous" sequences and successive "impressions" such as "sunrise with daylight"—these are the associationist principles on which Loisette's and other nineteenth-century systems operated. It was in part a psychologically informed expansion of Ramism, whose binary arrangements were also logically necessary. Ramus's order was based on a single relational principle, general → specific, the logical necessity of which would (according to the Ramists) aid the memory of whatever material was plugged into it. Associationist mnemonics simply expand the idea to include many other "necessary" relational principles: cause and effect, identity and diversity, part and whole, and so on.

Associationism also owes an obvious debt to Aristotle, whose *On Memory* was the concept's ultimate *fons et origo*. Recall Aristotle's description of natural memory as portrayed in chapter 1: memory is a search process, Aristotle argues, in which we "hunt for the successor" of the thing we are trying to recall, "starting in our thoughts from the present or from something else, and from something similar, or opposite, or neighboring . . . e.g., from milk to white, from white to air, and from this to fluid, from which one remembers autumn."[24] I still have no idea how Aristotle gets from milk to autumn, but the first two movements (from milk to white, from white to air) indicate that Aristotelian recollective movement denotes a process of rational relationships. Recall also *On Memory*'s abstract scheme in which a man searches a series of memories that Aristotle likens to a series of letters, A, B, C, D, E, F, G, and H. If the man needs to recall H, Aristotle says, he can begin at F and move through G. Or, further, if he wants to recall E, he can move backward from H through G and F; alternatively, he may begin at B and move through C and D. Such associative mnemonic chains, according to Aristotle, are always based on some logical relation or property, like similarity, opposition, adjacency, distance in time from the present—all of which presage Loisette's "Laws of Memory."

In both the Aristotelian and Loisettian systems, mnemonic association is quite different from the principle underlying the loci of the ars memoria. To reiterate a familiar point, the memory palace's associations are not logical but idiosyncratic, visual/spatial, and affective. In the eye of memory, most of us travel not between abstract concepts like Socrates and hemlock but within the vivid spaces of our own experiences and imaginings. And while Loisette's or Aristotle's associative ideas are designed to enable an almost algorithmic search for a particular piece of information, the affective spaces of the memory palace are designed to facilitate creative bricolage, an inspired wandering across multiple strands of information, allowing the rhetor to bring them together and connect them into something new. The nearest Loisette comes to using the more imaginative classical precepts is in his utilization of homophony to form correlative chains: for example, at one point, he offers the chain *cloth → sackcloth → Saxons* to remember that the Saxons were one of three tribes that conquered England. Otherwise, despite a surface-level resemblance between mnemonic loci and nineteenth-century mnemonic association, the two techniques are far apart from each other in spirit and in practice.

The other technique in Loisette's system is identical to the major system described earlier—converting numbers into consonants and forming words out of the ensuing consonant clusters. Loisette mentions but does not utilize the classical system of loci et imagines. For him, the art of memory is a historical reference point but not a living practice. Word association and conversion of numbers into letters are his preferred "modern" techniques. And he is not alone. In *Memory Systems New and Old*, Middleton provides an annotated bibliography of fifty-six "modern mnemonical systems" (i.e., nineteenth- and late-eighteenth-century systems), each devised and published by a different mnemonic lecturer.[25] The majority are variations on either Loisette's correlationist technique or the major system; some make use of aural techniques, such as rhymes and acrostics. Only seven of the fifty-six systems described by Middleton make use of something similar to the classical art of memory, which Middleton variably calls the "topical" or "locality" system, a reference to the topoi or loci—the places—of the art of memory.

However, even these modern locality systems operate on a principle of linear arrangement rather than a conscious harnessing of the affective spaces and images of the memoryscape. They are the uninspired descendants of Willis's carefully designed "repositories" or Lambert Schenkel's architectural schematics, only distantly related at this point to the classical memory palace. In addition, like the associationist technique, the locality system is designed to facilitate an algorithmic search for a particular piece of information, most often in the form of numbers, dates, or other rote facts. A few descriptions of these unimaginative locality systems, taken again from Middleton, will be illustrative:

1849, WILLIAM DAY, "THE NEW MNEMONICAL CHART AND GUIDE TO THE ART OF MEMORY"
The author . . . elaborated the topical method to the extent of locating one thousand consecutive objects in ten rooms. The ten rooms were named respectively—the Index Room, Dame's Room, Nurse's Room, Model Room, Riding Room, Library, Chapel, Conservatory, Waiting Room, and Portrait Room. The initials of each room represented the numerals 0 to 9. Each room had ten divisions, and ten objects were located in each division. . . . The first room, for instance, would have ten divisions, under the title of Dame, Nurse, Music, Rosebush, Lamp, Gentleman, King, Fireplace,

Painting; and each of these would be associated with ten other objects, having some association with them.[26]

1867, THOMAS A. SAYER, "AIDS TO MEMORY"

The locality system consists of ten places, with ten objects in each, arbitrarily arranged, the tenth object being a substantive supposed to suggest the number of the locality. A tree represented the first locality because its initial represented 1; a boat the second from its having two oars; a parlor table third because it has three feet; a horse with four legs represented four . . .[27]

1870, WILLIAM HILL, "LOCAL SUGGESTER"

[The arrangement] consisted of dividing the interior of a room into 50 spaces, and arranging a series of alphabetical words in each. To these words were connected the idea or fact to be remembered. Music, French, Quadrilles, &c., were taught by this method, rhyme also being used as an aid.[28]

These memory "spaces" are nothing like the loci of the actively traversed memoryscape. They are diagrammatic, dry, and impersonal. And the small hint of visual re-mediation remaining in these systems ("a horse with four legs represented four") is literalist. These systems are, again, designed to store information for rote recall. The imaginative memoryscape is left with nothing to do when presented with mnemonic forms such as "ten rooms . . . named respectively—the Index Room, Dame's Room, Nurse's Room, Model Room, Riding Room." These localities cannot even be said to enable information *management*, insofar as management implies not only raw storage but also a system for recall and integration.

Middleton does reference several "pictorial alphabets" similar to the mnemonic alphabets developed in the Middle Ages and popularized during the Renaissance by authors such as Johann Romberch. As a rule, however, the modern mnemonic alphabets are far less artistic than the naked bodies and mythical beasts that their predecessors exchanged for letters. Middleton also describes a system devised in 1875 by W. H. Courtley that taught French grammatical genders by "ingeniously associating [them] . . . with the Queen's head on a penny piece."[29] However, this penny mnemonic and the mnemonic alphabets are as near as nineteenth-century lecturers came to producing a memory art grounded in principles of visual transformation. None of them, as far as I can tell, recommend employing personal imagination and one's own past to create places, images, and associations, as the classical sources do. Most importantly, none of these systems recognize the connection between artificial memory and the invention of knowledge, which was the entire point of ancient, medieval,

TABLE 4.1. Words Most Frequently Used in 115 Memory Treatise Titles (1780–1888)

memory 60	phreno/typics 7	applied 4
mnemonic/s 22	technica 6	dates 3
art 14	method/ic 6	forgetting 3
system/s/atic 14	improve/d 6	helps 3
new 9	artificial 5	instantaneous 3
history 8	chronology 5	natural 3
memoria 8	science/s 5	
aid/s 7	language 4	

and many early modern mnemonic arts. The link between mnemonics and creativity is nonexistent in nineteenth-century memory culture.

This cultural amnesia is, again, perhaps unsurprising. Their systems influenced by protopsychological theories of associationism, lecturing mnemonists such as Day, Sayer, Loisette, Stokes, Woollacott, and Brayshaw thought of their mnemonics as *scientific* and psychologically informed techniques. The nineteenth and late eighteenth centuries were nothing if not self-consciously scientific. In his "Bibliography of Mnemonics, 1325–1888," George Fellows lists 115 memory texts published between 1780 and 1888. Examining the most frequent words in these 115 titles (table 4.1), one detects the scientific postures adopted by the traveling memory teachers and regional pedagogues who wrote them. Apart from "memory," the most frequent words in these titles demonstrate an attempt to turn artificial memory into a technical pursuit: "memoria technica," "method," "applied," "phrenotypics," "science," "new," and "systematic." Even the word "mnemonic/s" itself points to a new rationalist mind-set about artificial memory. "Mnemonic/s" is rarely used in memory treatise titles prior to the eighteenth century. Of the hundreds of treatises published between 1430 and 1700, only five utilize that Greek root: the anonymous *Gymnasium Mnemonicum* (1610), John Henry Alsted's *Systema Mnemonicum* (1610), the anonymous *Artis Mnemonica Explicatio* (1611), Henry Herdson's *Ars Mnemonica* (1651), and John Willis's *Mnemonica, or the Art of Memory* (1661). All the others are *ars reminiscindi* or *artificiosae memoriae*. In 1730, the first treatise to use the word "mnemonics" in seven decades is published: *Mnemonics Delineated in a Small Compass and Easy Method, for the Better Enabling to Remember What Is Most Frequently Wanted, and Most Difficultly Retained or Recollected.* This text seems to mark a turning point in the word's popularity, for in the middle of the eighteenth century, "mnemonic/s" and "mnemotechny" become increasingly popular in the titles of the memory treatises. It is as though practitioners of artificial memory, responding to the centrality of science in the surrounding culture, felt a need to *technologize* their techniques. They seem to have grasped onto the hitherto unpopular term "mnemonic" to signal that their arts, too, are grounded in scientific principles.

Artificial memory, then, was back on the intellectual map in the nineteenth century. It was not, however, the artificial memory of the ancient world. Mnemonics had become synonymous instead with psychological principles emphasizing necessary correlation and succession. The affective loci et imagines of Cicero and *Ad Herennium* had been eclipsed by systems promoting the rote memorization of facts, figures, and numbers. This nineteenth-century memory culture was the milieu in which mnemonics came to denote the sort of rote recall and memorization performance synonymous with the term today. Most significantly, in this culture artificial memory continued to be severed from its original purpose of facilitating invention. Rhetorical memory, in short, was made wholly *methodical* and technical in a way that even Ramus did not intend.

Though there is ample evidence for the popularity of these bowdlerized mnemonic arts, the number of memory treatises published during the 1800s nevertheless remained lower than the number published during the memory arts' prime in the early 1600s. Viewing this trend in the context of increasing literacy rates and an ever-expanding publishing industry, it appears that the genre had simply stalled out by 1700, thereafter beginning its decline into the prosaic improve-your-memory tradition that has sustained itself in the twenty-first century. An ignominious end, so it seems, for a tradition once valued by Cicero and Thomas Aquinas for its creative and epistemological significance.

Ars Combinatoria: From Mnemonic Alphabet to Symbolic Logic

Before introducing the next thread in the history of the memory arts' modernization, a bit of theoretical housekeeping is in order.

In essence, the memory palace technique was a practice of visual re-mediation, of converting information into images. It was also, however, a practice of information compression, a term that I have used throughout the book but have not paused to explain. Visually transforming the complex threads of a court case into a single affective image, for example, always operates on an ancillary principle of information compression or reduction. In the previous chapters, I treated re-mediation and compression/reduction as analogous principles, arguing that early modern scholars valued the mnemonic tradition not only for its precepts about managing information but also for its precepts about transforming or reducing complex information into a comprehensible image, model, or "mirror" of the universe of knowledge. Re-mediation and reduction, to be sure, can function as synonymous metaphoric descriptions of what the memory palace *does*, but in the context of other artificial memory techniques, one term often will be more apt than the other. Put another way, we needn't oppose these conceptual terms so much as recognize that some mnemonic arts will emphasize one over the other. Precepts about mnemonic imagery and palatial memoryscapes emphasize visual *re-mediation* even if they also generate info compression by default. Mnemonic alphabets, in contrast, reverse the emphasis: by associating a set of information with a single letter or symbol, they accentuate the principle of *compression* over that of imagistic transformation. (Pictorial alphabets like the one by Thomas Bradwardine attempt to emphasize both coding schemes at once.)

As I noted in chapter 2, the idea to index a set of information to a single letter, as an aid for information management and recall, seems to have originated or at least been formalized in the medieval monasteries. In the later Middle Ages, the Majorcan polymath Ramon Llull recognized that these basic indexing symbols could, like any letters or symbols, be combined to generate larger information amalgamations. Llull also realized that if he assigned exact information to each symbol, the subsequent combinations avoided the slippage of signification that haunted all writing systems. His resulting art of associative and combinatorial symbology—the ars combinatoria—thus evolved the mnemonic alphabet into one of the earliest prototypes of an indexical, combinatorial information system. From a twenty-first-century vantage point, it may seem inevitable that Llull's system of symbolic association and combination would influence the forerunners of computational logic that emerged during the Renaissance and the Enlightenment. At the time, however, Llull's chief motivation for developing his ars was an explicitly religious one.

Writing at the turn of the thirteenth and fourteenth centuries, Llull reveals his medieval Catholic identity as much as his nascent scientific one in his technique. (The popular science writer Martin Gardner once called the Llullian art a fascinating mixture of science and nonsense.)[30] Living in Majorca soon after the Reconquista but before the Jews were expelled from Spain, Llull was motivated to create his combinatorial technique by a desire to convert these other members of the Abrahamic faiths to the truths of Christianity. He believed strongly that the world and all it contains—both natural and spiritual—point to and confirm the veracity of the Catholic faith by merit of the world's logically constructed existence. (One way to understand Llull's belief system is to compare him to contemporary apologists who have attempted to support God's existence by pointing to the "fine-tuned universe," the various cosmological constants that if altered by even a fraction would have stopped planets from forming, life from evolving, and so on.) Lacking knowledge of contemporary cosmology, however, Llull had to discover for himself how to demonstrate the logic of God's universe, in an objective way, to an ideologically hostile audience.

The best way to "confound the errors of the infidels,"[31] he eventually realized, was this: to convert the logical but complex workings of the natural and spiritual worlds into a simple model that reduces God's universe to a few basic elements with which it might be rationally questioned and discussed, bit by bit, in a way that confirms the necessity of the Catholic God. "Disputation," Llull states in *Proverbs of Ramon*, "requires an artificial order which is the image of the natural [one]."[32] His "art" was that artificial order—a simplified image, model, or mirror of natural and spiritual existence. The representative units to which Llull reduced and with which he deliberated about the Christian universe were indexed letters, drawn from the tradition of mnemonic alphabets.

In its final form, Llull's ars combinatoria reduced the natural and spiritual world to nine letters. Indexed to these nine letters were fifty-four abstract and concrete topics/subjects and questions regarding them:[33]

B   goodness; difference; whether?; God; justice; avarice
C   greatness; concordance; what?; angel; prudence; gluttony
D   eternity; contrariety; of what?; heaven; fortitude; lust
E   power; beginning; why?; man; temperance; pride
F   wisdom; middle; how much?; imaginative; faith; accidie
G   will; end; of what kind?; sensitive; hope; envy
H   virtue; majority; when?; vegetative; charity; ire
I   truth; equality; where?; elementative; patience; lying
K   glory; majority; how? with what?; instrumentative; pity; inconsistency

Each of these letters, with their indexed associations, was to be placed into Llull's famous combinatorial wheels and tables (figure 4.2). By following the permutations of the wheels and tables, the Llullian artist could generate and thus investigate questions or propositions about any subject in existence—"for the purpose of investigating the truth," Llull states.[34] The most basic combinations would generate abstract concepts: good difference, glorious concordance, the beginning of wisdom, eternal duration (beginning/middle/end), and so on. These concepts could then be explored in and of themselves. More complex combinations generated more detailed questions/propositions about more specific material: When is difference good? How much concordance is glorious? Where is duration eternal? Whether man's duration is eternal? What difference exists be-

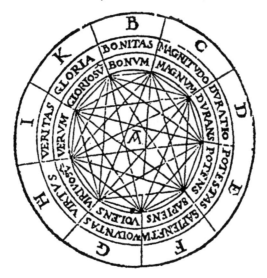

FIGURE 4.2. Llull's combinatorial wheels. (Printed in Cramer, *Words Made Flesh*, 36.)

tween God and angel? What difference in wisdom exists between man and vegetable? What is the difference between gluttony and prudence? Is there any concordance between God's justice and man's justice? And so on.

To contemporary eyes, the questions and propositions generated by the art may seem limited in scope. However, to Llull's mind, such formulations would have prompted all the relevant issues a Christian might need to address when debating the infidels. Indeed, anyone familiar with late medieval theology will recognize that Llull's combinatorial topics— the virtues, the vices, the principles of duration or concordance or magnitude, and the ladder of creation descending from God and the angels, through humans, down to the material world—are among the most important topics that occupied the late medieval mind.

Lull claims at the beginning of *Ars brevis* that his alphabetic index "must be learned by heart."[35] In *Ars generalis ultima*, a longer treatment of his system, Llull derives the faculty of memory itself from the rules and principles of the art. The scholarly consensus is that his combinatorial alphabet served an explicitly mnemonic purpose and that the system's reduction of complex information was what made it mnemonically efficient. Llull had designed his art, after all, for clerics, monastics, laymen, and any Catholic faithful who wanted to enter into religious disputation with the Jews and Muslims of southern Europe. For that reason, he wanted his system to be easily remembered for suggesting and generating questions about God's universe—not only for the sake of efficiency but also for the deeply rhetorical purpose of apologetic outreach. As an apologetic practice, the Llullian art thus also retained the classical and medieval link between memoria and inventio. Although Llull does provide answers to many of the questions generated by his combinatorial art, the system as such provides no answers to its questions nor any defenses of its propositions. That effort was left to the individual Llullian artist. When constructing answers or defenses, he would need to take into consideration his personal grasp of scripture, his apologetic context, and the disposition of his interlocutors, who may respond better to some points rather than others. In short, applied within its proper apologetic context, the Llullian ars combinatoria, like the memory palace technique, facilitated creativity as much as it enhanced the memory.

Despite Llull's religious motivation, the principles of info compression and info combination underlying his art were easily untethered from Catholic dogma and apologetics. The idea to reduce qualitative information to a single unambiguous symbol was destined to exert influence beyond the religious world.[36] In *Logic and the Art of Memory*, Paolo Rossi goes so far as to read the history of the combinatorial arts as a parallel thread to the history of mathematics. Popular throughout the late medieval and early modern world, the combinatorial arts—often called the Llullian art or the *ars Raymundo*—were commented on at length by a variety of scholars, nearly all of whom adopted the art not for its apologetic value but for its systematic potential to reduce complex information to a few basic building blocks.

Many of these scholars were involved too in encyclopedism, natural philosophy, alchemy, the mnemonic arts, or other practices exemplifying the taxonomic impulse portrayed at the beginning of chapter 3. Some were secular, some religious, but all were deeply interested in systems that could both manage the knowledge discovered during the Renaissance and allow scholars to construct unified images or models of this knowledge. Some of these thinkers, like Lambert Schenkel and John Willis, looked to the loci of the memory palace for inspiration; others, such as Athanasius Kircher, looked to Llull's combinatorial art; still others attempted to create a unified system out of multiple systems, such as Daniel Georg Morhof, whose *De Acuta Dictionie* combined encyclopedic methods with Llull's combinatorial art;[37] and, of course, Giordano Bruno infamously layered mnemonic imagery onto Llull's imageless wheels and tables. Some of these systems were designed only to manage information; others, like Bruno's wheels or Kirchner's *Ars Musarithmica* (a combinatorial device for creating polyphonic church hymns), were meant to generate knowledge as well as manage it. Across the board, however, the combinatorial arts were influenced by the same modernizing spirit that altered mnemonic and, indeed, rhetorical practice as a whole from the late 1600s into the Age of Enlightenment— which means that the ars combinatoria, like the art of memory, eventually became dissociated from the rhetorical and mnemonic traditions.

Modern combinatorics were received positively by some Enlightenment figures and negatively by others. As regards the negative reception, a subset of Llullists had apparently begun to use their combinatorial art for nothing more than "pomp and the ostentation of knowledge," as the occult philosopher Cornelius Agrippa complained in 1600.[38] Francis Bacon mentions the Llullian art twice and both times agrees with Agrippa that its users merely attempt "to gain the admiration of the ignorant than to find out the truth." States Bacon, "This method [the combinatorial art] uses a smattering of science so that an ignoramus can make show of a non-existent erudition. The art of Lull, and the *Typocosmica* which someone has recently invented are arts of this kind. Both consist of an undigested mass of terms from the various arts which are used to make someone who knows the terms sound as if he knows what they mean."[39] The combinatorial arts would indeed allow someone who had memorized a set of terms or concepts to combine them in a nearly endless diatribe— whether or not he knew what the terms and their combinations actually meant. Ironically, Bacon levels the same criticism against combinatorics here that contemporary critics level against artificial intelligence: that AI's "understanding" is not understanding at all but merely an exhaustive comparison of combinable labels and classes preassigned by a programmer or constructed ad hoc through various regression models. One scholar has described the Llullian art in similar algorithmic terms as a "systematically exhaustive consideration of all possible combinations of material, reduced to a symbolic coding."[40] Across a millennium of technological development, the ars combinatoria and contemporary AI thus meet a similar skepticism—that true understanding and discovery, to paraphrase Bacon, require more than an ability to encode and regurgitate information amalgamations through some automated process.

Contra Bacon, however, the combinatorial art's potential for information encoding and decoding was precisely what led Gottfried Leibniz to receive it more positively. Leibniz was a philosopher who lived in Germany from 1646 until his death in 1716. He is principally remembered today as the codiscoverer, with Isaac Newton, of differential and integral calculus. What impressed Leibniz about combinatorial letters was their resistance to semantic slippage due to their explicit coding. The Llullian symbols were not typical linguistic signs, Leibniz realized. Rather, as described earlier, they compressed and indexed specific, pre-encoded information. When the symbols were combined, their permutations thus generated increasingly complex info amalgamations without sacrificing semantic specificity. Inspired by Llull's system, Leibniz undertook the project of compressing all qualitative knowledge into combinatorial symbols so that one could perform a sort of calculus on nonnumerical information. This grand idea—a limited set of symbols-cum-concepts, capable of being combined into a nearly endless array of complex amalgamations— was elaborated by Leibniz in his 1666 dissertation, *Dissertatio de arte combinatoria*, in which Leibniz worked from Llull's system to posit a whole ordered ontology utilizing combinable symbols.

Leibniz would later disparage his dissertation as "immature," but his ruminations on Llull's combinatorial, indexical alphabet clearly foreshadow his *characteristica universalis*, or universal character, an ideographic writing that was to be the basis of, in Leibniz's words, "a new way of calculating, suitable for matters which have nothing in common with mathematics, and if this kind of logic were put into practice, every reasoning, even probabilistic ones, would be like that of the mathematician."[41] Leibniz's universal character was to be a set of symbols that, by virtue of its explicitly coded conceptual associations, could be "read" by all regardless of the language they spoke. It could thus, again, be used to undertake a sort of calculus of qualitative, nonnumerical concepts and issues. Leibniz explains further:

> For let the first terms, of the combination of which all others consist, be designated by signs; these signs will be a kind of alphabet. . . . If these are correctly and ingeniously established, this universal writing will be as easy as it is common, and will be capable of being read without any dictionary; at the same time, a fundamental knowledge of all things will be obtained. The whole of such a writing will be made of geometrical figures, as it were, and of a kind of pictures—just as the ancient Egyptians did, and the Chinese do today.[42]

Like many early modern and Enlightenment thinkers, Leibniz was transfixed by ideographic or logographic writing, imputing onto it an almost Romantic quality of transparent communicative immersion. He imagined that ideographic writing denoted essential, universally understood concepts and that it therefore avoided the slippery semantics and detached opacity of the Roman alphabet. The ability to communicate in a rational, transparent, and even mathematical way about "matters which have nothing in common with mathematics"—in other words, to reason quantitatively about qualitative information—surely relied, Leibniz thought, on the development of such a transparent communicative medium, a writing system grounded not on the rebus principle or other arbitrary standards but on combinable symbols, "a kind of pictures," indexed to essential concepts.

Leibniz, unfortunately, never completed his universal character. In 1714, he wrote to a friend complaining that people paid no more attention to the idea "than if I had told them about a dream of mine."[43] However, through Leibniz, the idea of a combinatorial symbolic alphabet greatly influenced the development of future intellectual projects, including semiotics, logical positivism, Boolean algebra, and any number of Enlightenment predecessors of symbolic and computational logic. As Florian Cramer has argued, both Leibniz's idea of a "universal character" and the Llullian art that inspired it are early exemplars of what today might be called a computational, algorithmic system.[44] Anyone who dabbles in data science will recognize in Llull's combinatorial alphabet a hint of the work of information science and machine learning. To tell a machine what to do with any given information set, programmers must reduce both the information and the machine's instructions to individual characters, which are then combined in more and more complexly structured programs—assigning names to variables, passing arguments into functions, and passing functions into other functions, to use the language of computer science. As a simple example, before I can run a quantitative analysis on a qualitative data set—say, a Jane Austen novel—I first need to reduce the entire novel to a single indexed or "assigned" character or set of characters:

$$E = \text{open}(\text{'Emma.txt'}, \text{'rU'}).$$

The novel thusly assigned, E now becomes the indexed symbol for the entire novel *Emma*. I can then combine or pair E with other letters or words that are themselves indexed to various information structures, the combinations allowing me to treat the novel as a quantitative item. For example, if I were using the popular Natural Language Toolkit to "tokenize" the novel—that is, to turn every word in the novel into a single item in a long list, so that the words can be counted and computed—I would combine E with the simple line **wordpunct.tokenize** in the command line, the latter "symbol" standing in for a whole module, or complex set of machine instructions:

$$E2 = \text{nltk.wordpunct.tokenize}(E).$$

Thus would the symbol E2 now be indexed to the entire novel *Emma* in its tokenized form

['Emma', 'Woodhouse', ',', 'handsome', ',', 'clever', ',', 'and', 'rich' . . .],

while E would still be indexed to the novel in its nontokenized form. If I were curious about the contexts of a particular word in the novel—"love," say—I could now combine the symbol E2 with the term **concordance** (which, again, would itself be a symbol indexed to a much more complex set of machine instructions that acts on E2, the tokenized novel) to produce a list of all the sentences containing the word "love."

E2.concordance("love")

. . . Mr. Knightley loves to find fault with me . . .
. . . Miss Churchill fell in love with him . . .

Without squinting too much, it should be possible to discern a conceptual resemblance between the combinatorial arts and the operations of the command line, which, in the majority of programming languages, make use of the same efficiency-maximizing principles of info compression, info indexing, and info combination. Thus can a line of influence be traced from mnemonic alphabets—in which a letter or symbol denotes a quantity of knowledge—to the formal ontologies of information science. In the middle of this line stands the mystic Ramon Llull and his unique idea that mnemonic alphabets and the information for which they stand might be combined in myriad ways not only to manage complex permutations of knowledge but also to generate new knowledge altogether.

Lull's use of mnemonic principles and Leibniz's use of Llull's principles also reveal the ease with which mnemonic precepts can be absorbed into larger projects to a point where the mnemonic precepts all but disappear *as active mnemonic precepts*. In the early 1300s, the connection between mnemonics and Llull's combinatorial wheels was still explicit. However, when filtered through the ars combinatoria's early modern updates by men like Athanasius Kirchner, then filtered again through Leibniz's scientifically oriented scholarship, the connection between mnemonics and the idea of a "universal character"—a symbolic system to encode and calculate qualitative information in a quantitative way—becomes increasingly faint. Today, the suggestion that mnemonics have anything to do with information technology or data science sounds a bit odd. When was the last time anyone thought of the Google search bar as a mnemonic device? Unlike the Llullian art, which highlighted its principles from a mnemonic point of view, digital information systems tend to mask their combinatorial, encoding/decoding operations. They work best, we feel, when the underlying process by which they re-mediate qualitative information (like language, music, and image) into quantitative form—before re-mediating that information back to us in qualitative form—fades into the background, taking on the cloak of invisibility as it facilitates some other intellectual work. It is as though a newer ars—the art of the easy-to-use graphic interface—has been layered onto the combinatorial wheels, relieving the user of the conscious mnemonic work demanded by the ars combinatoria. It is more efficient, certainly, but this new graphic ars robs the user of any understanding of how knowledge is being recalled, integrated, or generated. Indeed, at the digital interface, the user has no sense of knowledge being *recalled* or *combined* or *generated* at all—it is merely there, *given* at the click of a mouse. Reclaiming the graphical user interface as a mnemonic device is going to be a challenge; its raw efficiency works against a rhetorical renovation.

CHAPTER 5

Theory and Practice of a Digital Ars Memoria

At the end of *Graphesis*, a book on the grammars and ideologies of data visualization, Johanna Drucker offers a challenge to residents of the digital world:

> The expansion of access to any and all stored data that can be repurposed and remediated nearly boggles the mind. . . . The ability to think in and with the tools of computational and digital environments will evolve only as quickly as our ability to articulate the metalanguages of our engagement. We have to have a way to talk about what it is we are doing, and how and to reflect critically and imaginatively if tools of the new era are to be means to think with, rather than instruments of a vastly engineered ideological apparatus that merely has its way with us. . . . Where are the manuals of rhetoric for the electronic age? What grammars will take their place beside those that stood for years . . . ? What treatises in rhetoric will expand the principles of ethos, pathos, and logos from Aristotle or build on Quintilian's concepts of invention, arrangement, style, presentation, memory, and action in ways appropriate to the media of our time?[1]

Drucker's challenge is, of course, not so much a challenge as a call to continue intellectual activity. As early as the 1960s, Marshall McLuhan was already developing a grammar and rhetoric of the electronic age, long before smartphones and personal computers came into existence. More recently, Richard Lanham, Collin Gifford Brooke, Edward Tufte, Susan Delagrange, and many others have furthered the project of constructing digital grammars and rhetorics. Tufte is of course the great formalist and stylist of graphical data representation. Delagrange's work has focused on the canon of arrangement in the context of digital media. Brooke's *Lingua Fracta* is an explicit attempt to refigure all five canons of classical rhetoric for a digital ecology. Drucker's *Graphesis* offers a grammar of information

visualization, combining Tufte's analysis of form with a postmodern skepticism about the semantic transparency of information display.

The final two chapters of this book align with this digital rhetorical
tradition, answering Drucker's challenge by expanding the principles of
memoria in particular "in ways appropriate to the media of our time." As
I explained in chapter 1, current scholarship on rhetorical memory, even
work with a digital bent, tends to overlook the history of the fourth canon
and its allied mnemonic tradition. The preceding chapters have retold that
history from a variety of perspectives and sources. It is an interesting narrative in its own right, but the fourth canon's history should be retold also
so that it can inform its contemporary, digital manifestation. As the history
has shown, the memory arts need not undergo a wholesale renovation to
find relevance in the electronic age. A constellation of precepts regarding
the compression, management, integration, and visualization of information, the mnemonic tradition has a digital relevance that glimmers in an-
ticipation from the *Dissoi logoi* onward—through Cicero, Hugh of Saint
Victor, Thomas Bradwardine, Ramon Llull, and even reformers like Petrus
Ramus and Lambert Schenkel. These final chapters therefore continue to
rely on the fourth canon's history even as they adapt the mnemonic arts
to the contemporary cyberscape.

I have suggested throughout the book that the classical memory-palace
technique—the original art of memory in its Ciceronian/Herennian
form—is the most valuable mnemonic art gifted by history. This ancient
technique emphasizes the link between knowledge construction and a
disciplined memoryscape, within which information is re-mediated into
or associated with visual, affective forms. These allied precepts tend to be
scattered or reemphasized in other mnemonic arts. In the Middle Ages,
for example, the connection between memoria and inventio was left intact, but the mnemonic practice linking them was memory of text as such
rather than the visual transformation of text. Early modern systems revived the visual precepts but downplayed the affect and idiosyncrasy that
gave classical mnemonic imagery its power. Other early modern and Enlightenment systems bowdlerized the ars memoria, severing the link between visual memory and creativity. Only the classical sources and the
treatises most influenced by them contain the entire mnemonic kit relevant to rhetorical praxis in the electronic millennium.

"Now the keenest of all our senses is the sense of sight," states Cicero.
"Therefore, things perceived by our hearing or during our thought processes can be most easily grasped by the mind, if they are also conveyed
to our minds through the mediation of the eyes."[2] The insight behind visual mnemonics is that the creative mind works better with visual models

than with text or information as such. Cicero and *Ad Herennium* thus suggest re-mediating information—things perceived by "hearing" or during "thought processes"—into visual form. The art of memory was and remains a technique for translating the semiotics of language and thought into a semiotics of sight and dimension. Vitally, the purpose for transforming thought into sight, the classical sources assert, is to facilitate the invention of discourse within a rhetorical context: thus *Ad Herennium*'s well-known praise of memory as a *thesaurum inventorum*. The memory palace technique converted information into emotionally linked imagery because such imagery, the orators recognized, more readily accommodated the bricolage—the browsing through, integration, and application of fragmented material—that was synonymous with rhetorical activity. It made it easier for the orator to bring together multiple strands of knowledge to create something new and persuasive in any given context. The creation of mnemonic imagery was never a practice of accurate representation for the classical orator. Inventio was the art's reason for being—an important point for rhetorical theory, then and now. In the digital age, scholars such as Drucker have similarly exhorted humanists using data visualization to "break the literalism of representation" through both social and formal critiques of visual knowledge.[3] Likewise, Susan Delagrange argues that new media interfaces should not be celebrated as things enhancing the "liveness" of reality, providing "a transparently 'real' experience ... [that] erases the frame and appears to provide unmediated access to content," but rather be theorized as technologies that can potentially make users aware of "hypermediacy," the ways in which the graphical interface calls attention to its own mediation.[4] Digital rhetorical theory will not give quarter to terms such as *accuracy, transparency, truth,* or *precision* when it comes to the visualized data on our screens. However, by embracing the ancient practice of memoria and by shifting the discursive frame from *visualization-as-representation* to *visualization-as-invention*, I argue, humanists can enact a constructionist critique without foreclosing on the value, necessity, and inevitable usage of visual information displays.

Why valuable? Necessary? Inevitable? The key insight behind classical mnemonics remains valid: imagery and visual models make data comprehensible and thus more useful than raw data themselves (particularly in large quantities). To integrate a "collection of heterogeneous and autonomous data sources," states computer scientist Tiziana Catarci, one needs "a uniform interface" to provide access to the diverse data.[5] One needs, in other words, a singular visual port through which data flow to the user as comprehensible, manageable knowledge. It is thus not surprising that the classical mnemonic insight is reaffirmed daily in the discourse of com-

puter and information scientists. Recall the early computer engineering
article cited at the beginning of this book: James Wise et al. argue that the
key to "read[ing] and assess[ing] large amounts of text" is to transform
documents "into a new visual representation that communicates by image
instead of prose." Comprehending gigabytes of textual information, they
state, is best facilitated by converting raw text into "a spatial representation which may then be accessed and explored by visual processes alone."[6]
Their resulting visualizations transform documents into a "thematic terrain" of conceptually related text clusters, portrayed as linked nodes that
presage interactive network graphs. Work in interface design likewise acknowledges the importance of robust visual metaphors and systems for
users wandering the dense thicket of files saved on their devices. Catherine
C. Marshall states that an important goal of twenty-first-century operating systems should be to develop two sorts of visual interfaces: (1) "digital
places and geographies" that treat different data differently and provide
novel interfaces for, for example, information accessed rarely and objects
accessed daily; and (2) "automatically generated visualizations that provide us with an overall gestalt of what we have" across the entire database
structure or any given slice of it.[7] Computer scientists Eric Freeman and
David Gelernter reiterate the latter point. "An important aspect of managing information," they state, "is the capacity to construct a 'big picture'
view of that information." They continue: "For example: a time series of
mutual fund closing quotes can be summarized in a historical graph. . . .
'Summarized' can (and ought to) be an exceptionally powerful function if
we define it imaginatively."[8] *Imag*inative summaries of data, big pictures,
overall gestalts, digital places and geographies, representations that communicate by image—visual/spatial metaphors and literal pictorial models
fill the data science literature. Beyond graphs, interfaces, and other visualizations, one even finds basic formats such as the spreadsheet grid—a
screenified version of medieval mnemonic systems—described as mental
aids that allow users to absorb information hard to comprehend in its un-
visualized form: "The reasons spreadsheet software is more approachable
than R/Python," states Kaggle data scientist Rachael Tatman, "is that you
can directly see and manipulate the data structure." She adds, "There's so
much conceptual scaffolding in just the idea of a grid."[9]

The importance of being able to "see and manipulate" information is
the common conceptual ground linking the mnemonic tradition with
the contemporary work of data science, interface design, and, most importantly for this chapter, information visualization. From the columnar
spaces and affective imagery of the Herennian memory palace, through
the text grids of the monastics, to the pictorial alphabets, the lovely maid-

ens, the schematic loci, and even, to some extent, the Ramist diagrams of the early modern period, the historical arts of memory—arts of info visualization and info manipulation—find their progeny in the visual interfaces that inundate our screens. A digital canon of memory and a rhetoric of data visualization will therefore be, if not identical, at least allied components of digital rhetorical theory. Humans are doing on the screen today what the eyes of their imaginations did two thousand years ago in the political squares of the Mediterranean; indeed, humans are doing on the screen today what their minds have been doing "naturally" since the species first evolved—converting information into imagery. Hence, there is an inevitability to and persistent value of visual data display.

Theory I: Data Visualization as Memory, Natural and Artificial

As distinguished in chapter 1, there are two senses in which the mind/ memory converts information into imagery: the "natural" way and the "artificial" way. Classical sources differentiate the two, defining the latter as a method of harnessing and thereby improving the former. Although I stressed this difference at the beginning of the book, it should by now be clear that the memory palace technique is not distinct from natural mental processes but rather is a conscious manipulation of them. *Ad Herennium*'s comparison to athletic training remains clarifying. The rhetor improves her memory through an art of memory the same way an athlete improves her body through physical exercise. Artificial memory can thus be defined as *applied* natural memory, just as athletic training might be defined as applied anatomical movement. The digital mnemonic arts, too, can be understood as applied natural memory.

Like the imagery and pictorial alphabets printed in early modern treatises, the imagery of the digital arts are created externally rather than in the mind. Nevertheless, the mnemonic forms in both cases represent secondary (artificial) rather than primary (natural) human knowledge; they are, in other words, deliberately created rather than instinctively imprinted forms of knowledge. Of course, iconoclasts and iconophiles throughout history have debated the nature of the divide between primary and secondary knowledge, between our immediate perceptions and our "double objects" or "shapes of consciousness" (G. W. F. Hegel), between us and our "dialectical images" (Walter Benjamin), between us and our "extensions" (Marshall McLuhan), and between us and our "literary representations of reality" (Erich Auerbach). Avoiding those murky philosophical waters, I posit as a purely descriptive point that natural/ primary memory and artificial/secondary memory are both processes that make phenomena intelligible to humans through tangible and often visual models. The two might be distinguished, then, as the classical treatises distinguished them (and on practical rather than deep ontological grounds): by the degree of control, purpose, or creativity exercised over the models produced. The more creative control involved in the forming of the model, the more artificial or secondary it becomes. Analyzing a character in Petronius's *Satyricon*, Erich Auerbach says that the character's whole social world is described by Petronius not "as objective reality, but as a subjective image, as it exists in the mind of [the character]."[10] The character's "subjective image" of his social world and its inhabitants would be, were he real, a natural/primary imprinting on his mind. Petronius's literary rendering of it represents a deeply creative act and is therefore an example of an artificial/secondary imprinting; when reading the *Satyricon*, a reader's own mental image of this image would exist, in my view, as an artificial imprinting of its own. However, one could argue that images conjured in our minds when reading (or even when reflecting secondarily on our own social worlds) exist in a liminal space between natural perception and artificial creativity. To reiterate, the deep nature of the difference is not precisely the point. The point, for rhetorical theory, is that the more *creativity* and *active agency* involved in image formation, the closer we move toward artifice and all the rhetoricalness that artifice implies.

Humans have little if any conscious control over how their brain-body complexes filter experience into the sensory phantasms called *memory*— and not much control over how they integrate those phantasms into a thing called *meaning*. We have not the faintest clue how our neurophysiology interfaces with the flux and flow of the physical universe in which it is embedded—the universe's forces, wavelengths, chemicals, particles, materialities—in a way that converts those fluxes into sensible forms in the eyes of our imaginations. Although it addresses the issue with a philosophical rather than rhetorical interest, Thomas Nagel's "What Is It Like to Be a Bat?" is nevertheless instructive. Nagel argues that all sensing entities—including humans—can be understood as "neurophysiological constitutions" that interface with the universe's flows, fluxes, and particulate forces in dissimilar ways, attuned to and exploiting some forces while tuning out others:

> Now we know that most bats (the microchiroptera, to be precise) perceive the external world primarily by sonar, or echolocation, detecting the reflections, from objects within range, of their own rapid, subtly modulated, high-frequency shrieks. Their brains are designed to correlate the outgoing

impulses with the subsequent echoes, and the information thus acquired enables bats to make precise discriminations of distance, size, shape, motion, and texture comparable to those we make by vision. But bat sonar, though clearly a form of perception, is not similar in its operation to any sense that we possess, and there is no reason to suppose that it is subjectively like anything we can experience or imagine.[11]

Both the bat and the human are bombarded every nanosecond by countless forces and met by countless particles and wavelengths; each creature has evolved a certain constitution to make sense of those forces, to reduce and re-mediate them into sensible (and, for humans, primarily visual) models, first as the flash of subjective perception, then as the affective phantasms of the memoryscape. We needn't tackle Nagel's interest regarding the mutual intelligibility of neurophysiological constitutions to appreciate his theory of the human qua interface or apparatus—one among many—whose most instinctual act is to process the universe according to the characteristics of its evolved constitution, its embodied sensorium. Because it is old hat to compare a mind to a computer, perhaps "process" is not the most apt verb here. Comparing the mind-body complex to an interface, a more rhetorically generative metaphor, we might posit the individual not merely as a site of data processing but also as a more dynamic point through which data flow and within which data transform into human-readable format. However, to reiterate the salient point, humans have no real control over how their constitutions interface with and automatically transform the universe's raw data into comprehensible sensory models, which we can then access via some unspecified brain-body network.

What our neurophysiologies do naturally, however, becomes less inscrutable when we do it consciously or "artificially." Humanity's Promethean predilections have compelled our species to duplicate the natural activity of mind and memory with *active* attempts to model the universe with comprehensible images. And only a small dose of critical self-reflection can reveal the ways we re-mediate, reduce, and model the fluxes of the universe with our own peculiarly human semiotic habits. Though the primary knowledge within our minds and memories is largely unknowable—both in its formation and its existential substrate—the secondary knowledge we create is more open to scrutiny. Indeed, the preceding study of the mnemonic arts has been a study of secondary knowledge construction, an examination of one way humans have learned to convert information into images to be readily interfaced with, integrated, and used to coordinate real-world activity. These artificial mnemonic forms, like all forms of secondary knowledge, are thoroughly constructed and for that reason thoroughly rhetorical.

Theory II: Data Visualization as a Rhetorical Art

To be sure, some artificial mnemonic forms signal their rhetorical quality more than others. The creative imagery of *Ad Herennium*, for example, made no effort to conceal its imaginative constructedness. No classical rhetor mistook ram's testicles, blood-smeared bodies, and the affective spaces of memory for transparent information displays. The same can be said for Giordano Bruno's wheels of pagan imagery, Peter of Ravenna's maidens, and Thomas Bradwardine's strange numbers and letters. These were all mnemonic cues, products of a creative ars valued above all for their rhetorical utility. What mattered was not their truth-value or ontological accuracy but their ability to facilitate robust recall, integration, and deployment of information to generate something new.

None of that can be said, however, for network graphs, infographics, file icons, interactive charts of all types, or any other digital data displays. The creative ethos of historical mnemonics can seem far afield when venturing into the gravitational pull of contemporary statistics, machine learning, and information visualization (which, together, are often given the title "data science"). Nevertheless, despite the pretensions of some techno-boosters, the same creative agency that went into the construction of memory palaces also goes into the construction of data visualizations. Proceeding as a series of concatenations, graphical data display begins by selecting some phenomenon in the world (i.e., by collecting "data," which necessarily means not selecting other phenomena) and turning the phenomenon into a quantitative or numerical form via an agreed-on measurement system or statistical process; it then continues by changing the resultant numbers into some imagistic representation, and the image is then interpreted via various flavors of empirical discourse. This re-mediational chain, or series of interfaces through which data flow and within which they change form, is of course rife with epistemological problematics, and the best data scientists admit it. When representing the world and all its randomness in discrete numbers, and when representing numbers in graphic form, everything is always a proxy for something else. Distortions inevitably occur. However, in my view, data visualizations are "distortions" only insofar as the scientist creating them fails to acknowledge her role as creative artist and rhetorical decision-maker; and most scientists readily acknowledge the creative element in their data models, visual or statistical. "Data represents the traces of real-world processes," remark Rachel Schutt and Cathy O'Neil, industry experts and authors of *Doing Data Science*; however, "you, the data scientist, the observer, are turning the world into data, and this is an utterly subjective, not objective, process."[12]

To be sure, some data scientists remain more sanguine than others about visualization's ability to tell, if not the whole truth, at least most of the truth about data (and whatever underlying phenomenon they have been designed to capture). Edward Tufte, for example, poses the problems of data conversion as challenges to be met rather than inherent glitches undermining the whole procedure. He provides a simple equation—the "lie factor"—to test the accuracy of a graphical display. A graphic's lie factor, Tufte explains, equals the size of an effect shown in a graphic divided by the size of the same effect in the underlying data.[13] The lower the lie factor, the better the visualization. Tufte's work seeks to ascertain "general principles that have specific visual consequences, governing the design, editing, analysis, and critique of data representation," principles that can lower visualizations' lie factors and "help to identify and to explain design excellence—why some displays are better than others."[14] "Some displays are better than others," meaning that Tufte's bedrock assumption is that with rigor and method a visualization's semiotic elements can approach—even if they can never attain—one-to-one correspondence with data ontology.

Johanna Drucker is less optimistic than Tufte. She argues that data visualization methods are too naïvely "realist" and are thus "a kind of intellectual Trojan horse, a vehicle through which assumptions about what constitutes information swarm with potent force."[15] Data visualization, she contends, too often "familiarizes" its (messy, subjective) underlying data through the persuasive force of raw visual effect as well as through the accuracy-refining discourse championed by scientists like Tufte. Due to their visual rhetoric and the attendant rhetoric of accuracy, data visualizations obscure the reality that all data are, in Drucker's words, "capta," taken from phenomena but not inherent in them, and shaped by the biases, assumptions, and experiences of the observer qua constructed subject.[16] From the capture of data, through their numerical conversion, to their visual display, such biases can only multiply across the data-visualization process, according to Drucker.

There is, of course, a middle ground between Tufte and Drucker. One can admit that all data are capta without foreclosing on either the usefulness of visual models or the fact that some models *are* more accurate and useful than others. Playing on a claim forwarded in the *Foreign Affairs* article "The Rise of Big Data" by Kenneth Cukier and Viktor Mayer-Schönberger—the claim that "big data" allow researchers to approach "*N*

= ALL" in their models—Schutt and O'Neil state that a researcher may indeed "somehow capture the world" with data collection, echoing Drucker's term, but that a researcher only ever captures "certain traces of the world," echoing the spirit of Drucker's critique.[17] Other traces will remain uncaptured and unrepresented. N can never equal ALL. The model never tells the whole, transparent truth. The image always has a well-defined frame. Nevertheless, Schutt and O'Neil accept this critical point without denying the value of (careful, ethical) data science, model building, and graphical information display for solving real-world problems. "We now have tons of data on market and human behavior," they remark. "As data scientists, we bring not just a set of machine learning tools, but also our humanity, to interpret and find meaning in data and make ethical, data-driven decisions."[18]

Whether we want to critique or minimize the distortions inherent in the movement from data capture to data display, the theoretical point is that these distortions are precisely what reveal data visualization to be a rhetorical art. It is in the distortions that we see the creative hand at work. Walking a line between Tufte's and Drucker's stances, a digital canon of memory would take a position roughly similar to that of Rachel Schutt's, Cathy O'Neil's, and many other working data scientists' view. It would recognize the distortions inherent in the process of information display but would not frame them as "distortions"[19] so much as creative alterations necessary to re-mediate complex phenomena into a form humans can contemplate and use to coordinate activity (necessary for the creation of a mnemonic cue, in other words). From the standpoint of rhetorical theory, a digital canon of memory would highlight these alterations not only for what they reveal about epistemology but also for what they reveal about the practical work of data alteration—what the process *does* to data, and why, and how—so that digital rhetors feel comfortable joining in the creative work of collecting, categorizing, cleaning, modeling, and visualizing data. A digital canon of memory would highlight data distortion, in other words, for what it reveals about digital *practices*. The practice of transforming the world into data and data into imagery should not be taught as though it entails black-box thinking, as many critics suggest; rather, it should be taught as a rhetorical ars demanding a critical accounting for various methodological parameters set and active decisions made within specific contexts. "Algorithms," Matt McAlister remarks, "are often characterized as dark robotic machines. . . . But when you open them up and look at their component parts, it becomes apparent how human-powered they are."[20]

Take the example of network graphs. These visualizations encode something in the qualitative world—text, in the case I explore here—into numbers and then into image. Each step of the process requires creative human input and decision-making, informed by some explicit goal. It is a rhetorical as much as a technical undertaking.

Text networks visualize a text's semantic connectivity: Which words are connected to what other words, and how often? The word *connected* is obviously vague. Connected in what way? Before I can re-mediate text into image, that question must be answered in a series of formal decisions. The first decision highlights Drucker's point about "capta": What features of the text world will I select, and what features will I ignore? What words in the text will I in fact capture and convert into the underlying data of what will become my text network? I have the option to port every single word in the text into the network. Anyone who has dabbled in natural language processing, however, knows that would be a poor decision. Stopwords such as "the," "of," "or," and "and" will dominate any lexical results by virtue of their sheer frequency compared to content words. They will become the most prominent nodes in the network no matter how I set other parameters. Selecting the whole text is rarely a viable option—just as mapping the whole territory would make for a useless map (more on that later). N can never equal ALL. So, if I am not selecting the whole text, what selections and deflections should I make? Should I remove all the stopwords, as delineated in any number of stopword-removal lists available in natural language processing resources? Should I create a custom stopword list, removing "the" and "of" but retaining auxiliary verbs such as "is" and "was"? Critical thinking about the *goals* I have for the text network should guide my decision to apply a large, indiscriminate stopword list or to create a limited, bespoke one. Why am I creating this particular text network in the first place? What questions do I want to answer, or what problem am I attempting to solve? Articulating these preliminary goals is ultimately the most important step that precedes any data-visualization process. Think of yourself as an orator preparing her memory palace for a specific court case or senate debate; the exigencies of tomorrow's performance will determine the nature of the mnemonic imagery and their associations.

In addition to deciding which words to capture and which to ignore for my text network, I also need to figure out what *counts* as a word in the first place. Do I divide compound nouns and proper names—such as "police station" or "parking lot" or "Principal Skinner"—into two words? Or do these count as single words? Similarly, do I treat inflections and derivations as different words? Or do I reduce—in linguistic terms, do I stem or lemmatize—inflections and derivations into single roots? For example,

TABLE 5.1. Underlying Spreadsheet of a Text Network (from a Student Essay on Genetically Modified Food)

1	A	B	C	D	E
2	Concept	Concept	Frequency	Average distance	Shortest distance
3	gene	transfer	1	1	1
4	genetic	makeup	1	1	1
5	genetically	altered	3	1	1
6	genetically	cells	1	2	2
7	genetically	corn	1	2	2
8	genetically	crops	1	2	2
9	genetically	material	2	2	2
10	genetically	materials	1	2	2
11	genetically	modified	8	1	1
12	genetically	organisms	3	2	2
13	genetically	particles	1	2	2
14	gluten	raj	1	1	1

should I count "study," "studies," and "studying" as three different words, or should I lemmatize these forms into the root "study"?

Along with deciding what words to count and what counts as a word, I need to delineate the lexical gap that will end up defining the network's semantic connectivity. Put more simply, because a text network converts a text's words into a collection of nodes and edges, I need to decide what lexical distance should in fact produce a node/edge connection. Should I adopt a two-word gap—that is, should words appearing side by side produce a node/edge connection? Or should I adopt a wider three-word gap? A four-, five-, or six-word gap? That is, how wide a net do I cast in order to measure the abstract concept of lexical/semantic connectivity?

All these and other questions must be answered in order to lay the groundwork for a text-to-numbers-to-network conversion. In Auto Map, Gephi, and similar network tools, the initial text-to-numbers conversion generates a spreadsheet that displays two words in each row, the number of times the words are "connected" in the text, and the average and shortest "distance" between the two words. Table 5.1 contains a brief example created from a student essay on the labeling of genetically modified food, which I return to later in the chapter.

With the words of the text converted into a numerical spreadsheet, it is now possible to visualize the spreadsheet as a network graph. Once more, this task requires active input. Many decisions must be made when converting a spreadsheet into a network, but I will discuss only one here. The most important decision, in my view, is what algorithm will be used to visualize the nodes' connective significance. Different algorithms emphasize different sorts of significance, because what network graphs display,

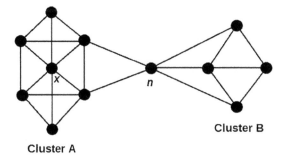

Cluster B

Cluster A

FIGURE 5.1. Degree centrality (x) and betweenness centrality (n)

through size or coloring, is how important or "central" any given nodes are within a network as a whole, and there are obviously different ways to measure centrality. For a text network, I would need to decide which measurement is best suited to visualizing the concept of lexical centrality within a text's entire meaning-making structure.

The most common centrality equations are *degree centrality* and *betweenness centrality*. Degree centrality measures the total connections a node has to other individual nodes; a node with high degree centrality will simply be a node connected to many other nodes. Betweenness centrality measures how often a node is connected to other nodes that themselves have many connections; a node with high betweenness centrality will in essence be a passageway between clusters within the network. In figure 5.1, for example, node x has high degree centrality but lower betweenness centrality; node n has high betweenness centrality but lower degree centrality. In the context of a text network, a node with high degree centrality is a word used in connection with myriad other words. This would simply tell me that this word is used frequently in a text. A node with high betweenness centrality, on the other hand, is a word used frequently *but in conjunction with other words* that also connect to many other nodes, forming community clusters on either side of the word/node. High betweenness centrality tells me that this word is used not only frequently and in many contexts but also in connection with *other* words that *also* do a lot of semantic work in the text. A word with high betweenness centrality is a word through which many meanings in a text circulate, deployed to discuss first this and now that topic or subtopic. Betweenness centrality would thus in many cases be the better equation to apply when creating a text network; it more closely represents what literary or rhetorical scholars likely mean when talking about a text's meaning-making structures. (As a practical matter, the network would visualize nodes/words with high be-

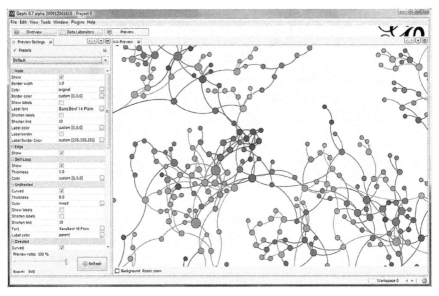

FIGURE 5.2. The interactive space of Gephi

tweenness centrality by increasing the nodes' sizes and by color coding distinct clusters around them.)

Importantly, with a network visualization tool such as Gephi, I can experiment with many centrality measurements, visualizing the data first this way, then some other way, tuning the parameters this way and that to see how they affect not only the network but also the way I might interpret the underlying text. (I have not even considered here the importance of force-directed algorithms, the parameters by which we decide how the clusters are visually separated in the interface.) This is perhaps the most vital point for digital rhetoric: that visualizing text as a network is a starting point for inquiry, a practice by which we gain not a final and total perspective but multiple visual perspectives on the underlying text. The vast majority of visualization tools facilitate this sort of interactive, imagistic play (figure 5.2). I'll return to this key point later on. But it's worth recalling here that classical mnemonic imagery was used also as a starting point for knowledge construction. The art of memory, I wrote in the first chapter, did not result in a definitive visual model in the mind, a palace built with immutable and immutably associated imagery representing static information. Rather, like letters on wax tablets, mnemonic images were ever changing as the orator made new connections or found new uses for old knowledge—"for the images, like letters, are effaced when we make no use of them," as the author of *Ad Herennium* wrote.[21] It was the principle of interactive visualization that linked memoria and inventio in the classical world. The same should be said today about data visualizations, particularly when it comes to the interactive spaces offered by programs like Gephi.

The point of this text-network walk-through is not to provide a tutorial but rather to reveal (especially to humanists skeptical about the intrusion of visual, quantitative methods) that data visualization is not an epistemological black box hiding nefarious ideologies, neoliberal or otherwise.[22] It is, instead, a deeply creative and rhetorical undertaking. To repeat the argument, the creativity that went into crafting mnemonic images goes also into creating data visualizations. Like any secondary/artificial form of knowledge creation, data visualization involves precepts and practices; these are knowable and learnable. Data visualization is thus aptly described as a rhetorical ars. Users must take particular actions and make various choices informed by their intellectual and rhetorical goals. These choices produce data alterations and provide points of entry for anyone wanting to understand, critique, or join in the digital knowledge construction process. Far from being black boxes, visualization methods do not function without judicious input at each transformational stage—from world to data to numbers to image. The process of knowledge creation and its potential biases are laid bare for anyone willing to learn and analyze it. Fashioned with selections and deflections, data visualizations are as self-consciously assembled as any classical memory palace or any other form of secondary human knowledge. Like the ancient ars memoria, then, the digital memory arts will re-mediate information into visual form to facilitate info recall and info integration in service of rhetorical and other intellectual activity.

Contra the more objectivist views of data visualization—such as Tufte's—the digital memory arts will not be too concerned with developing perfect, semiotic correspondence between data and graphic display. To be sure, digital rhetors should find ethical value in detecting or ameliorating a visualization's lie factor whenever possible. As a general rule, however, their primary impetus will be to enact a constructionist critique by doing with data displays what classical orators did with imagines in their memory palaces: deconstruct and reconstruct them, assemble and reassemble them, and teach others to interact with visualizations in various ways, all with an eye toward generating new perceptions of and contact points among the underlying information. Historically, mnemonic imagery was a means to an end, the starting point rather than the final product of inventio. All practices within a digital canon of memory should flow from this basic point. Following the Greeks, Romans, and monastics, the accuracy of the digital mnemonic cue will be less important than the (many) ideas that the cue generates and the rhetorical uses to which it can be put. Of similar importance will be to develop precepts about "visualizing" not only information but also the decisions that informed the initial data categorization and parameter tunings that produced the final form of the visualization itself. How might one visually acknowledge, *within* the network, the centrality measurement one has used to *build* the network, for example? (Good data scientists already follow similar precepts by, for instance, producing box plots, error bars, and other images that visualize statistical uncertainty in their data.) A digital memoria, in short, will frame data visualization as a creative practice of data bricolage rather than as a method for mastering the world's unbounded data streams. "Nothing is more beautiful than to know all," wrote Athanasius Kircher about his ars combinatoria.[23] To which the rhetorician replies, "Nothing is more beautiful than to know things many different ways, and to show one another how we came to know them."

Practice I: Text Sense and Text Networks (Images for Words)

Classical treatises recognized two types of mnemonic imagery: imagery for words (*memoria verborum*) and imagery for general content (*memoria rerum*). Adapting this ancient distinction, *memoria verborum* can be associated in digital spaces with visualizing text in particular, whereas *memoria rerum* can be associated with visualizing any other type of information, from geographical coordinates to economic data to demographic facts and so on. Given the ubiquity of visualization tools—both static and interactive—endless opportunities exist for applying these tools as mnemonic and explicitly rhetorical devices. I provide two examples in this and the next section, one for *memoria verborum* and one for *memoria rerum*.

By definition, *memoria verborum* will be deeply intertwined with the practices of writing and analyzing text. (Although I focus on writing in this section, everything said can be applied, with minor variation, to reading and literary analysis.) For text-visualization strategies to make mnemonic sense, however, we should first consider the relationship between written composition and natural memory.

Although the popular imagination no longer associates writing with memory, psychologists and compositionists have recognized that the strength of natural memory (both short and long term) is central to the writing process. In her overview of research into memory operations during composition, Deborah McCutchen explains that the dexterity with which a writer generates text is circumscribed by her short-term or working memory.[24] Numerous studies have found that, across demographic groups, a strong working memory is associated with the production of more rhetorically and stylistically rich texts. The stronger the working memory, these studies conclude, the greater the ability to connect ideas at the scale of the sentence, the paragraph, and the whole text. Skilled writers also possess the ability to access long-term memory in the midst of composition, recalling information related to genre conventions and discourse forms.[25] The management of text-level linguistic elements in working memory and the simultaneous recall of genre information from long-term memory are vital applications of natural memory during the writing process. None of this should be surprising to writers familiar with the exertions of mind required to juggle the many "units and relationships," as Patricia Sullivan and Richard Young describe them,[26] of a complex text being composed.

Christina Haas posits the phrase "sense of the text" to describe the mental process by which writers "develop some understanding—some representation—of the text they have created or are creating."[27] This representation includes not only the linguistic and genre elements highlighted by McCutchen but also an overall "understanding of the structure of [a text's] arguments"—that is, its overall rhetorical assembly. Haas is explicit about the role played by memory in the development of text sense. It comprises "both a spatial memory of the written text," she argues, "and an episodic memory of its construction."[28] Text sense denotes a mnemonic entity distinct from but modeling the actual written artifact. The development of text sense, in other words, is a writer's attempt to recall the thematic and lexical shape of a text in progress in order to facilitate revision and further invention. Research in psychology provides a foundation for the concept. It has long been accepted, for example, that humans make sense of written content with recourse to visual imagery and mental models,[29] a point that will be obvious to anyone with an active reading life. Haas simply shifts focus from the mental modeling of a text's content to the modeling of the text as such. Furthermore, a long-standing theory in psychology is that all human reasoning is not solely a linguistic phenomenon but also relies to some extent on mental imagery[30] and spatial models.[31] It would stand to reason that whenever writers think critically about textual development, a mental model of the text's layout plays a role in their thinking. (The idea of text sense rings true in my own experience as a writer.) Interestingly, Haas's idea of text sense echoes the text-based mnemonic arts of late antiquity and the Middle Ages, arts that eschewed imagery and endorsed crafting mental images of the text as such. Quintilian's segmentation system, Augustine's numeric ordering of Psalms, and Hugh of Saint Victor's text grids were all designed to aid the development of "some representation" of a text being engaged with—something our minds do naturally, according to Haas, when producing text sense. Insofar as text sense facilitates invention, it is similar in particular to medieval mnemonics, which enabled monks to see within their minds the text of the Bible while praying or preparing a sermon. Developing a sense of the text for its own sake was and is not the point; the point is to create something new within it or from it (in the form of citations, revisions, and so on).

However, as I suggested in chapter 2, and as many rhetors knew and warned, a mnemonic sense of text qua text—even a textual image placed at the service of creativity—is not a particularly efficient memory aid. "Although men invented writing," a Renaissance author keenly observes, "they could not remember everything they had written." They therefore went about inventing "a subtler art so they were able to remember things without any kind of writing."[32] As long as text or any raw information appears before the mind's eye, the memory's attempt to develop a robust sense of it is destined to be less successful than it might be were the thing clothed in a more distinguishable form.

Today, the deficiency of writing as a mnemonic aid—a deficiency recognized during the classical and early modern eras and downplayed in the word-centric Middle Ages—is likely exacerbated in the context of the digital screen. In one of her studies, Haas explores the development of text sense by observing writers using pen and paper versus writers using a word processor. Writers using pen and paper, she discovered, reported to have developed text sense more easily than writers using a computer. Because text sense exists as a mnemonic artifact distinct from the text itself, Haas speculates, the ability to interact materially with a text likely facilitated the construction of a more detailed, three-dimensional mental model of it. Haas lists distancing, pointing, changing perspective, and tactile manipulation (e.g., spreading pages on a table) as physical interactions that writers using pen and paper employed to help them develop a clearer mnemonic image of their texts in development. Such interactions were not possible for the electronic writers, who complained about the difficulty of "getting a perspective" on their born-digital texts.[33] The following remarks, Haas reports, were made by the electronic writers who found it difficult to develop text sense when composing on a computer:

> "I have to print it to get a perspective on it."
> "Seeing it on the screen isn't really seeing it."
> "It's hard getting your center of gravity in the writing."
> "My text is hard to pin down online."
> "I get a printout just to see that it's developing right."

"When I write on the computer, I have a hard time knowing where I am."

"I can't get any distance from it when it's here." [points to the screen]

"I need to see if it's still on track."[34]

The spatio-visual metaphors are obvious: "get a perspective on it," "center of gravity," "hard to pin down," "to see that it's developing," "knowing where I am," "get distance from it," "still on track," and, most fascinatingly, "seeing it on the screen isn't really seeing it."

In my view, the fact that writers instinctively talk about texts in dimensional terms validates the idea that whenever they sit down to compose, their creative minds are demanding something visual to set before the *oculus imaginationis*. I tend to agree with Haas that the three-dimensionality of pen and paper better satisfies that demand than the two-dimensional space of word processors (though I agree more with the classical rhetors, that even a physical text at some point will become difficult "to get a perspective on"). However, the reality is that the vast majority of writing today occurs in the flat space of the digital screen and, in particular, the flat space of the word processor—which has changed little since its development in the 1980s. Circa 2019, word processors still fail to encourage anything like the text-visualization strategies recommended in classical rhetorical treatises. Although writers seem to possess a natural impulse to develop text sense—to visualize the "units and relationships" of a text while composing it—the word processor, as a medium and an interface, severely limits the techniques by which natural text sense might be enhanced. Media and interfaces are not neutral, after all; they are active participants in the contact between information and a cognitive subject. They shape how a subject sees or does not see information, expediting certain types of access while impeding others.[35] For all its sophistication, the word processor remains a space of text qua text, a flatland of two-way scrolling. Under its influence, writers visualize their texts futilely with indefinite loci such as "up there" or "down there" or "over on that other page." This is not a very robust technique. The mnemonic lesson learned by Cicero in the context of papyrus remains doubly pertinent in the context of the digital screen: the creative mind works better with visual models than it does with raw words. What is required, then, in terms of digital mnemonic practice, is to re-mediate the digital text into visual form, the end goal being to facilitate more sophisticated invention and revision strategies.

One such visualization strategy was introduced just a moment ago: the text network. As a rhetorical art, the creation of a text network does not generate an accurate or complete representation of the text as a whole but rather prompts new approaches to revision and invention. Stephen Ramsay's idea of "algorithmic criticism" is relevant here: when converting text into a new visual form, Ramsay states, "potential readings" that had once been hidden should emerge into view. Further alteration of the text itself should at some point become "unavoidable" once we step down this path of visual alteration.[36] In the case of text networks, they allow a writer to see her text not as a two-dimensional surface or a series of autonomous words but as a more dynamic and visual object consisting of connected lexical clusters through which ideas and meanings circulate (somewhat like the loci of the ancient memory palace).

Each node cluster within a network visualizes a collection of frequently associated words—what might be thought of as a topic, or a theme, or an area of focus. Visualizing a text as nodes and edges allows the writer to see how these thematic areas are (or are not) connected to one another. It allows her to see how meaning circulates in her text and to move through the cohesive meaning-making structures she has crafted thus far—the text's patterns, its connections, its transition points, and the intratextual relationships of its lexicon. While writing, it is nearly impossible with working memory alone to recall all the semantic clusters one has constructed; it is even more difficult to recall how one has linked and transitioned between them. The value of a text network is that it visualizes this semantic connectedness. Network graphs allow users to interface visually with a text's linguistic morphology, to move through it, to get various perspectives on it—and, most importantly, to reimagine it. Because most network tools are interactive, they allow users to (re)arrange the nodes and clusters into different assemblies and proximities (see, again, figure 5.2). What do the new assemblies suggest about the text's potential next draft?

Because the interface of the book does not permit easy discussion of network tools' interactivity, I will not pursue the point further. However, even as a static object, a text network can still aid a writer's creativity. Figures 5.3 through 5.5, for example, display a text network of a student essay on genetically modified (GM) food and the labeling of said food (each figure zooms in at different points on the same network). Again, if the writer were viewing this network in its original interactive space—Gephi—he could point and click through the existing clusters, play with parameters to visualize denser or sparser clusters, or create new clusters with various centrality algorithms, all in search of some novel perspective to inspire new directions for the composition. Even these static visuals suggest a couple of ideas, though. Because this network visualizes nodes with high betweenness centrality, the centrality of "raj" and "lilliston" in

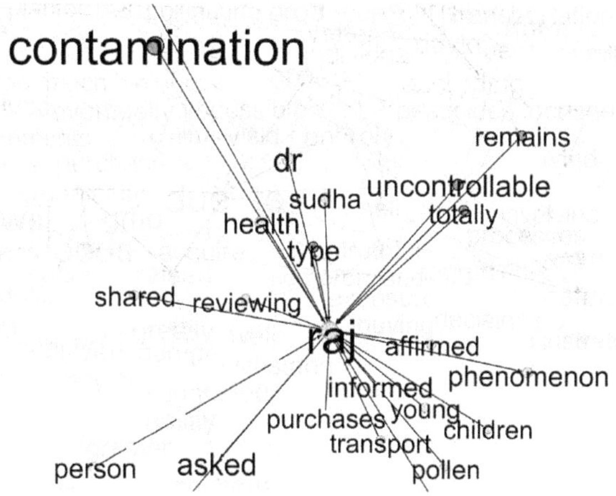

contamination

remains

dr
sudha uncontrollable
health totally
type

shared reviewing

raj affirmed

informed phenomenon
purchases young
transport children
person asked pollen

FIGURE 5.3. Text network of a student essay on genetically modified food (zoomed in)

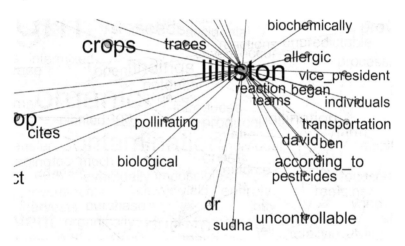

biochemically

crops traces

allergic

lilliston vice_president
reaction began
teams individuals

op
cites pollinating transportation

davidben

biological according_to
ct pesticides

dr
sudha uncontrollable

FIGURE 5.4. Text network of same essay (zoomed in to a different area of the network)

separate clusters is interesting (figures 5.3 and 5.4). Lilliston and Raj are two key sources employed in the essay. Their centrality in separate clusters suggests that the sources are not used in close conjunction; they occupy separate loci in the overall textual space. Each source is connected with another "dr."— "sudha"—but they do not connect with each other through that node/word. Perhaps this separation is purposeful, dictated by the simple fact that each source attends to a different aspect of GM-food labeling. On the other hand, perhaps these clusters call to mind an opportunity for greater interplay between the two sources. Perhaps the

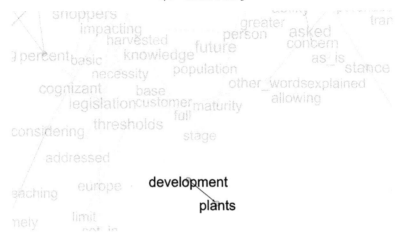

FIGURE 5.5. Text network of same essay (zoomed in to a different area of the network)

writer has missed important connections between the "lilliston" and "raj" sources, of which an exploration might improve the essay.

Another idea suggested by these static visuals is that while most of the words in the network are connected, even if by multiple degrees of separation, Gephi has returned several word clusters that fail to connect to any of the other words in the essay. One of these clusters (figure 5.5) contains two words that, given the essay's content, seem like they should occupy a more central location within the text network: "development" and "plants." How wide a net the writer cast while creating this network— that is, if he defined "lexical connection" as a one- or two-word gap rather than a five- or six-word gap—might explain why these words are disconnected in this particular visualization. However, once again, perhaps this little lexical island will prompt the writer to return to these terms with a more critical mind-set, asking himself if they should be deployed more often or used in connection with other key terms in the essay. Perhaps he has missed out on another opportunity to construct more explicit connections between ideas. In my mind, again, it seems like the words in this disconnected cluster should occupy a more interconnected space in an essay on the labeling of genetically modified food.

These are two simple examples of how a text network can assist the development of text sense and prompt invention strategies. If one relied on working memory alone, it would be difficult to develop a sense of a composition's terminological and thematic morphology at this granular scale. Text network interfaces make it easier. Transforming a text into a network graph shows writers which words or phrases do the most work in their texts, which words work together, and which words never or rarely cross paths. They are like dynamic dispersion plots, inviting writers to move between idea clusters just as orators moved between loci in their memory palaces. Gaining a perspective on this meaning-making movement is vital to developing a sense of the text, but it would be difficult to do so by juggling words in one's mind, placing them in vague mental locations, and attempting to recall as much of the edifice as possible while writing. Text networks provide an image of the lexical edifice, and interfaces such as Gephi's allow writers to interact with it and reimagine the connections discovered within it. They allow the writer to get a handle on the through line between the smaller (words) and larger (themes) components of her text. "The *whole*," Bruno Latour says about digital transformations of data, "is now nothing more than a provisional visualization, which can be modified and reversed at will, by moving back to the individual components, and then looking for yet other tools to regroup the same elements into alternative assemblages."[37] Although Latour is writing about digital, quantitative datascapes in general, his comment applies even to as humble a visualization as a text network of a student essay.

Practice II: Digital Maps (Images for Things)

I have implied throughout the chapter that a digital canon of memory will enact more so than discuss its critical stance regarding the rhetorical (as opposed to the "accurate") aspects of data visualization. Creating and exploring a text network is one such enactment: it enables a writer to think critically about and experiment with her composition's lexical and semantic shape. A network graph is the beginning of creativity, not an end product; its primary goal is not accurate representation but rhetorical invention.

When constructing *memoria rerum*, the possibilities for enacting a visual critique become even greater. The creation of images of all other sorts of information beyond written text invites rhetors to tap into the surfeit of geographic, climatological, historical, biological, demographic, social, and economic data readily available online. Much work in social analytics and other data sciences, in my view, is already producing rhetorically-aware data visualizations, emphasizing that their imagery can (and must necessarily) be as biased as any narrative, that their imagery hides as much as what it reveals, and that a visual model should be used as one element in a larger analysis rather than as a final representation whose conclusions speak for themselves. Data visualization "exists in between art and information," state data scientists Schutt and O'Neil. "An education that

FIGURE 5.6. Los Angeles, viewed through the Google Earth interface

doesn't take [design principles] into account, as well as the principles of journalism and storytelling, and only focuses on tools and statistics is only giving you half the picture. Not to mention the psychology of human perception."[38] In the same spirit, I want to look in this section at digital maps as one potential type of data visualization that can enact a humanistic critique, provide a narrative, and emphasize its role as the beginning rather than the end point of inquiry—the creation of a particular story (one among many possible stories) rather a trumpeting of final data mastery.

We begin with the Google Earth interface (figure 5.6). The view of a geographical location through the lens of Google Earth might seem to offer an objective, almost godlike image of a space. I can zoom down to the streets of Manhattan, Los Angeles, and Moscow, or, a second later, I can scroll over the world's most remote locations, from Utqiaġvik, Alaska, to clearings in the Amazon jungle. Nowhere on Earth is hidden from Sergey Brin's eyes in the sky.

However, even these high-definition satellite images conceal the most important information emanating from any given space. When we shift interfaces from Google Earth to Google Maps (figure 5.7), the overlaid search bar reminds us of all the things going on in locations that satellite images do not show: traffic patterns, hotel costs, gas prices, the mileage between points, the types of businesses housed in any given build-

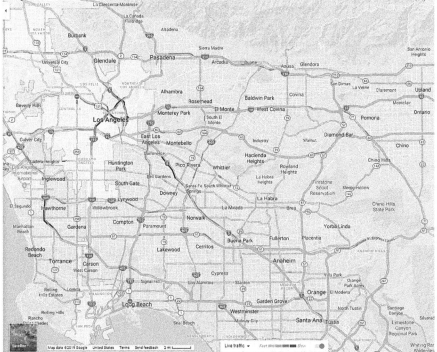

FIGURE 5.7. Los Angeles, viewed through the Google Maps interface

ing, and so on. Even this information barely scratches the surface. Also hidden from satellite imagery is information related to climate patterns, voting patterns, criminal activity, population density, racial composition, government zoning, water usage, energy usage, home prices, and elevation contours—the entire expansive set of social and physical data that saturates any given place. Naturally, were we interested in exploring these data and their intersections, natural memory alone could never hope to recall, juggle, or utilize it all at any one time. With a digital map interface, this becomes more feasible. In conjunction with Google's and other specialized data sets, interfaces such as Google Maps allow a user to view not only the physical place but also all the relevant information about the place that is typically hidden by traditional maps and even high-def satellite images. The benefit of the digital map is that, like all visual mnemonic forms, it recalls, re-mediates, and integrates these data into a single imagistic and interactive space.

Of course, we must remember the lessons of the critical cartographers. Even the Google map is not the territory. J. B. Harley reminds us that the map is always a construction, a motivated representation, designed by humans to show some things and to not show other things.[39] Just as Kenneth Burke analyzed language as a process of selection and deflection—of terministic screens—so, too, have critical cartographers recognized the selections and deflections inherent in purportedly objective representations of space. Their critique is elementary. Long before critical cartography, authors such as Lewis Carroll and Jorge Luis Borges had acknowledged in fictional rather than theoretical terms the map/territory distinction, the notion that a map fully faithful to the world simply recreates the world and is therefore both impossible and useless. As Borges states in his fictional treatise "On Exactitude in Science,"

> In that Empire, the craft of Cartography attained such Perfection that the Map of a single Province covered the space of an entire City, and the Map of the Empire itself an entire Province. In the course of Time, these Extensive maps were found somewhat wanting, and so the College of Cartographers evolved a Map of the Empire that was the same Scale as the Empire and that coincided with it point for point. Less attentive to the Study of Cartography, succeeding Generations came to judge a map of such Magnitude cumbersome.[40]

How else would maps work without selecting certain elements of a territory and deflecting everything else? Like most critical endeavors, critical cartography makes an ethical point more than an epistemological one. It encourages scholars to consider *who* and *what* are removed from officially sanctioned maps and to ask whose interests are served or ignored by those deflections.

Despite its salutary ethical and political motivations, Harley's critical work nevertheless suggests a strong form of relativism—when it comes to maps, we might conclude, there is no *there* there, only inscriptions of power. Donna Haraway's "Situated Knowledges" can be read as a corrective counterweight to such relativistic interpretation. Although it never mentions mapping explicitly, Haraway's argument remains relevant with its epistemology of partial, local perspectives. Any strong form of relativism, Haraway claims, is simply the "mirror twin" of totalizing scientist objectivity. Both relativism and totalization "deny the stakes in location, embodiment, and partial perspective; . . . both [are] 'god tricks' promising vision from everywhere and nowhere equally and fully."[41] Countering both impulses, Haraway theorizes an "epistemology of partial perspectives," of "local knowledges" or "webbed accounts" that "resist the politics of closure" and encourage instead a "politics of interpretation, translation . . . and the partly understood."[42] In other words, Haraway's epistemology transforms the godlike view "from everywhere and no-where" into an embodied view from multiple perspectives in dialogue. J. B. Harley destabilizes the map as a totalizing, purportedly "neutral" view of a space. Following this destabilization, Haraway steps in to replace the old totalizing view with a new multiplicity of views. (Harley does at times inch nearer to Haraway's view, writing that the "logic of the map" should not idealize a space but create "alternative visions of what the world is, or what it might be.")[43] Giving life to such multiple visions, says Haraway, must begin with a reclamation of vision itself—exchanging the view from nowhere for "varied apparatuses of visual production."[44] Vision does not present consciousness with "already processed and objectified fields," Haraway states; rather, it is a mediating interface. And there are many interfaces through which one might mediate the world. The trick is to not confuse any particular interface—any particular view—with the one view to rule them all, as do the strong forms of relativism and scientific objectivity. To view otherwise is to foreclose on alternative visions of space and place.

More recently, Harley's and Haraway's imaginary conversation echoes in Jeff Rice's *Digital Detroit*, in which Rice likens his movement through—his interfacing with—the material/digital space of the Motor City as a "virtual map of abstract possibilities."[45] Quoting Matthew Fuller, Rice claims that his virtual map embodies a "media ecology, . . . mobilizing and mapping, using the perspectivalism of particular approaches, materials, and ideas as they intersect." Rice's virtual map "write[s] spatial encounters as an invention practice" that attends to and looks for "the possibilities of spaces." In the era of Google Earth, Rice and other scholars of media and rhetoric have recognized that the key to using new media for invention rather than for reinscribing the old totalizing visions is to *view* them in Haraway's sense—to disconnect the map from the territory, to "break the literalism of representation," as Johanna Drucker puts it,[46] and to use digital interfaces to pursue "partial" and "partly understood" perspectives, what Fuller calls "the perspectivalism of particular approaches."

By intersecting or moving between perspectives—by recognizing that every perspective is partial—one opens the door to the "possibilities of spaces." In the context of digital mapping, this means that every recalled layer is particular, temporary, and partial, to be selected or peeled back as the need arises so as to enable myriad orientations. While the selections (and thus deflections) of a paper map are set in stone, so to speak, interfaces such as Google Maps allow for fluid and ever-expanding selections, so that the deflections inherent in one selection can themselves be selected, and thus made visible, with the click of a mouse or a simple download. The only limit to what can be selected and visualized is the availability of data—and data abound. Digital map layering thus enacts Haraway's epistemology of partial perspectives. By design, maps constructed for industry or travel leave out many elements of a space; by design, digital maps in the hands of socially interested rhetors can return those elements to a space, including social, political, economic, and climatological information. Digital maps, in other words, are designed for *maximum selection*. Each selection is finite and incomplete, but digital interfaces allow multiple finite selections to be layered onto one another and compared, contrasted, oriented, and reoriented. Each selection offers a partial perspective, but by assembling the partial perspectives in and on a single image, one begins to construct not a "view from nowhere" but a view from many perspectives all at once. To be sure, the dangers of literalism and reification are always lurking in any interface. Viewed rhetorically, however, the interactive capabilities of mapping software remind users that mapping is an act of invention that resists closure—yes, we can look at a space *this* way, but we can also look at it *that* way . . . and so on. Visualizing and reorienting informational map layers is every bit an act of bricolage as is wandering through the memory palace in search of that one connection or bit of information perfect for a given rhetorical goal.

One way to produce a multiplicity of views of a space is to recall data related to the space's various socioeconomic conditions. Without assuming a priori the existence and precise coordinates of class boundaries, it is possible to view them, in their curious fluidity and stability, by orienting multiple perspectives. For example, one method I have used to visualize class boundaries is to gather, first, the addresses of the dozen or so most expensive homes in an area (using the sales website Zillow) and then, second, the addresses of public housing units (using local Human Services websites). These addresses can then be plotted with Google Maps to see where they exist in proximal space.

Having done this with numerous cities for both research and pedagogical purposes, I have often found one of two antithetical visions of American class boundaries: what I call the "grid boundary" and the "fortress boundary." Observe the visualized data—most expensive homes versus public housing—in Los Angeles, California, (figure 5.8) and New Orleans, Louisiana (figure 5.9). In New Orleans, the expensive homes stand near Tulane University and stretch in a U-shape from there along Saint Charles Avenue. However, as is visible, these wealthy plots stand relatively close to public housing sites. One multimillion-dollar home stands only a few blocks from a notoriously violent housing project.[47] Only two public housing units are far-flung from the expensive homes. Even then, the distances pale in comparison to the distances found on the Los Angeles

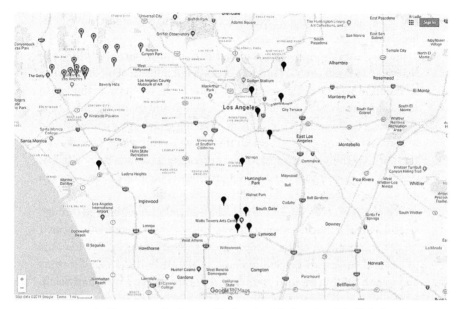

FIGURE 5.8. Most expensive homes (dot) and public housing (black) in Los Angeles, CA

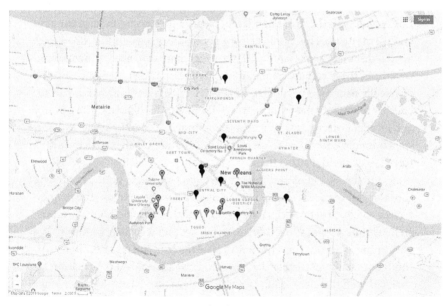

FIGURE 5.9. Most expensive homes (dot) and public housing (black) in New Orleans, LA

map. (Note the Los Angeles map is zoomed out to one mile, the New Orleans map to two thousand feet.)

In Los Angeles, millionaires gather in the northwest, into which the road grid does not extend. These homes are not individual plots of wealth so much as wealth enclaves, situated miles from the start of the urban sprawl and up to twenty miles from the eastern and southern ends of the city, where the housing projects cluster. Having grown up near and worked in the City of Angels, I can vouch that those twenty miles can take upward of sixty minutes to travel by car, depending on traffic: even with Los Angeles's famously vast freeway system, there is no direct route between downtown or south central and the wealthy northwest.

This is the grid boundary and the fortress boundary, visualized through sales data and public housing addresses. New Orleans represents the first type: the separation of the very poor and the very rich occurs *within* the urban grid. Spatial distances are much smaller than distances of income and wealth. Within the grid boundary, there are "no-go zones" and neighborhoods where "you just don't travel after dark." In these places, poverty and crime are a function of *street* rather than zip code or town. Poverty remains visible to the rich, and its effects will hit closer to home because they are quite literally closer to home (though not experienced directly). Los Angeles, on the other hand, represents a fortress boundary: the separation of the very rich and the very poor occurs beyond the urban grid. Spatial distances are as large as, if not larger than, distances of income and wealth. In these situations, members of the upper class need not ever be physically near members of the lower classes. Poverty is a function of zip code or town, so it never hits close to home for the rich, because poverty and its effects occur nowhere near their homes. Within Los Angeles's fortress boundary, poverty is largely invisible to the rich; they pass over it on freeways or avoid it altogether.

As interesting as this preliminary spatialization might be, the point here is not to "represent" a single dimension of a space but to use the map interface to construct multiple views of it. Within Google Maps, it is possible to continue recalling information from and visualizing information within the space. Let us stay with Los Angeles's fortress boundary. Although it would take other databases to view specialized information associated with the city—such as voting patterns or crime—Google Maps can still recall relevant data. For example, a search for full-service grocery stores reveals that both the wealthy northwestern areas and the downtown public housing units have access to stores with names like Trader Joe's, Whole Foods, Bristol Farms, and Sprouts Farmers Market; the south-central public housing units have access to stores with names like Food 4

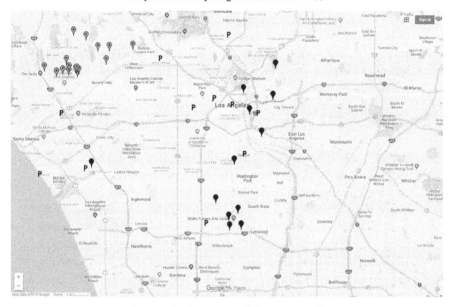

FIGURE 5.10. Distribution of police stations (P) in Los Angeles, CA

Less, Numero Uno Market, Smart & Final, and Vons. Another example is the spatial distribution of police and sheriff stations (figure 5.10). The distribution of law enforcement is not quite binary but nevertheless stark: downtown and south central are more actively policed than Beverly Hills.

I may or may not be trying to make a political point by visualizing these "multiple perspectives" on a space. Were I to continue recalling information from Los Angeles onto my (always partial) image of it, I would sooner or later confront a view that does not fit preconceived political narratives. For example, mapping the election results for the 2016 presidential race would reveal that both the poorer and the wealthier areas voted for Hillary Clinton over Donald Trump; mapping the results for California's Proposition 8—the 2008 gay-marriage ban—would reveal that the northwestern areas voted against banning gay marriage, while the poorer areas around the public housing units voted uniformly in favor of it. Such perspectival mapping, in my view, is best used to integrate data to meet a specific goal or to argue a specific policy issue; for example, in the cases above, these maps could inform city planners about the lack of food centers or provide activists with information about patterns of urban policing. Using map layers to verify a received ideology, on the other hand, will almost always hit a layer that complicates things. However, whatever the map's goal might be, it should be emphasized that mapping multiple perspectives cannot replicate the singular lived realities on the ground. Such realities mostly resist imagistic reduction: "the constructed experience of space," Johanna Drucker states, "cannot be presented in standard cartography any more than the variable concepts of temporality can be charted on a standard timeline."[48]

Nevertheless, framed as a rhetorical art, comparative map layering does at least illustrate a method for visualizing compound perspectives on a place. Taken together, these perspectives do not aggregate into some objective view of Los Angeles—indeed, if I were to place more than seven or eight layers onto my map image, it would quickly become unreadable, replicating on the screen the problem of memory overload, of "recreating the territory." The point is not data mastery or godlike objectivity; the point is, as always, to facilitate knowledge creation and discourse. By providing a view of Los Angeles from multiple perspectives, through multiple interfacing layers, with multiple "visual apparatuses," and by integrating these perspectives in an act of visual bricolage, map layering becomes an invention tactic—an art of memory in the classical sense. Any particular data layer, any association of layers, ignites discussion. Through exercises like the one above, we learn that although our minds can never know a place totally and objectively, we can always gain a new perspective on it.

Digital Iconoclasm Redux: Critique versus Rhetoric

Having considered two practices of digital memoria, I return in this concluding section to the interplay between rhetorical practice and digital iconoclastic critique introduced in chapter 3. Johanna Drucker and Wendy Hui Kyong Chun provide the main foils in the following discussion. I have found in their work the most challenging developments in the rhetoric of visualization, so their arguments are worth responding to in detail.

The text network displayed in figure 5.3 is a visual model. It is a rhetorical artifact making information more comprehensible through its visual conversion. It is not a full and transparent reflection of the whole text. Nevertheless, if the visualization has been constructed with particular goals in mind, it will facilitate an exigent analysis and provide suggestions for revision and inputs for decision-making despite being artificially constructed. There is much value in artifice. Its reason for being, after all, is inventio, not data mastery. Of course, digital iconoclasts would argue that the reduction of complexity into imagery is in itself a conceptual problem—more, it is one method by which ideologies reinforce themselves. The iconoclast does not draw comparisons between the visions on our screens and the arts of memory but between the digital vision and, say, the images of fascist propaganda. Of visual interfaces, Benjamin Bratton states critically that they "gather multiple events and effects into a conceptual whole as if they were a single thing." The interface, the image, is not for Bratton an *assemblage* of data the way I have been describing it. An assemblage of data is precisely what the interface is not: the visual interface makes it *seem* as though "a massively discontiguous assemblage line, bound together by exceedingly complex interfacial relays linking contents," is in fact a "single image," a "single pattern," a "convincing image of organization," when it is in fact an ideological reduction. Bratton is correct. However, as he himself admits, organized images of complexity are "instrumentally effective" and "affectively compelling," and they allow users to "compose cognitive maps."[49] These all sound quite useful to my ears. Of course, I do not deny that the digital interface—both literally and as metaphor—is implicated in violent forms of distributed social control. I would also argue, however, that without artificial views that convert complexity into human-readable format, we are left blind to potential knowledge that is salutary and valuable to human flourishing. There must be some middle, tactical ground to be occupied when it comes to the *reductive image*, both in terms of the principles of its existence and the ethics of its use. There must be at least some value in artifice, for, along with Latour, I do not think we can "do without images, intermediaries, mediators of all shapes and forms" if we are not to fly blind through the universe.[50]

Contra my (admittedly strategic, provocative) iconophilic stance, Wendy Hui Kyong Chun has argued that digital interfaces are problematic because they promise to reveal the whole text, to use the example of the text network, or "the whole elephant," to use Chun's own metaphor, when in fact, as Bratton argued, they disguise their distortions and hype partial representation as full and transparent reflection. Chun draws the elephant metaphor from the tale of the six blind men: "Each man seizes a portion of the [elephant] and offers a different analogy: the elephant is like a wall, a spear, a snake, a tree, a palm, a rope."[51] Each clings blindly to his own partial analogy as a full representation of the "true" shape of the animal. Working from this tale, Chun explains that any given visual interface is like one of the blind men claiming to have grasped the whole elephant when he has only crafted his own limited view of it—his own peculiar "ideology" about the elephant. "Software and ideology fit each other perfectly," she continues, "because both try to map the tangible effects of the intangible and to posit the intangible cause through visible cues. Both, in other words, promise a vision of the whole elephant. Through this process the invisible whole emerges as a thing, as something in its own right."[52] Chun's (and Bratton's) argument is no doubt an accurate critique of secondary knowledge in general and of data visualizations in particular. I do not question that people sometimes mistake visualizations for the underlying data, confuse the model for the reality, or, shifting the metaphor, misread the map as the territory. This is true not only for visualization in the technical and social sciences but also for all software interfaces in the social media ecology. People need to be reminded that the visions on their screens—visions not only of data but also, as I discuss in the next chapter, of themselves and one another—mask a complex hierarchy of abstraction layers that connect the user through the graphical interface, through a network of code (not to mention all the input/output devices), down toward the metal hardware. These abstraction layers, we must admit, are created by and legible only to the Western version of a priestly caste. It is worth asking why the priests have given us the visions they have given us and what they veil or reveal. I agree with Chun's metapoint that it is vital to reveal the screen as abstraction and to correct the conflation of visualization with "reality"—with a "doctrinal resolution" or "an image of totality" in Bratton's words[53]—both in our own work and in the culture at large. Such is the vital job of the critic. Indeed, as the scale of the terrain being mapped grows—as the elephant becomes larger and more potentially damaging—the significance of this critique grows as well. There is a substantive difference, after all, between visualizing a student essay to develop revision strategies and visualizing a trillion tweets to facilitate state surveillance. I do not begrudge the critical impulse when it comes to these latter types of visualization practices. As I said in chapter 3, I am using Chun and Drucker and other digital iconoclasts as strategic foils; I am not picking an ideological fight in earnest with my countercritique.

Nevertheless, the activity of critique—of "unmasking" the men in the tale to show they are not grasping the whole elephant—is not always and necessarily the same thing as rhetorical practice. Critique and rhetoric are simpatico pursuits, to be sure, but they are not synonymous ones. As I have attempted to demonstrate in this chapter, a digital fourth canon must facilitate practice, technique, and creativity; it must do more than offer a critique of the interface, the visualization, and the imagistic model if it is to contribute to digital rhetoric.

I argued in chapter 3 that Chun's and other digital iconoclasts' goal is to curb the production of visual secondary knowledge or at least to modulate its role in our hypermediated culture. They envision a practice of direct immersion into the world's "networked flows," an unmediated involvement in the local life of humanity and nature before our eyes. Pushing back against the Promethean desire to map the data flows that lie beyond our immediate apprehension, Chun asks what role our imagistic maps play in sustaining unethical social and political structures. Are such maps really necessary? "To what extent is our historically novel position not our ignorance and powerlessness, but rather our determination and our drive to know?"[54] Contra this iconoclasm, I would reiterate the basic fact that humans themselves are interfaces; they are not going to stop transforming the world into visual models any more than they are going to stop making memories. We will inevitably do artificially what our neurophysiologies do naturally: convert data into models, information into imagery, and territories into maps. There is an inescapable symmetry between natural memory and artificial mnemonics, between the unconscious conversion of physical experience into the phantasms of our memoryscapes and the conscious re-mediation of information into various mnemonic forms. Critique is necessary, to be sure, but rhetorical theory must also make room for an ethical praxis of data visualization. Critics who reveal the "contradictions" or "ideological effects"[55] of visualization—in natural or artificial form—provide a vital but incomplete bibliography for the rhetorician. If inventio lies at the center of rhetorical practice, as many scholars have claimed,[56] then knowledge construction is as important as critique to the rhetorician. Ancient orators, after all, did not observe the human capacity for speech and proceed to unmask what speech conceals or to deconstruct the ideologies of oratory (that was the job of the philosopher). Rather, they devised precepts for enhancing, harnessing, and utilizing that natural ability for specific contexts and purposes: poetry, law, politics, and, later, religious evangelizing. Similarly, the author of *Ad Herennium* did not unmask the workings of natural memory in a proto-Freudian discourse about memory's repression and fallibility; rather, he taught precepts that harnessed memory and put it to work for rhetorical practice.

Of course, the ethics of that practice are an important part of the picture. Like Thomas Farrell, I believe that praxis in the Aristotelian sense and praxis in the Marxist sense are not fundamentally at odds. The Aristotelian sense of praxis is more or less what I have been assuming about the classical ars memoria and now the digital: it is a "coherent mode of activity," in Farrell's words, "with its own internal standards of excellence"; it is a "craft," a "form of thoughtful action" that "derives from the real conditions of civic life."[57] The arts of memory have specific precepts, specific dos and don'ts, and specific ideas about how to harness memory to create knowledge, persuade others, and make decisions. In the context of digital memoria, we might even make room for a Tuftean evaluation of better and worse data visualizations. None of the art's precepts, activities, and standards, however, foreclose on the importance of that more critical sense of praxis: a questioning of the histories that have given rise to the social conditions and civic life in which memoria is practiced. In our more limited sense here, an Aristotelian, rhetorical praxis of memoria does not deny the value in critiquing memoria's precepts, ideas, and goals, and the value of asking how we derive our operative notions of "better" and "worse" data visualizations in the first place. These two sorts of praxis are—well, obviously—different practices, but they are not at odds. One needs the other to make room for human agency; the other needs the one to make room for the possibility of changing where human agency directs its energies.

Johanna Drucker's *Graphesis* walks a line between a praxis of critique and a praxis of practical, necessary activity. She is not an iconoclast. But she is nonetheless straightforward about her skepticism toward the naïve "realism" that, according to her, underlies the work and ethos of data visualization. Data-visualization methods, she states, are "a kind of intellectual Trojan horse, a vehicle through which assumptions about what constitutes information swarm with potent force. These assumptions are cloaked in a rhetoric taken wholesale from the techniques of the empirical sciences that conceals their epistemological biases under a guise of familiarity . . . they pass as unquestioned representations of 'what is.' This is the hallmark of realist models of knowledge and needs to be subjected to a radical critique to return the humanistic tenets of constructedness and interpretation to the fore."[58] Realist approaches to visualization must be critiqued, Drucker continues (and as I summarized earlier), because they deny the fundamental humanist idea that all observational data are shaped by the biases, assumptions, and experiences of the observer qua constructed subject. They forget that data are always "capta." Empirical approaches uncritically accept "that phenomena are observer-independent";[59] they trust that sophisticated approaches to data collection might provide scientists with Haraway's objective view from nowhere. As far as the naïve realist is concerned, Drucker argues, the creation of a visual or any statistical model of a phenomenon provides a mirror image of the phenomenon itself. Such is the naïve position the critic must unmask.

There are two methods to enact the critique, Drucker explains. The first is what I would call the *formal* method: it reveals the "ambiguity and uncertainty" that underlie the design of a supposedly objective data visualization and is similar to what Edward Tufte calls visual deception detection. The second is what I would call the *epistemological* method: it envisions new modes of visualization that not only return ambiguity to visual models but also in fact "use ambiguity and uncertainty as the basis on which a representation is constructed."[60] Each of these methods for enacting critique is essential to the praxis of digital critique; but each has drawbacks, in my view, in the context of rhetorical praxis.

One issue with the formal critique is that it is predicated on an uncharitable straw man of the information sciences. For every technology journalist trumpeting the $N = ALL$ rhetoric of data mastery, there is a working data scientist to combat that simplistic view of the field. I have already called attention to the data science handbook written by Rachel Schutt and Cathy O'Neil. Both authors are clear that data science is as much art as science, admitting the inherent subjectivity involved in data collection, categorization, integration, and visualization. Even Edward Tufte's guidelines for reducing a visualization's lie factor are in fact a response to the accepted fact that data can be distorted and ideologies reified through furtive, motivated visualization choices. Another related issue with the formal critique is that detecting and denouncing graphical deception, as Tufte has recognized,[61] is already part and parcel of good data science methodology and internal critique. It is such an old and common methodological critique—you can find data journalists voicing it on Twitter every day—that it no longer carries much critical force. To be sure, revealing how ideological biases emerge through seemingly neutral visual properties can be a worthwhile endeavor in many contexts. For example, Drucker analyzes how medieval genealogy trees visualized lines of inheritance and royal succession in a way that concealed the messy reality of bloodline overlaps: "assum[ing] common ancestors and direct lineages," Drucker states, the trees of succession told a "linear narrative of evolution" that reified and literally naturalized—via arboreal imagery—the legitimacy of a particular line of descent or inheritance, veiling what was in reality a complex field of contested rights.[62] A contemporary example of this style of critique would be the assessment of a truncated y-axis. A purely formal feature, the length of the y-axis can nevertheless shape the way an observer interprets a bar graph, line graph, or scatter plot. In the default setting, the y-axis ranges from a value of 0 to a maximum value that encompasses the range or potential range of the data. However, by playing with the value of the y-axis—by shortening or lengthening it—one can make differences in data seem much larger or smaller than they actually are. For example, a graph showing tax rates before and after the expiration of a tax cut might truncate or expand the y-axis to highlight or downplay the effect of the rate increase (figures 5.11 and 5.12). The monetary increase can look more or less severe, and thus more or less difficult to absorb, depending on the range of the y-axis's values. Each graph could be subjected to a formal critique to reveal the underlying ideological motivations lurking behind a seemingly neutral con-

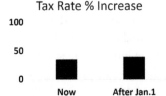

FIGURE 5.11. Tax rates before and after a tax cut expires (normal y-axis)

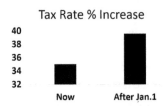

FIGURE 5.12. Tax rates before and after a tax cut expires (truncated y-axis)

figuration. The progressive would call attention to the truncated y-axis as a motivated attempt to make the tax increase seem more dramatic than it is; the libertarian would counter with his own critique.

To repeat, revealing the interplay of form and bias should be an important arrow in the critic's quiver. However, this style of deception detection is also rudimentary to the majority of data scientists. How the formal properties of a visualization can be tailored to fit biases, conceal underlying ambiguity, or affect how an audience interprets a visual model is all well-trodden ground in information science classrooms. Indeed, data visualization being nothing more than applied statistics, we need only observe the attitudes of statisticians to realize that the critique of data visualization is an update to the familiar "how to lie with statistics" genre of mathematical critique. And the critique is well taken by the "realist" side of the two cultures. "All models are wrong," statistician George Box famously proclaimed, "but some models are useful." In his article "Robustness in the Strategy of Scientific Model Building," Box elaborates on his point:

> Now it would be very remarkable if any system existing in the real world could be exactly represented by any simple model. However, cunningly chosen parsimonious models often do provide remarkably useful approximations.

... For such a model there is no need to ask the question "Is the model true?" If "truth" is to be the "whole truth" the answer must be "No." The only question of interest is "Is the model illuminating and useful?"[63]

Box's point, information scientists recognize, is even more pertinent to interactive, visually pleasing data displays than it is to purely mathematical models. The idea that "all models are wrong" has even been suggested as a core principle for an applied statistician's creed.[64] To be fair, Drucker herself recognizes that statisticians well know that the collection and interpretation of data is rife with ambiguity, and that all formal reductions of data hide as much as they reveal. However, in my experience, the point is obvious not only to professional mathematicians but also to anyone who has thought about the nature of data, information models, and truth. Humanists are often under the impression that data scientists and the educated public are more "positivist" or "realist" than they actually are. To be sure, there is a role in rhetorical pedagogy for a formal critique of data visualizations and the ideologies they promote; however, it should play a minor part in rhetorical practice, in the digital arts of memory—an early step, perhaps, in the larger project of developing rhetorically savvy, effective, and ethical visualization practices. Dubious visual models—models that veil contested interpretation through surreptitious visual choices—will always be with us. I am perhaps more optimistic than Drucker about how straightforward it is to unmask these visual deceptions.

Drucker's second method for enacting visual critique moves beyond revealing ambiguity in visualizations and instead imagines how we might "use ambiguity and uncertainty as the basis on which a representation is constructed."[65] Pursuing the thorny epistemology implicated in this critique would take me deep down a rabbit hole, so I want to limit my discussion here to a brief analysis of Drucker's final example of what an ambiguity-based, "observer codependent" visualization might look like.

The construction of visual representations from a base of ambiguity, as Drucker describes the process, seems to be an attempt to visualize (or make visually interpretable) the qualitative, phenomenal experiences that define the human subject and humanist inquiry. To incarnate her idea, she invokes the London physician John Snow, who, in 1854, ended a cholera epidemic by plotting all the cholera cases on a dot map and discovering that most of the cases clustered around a water pump on Broad Street. The dot distribution on Snow's map allowed city officials to track the source of the epidemic to this single pump. Describing Snow's map as "useful" and "crucial to analysis"—"its clarity and succinctness served an important purpose"—Drucker then poses a curious question: How might we complicate the map with observer-codependent ambiguity? Although Snow's map was "sufficient" to the purpose of tracking the origin of the cholera, Drucker argues that his map nevertheless deflected the entirety of the human, subjective terrain that surely accompanied the disease. We could thus "revisit [the] map," she states, "and use it to express" the human response to the phenomenal experience of the epidemic. For example, "what if we take the rate of deaths, their frequency, and chart that on a temporal axis inflected by increasing panic. Then give a graphical expression to the shape of the terrain, that urban streetscape, as it is redrawn to express the emotional landscape. Then imagine drawing this same streetscape from the point of view of a mother of six young children, a recent widow, a small child, or an elderly man whose son has just died?"[66] Such a display of embodied panic, Drucker explains, would be an instance of an ambiguity-based visualization, of "the graphical expression of humanistic interpretation" (insofar as panic is an unfiltered human response that differs in ambiguous ways from individual to individual based on their embodied subjectivities).[67]

Drucker's effort here to visualize not "data" but an embodied response to the phenomenal world is intriguing. The traditional first step when visualizing panic would be to "parameterize" (to use Drucker's term) or "operationalize" (to use Franco Moretti's term)[68] the abstractness of embodied panic into a numerical form $PANIC = x + y_2$, where x and y = numerical proxies of one sort or another. But in Drucker's view, such a parameterization would by design trade a humanistic approach for a scientific one. To paraphrase her overall argument, parameterization *of* experience misleads us to view the parameterization *as* experience. It conceals the fact that all phenomenal "data" are in fact "capta," "taken, not given," because "no data pre-exist their parametrization."[69] There is no such thing, Drucker argues, as *raw data*. Data do not precede interpretation but themselves construe the phenomenal world as experienced through a particular constructed subjecthood. "Data are constructed as an interpretation of the phenomenal world, not inherent in it," Drucker states. A humanistic, ambiguity-based approach to data visualization would thus be "rooted in the recognition of the interpretive nature of knowledge," which I take to mean that all visualizations emerge from the experience of a phenomenon informed in turn not by a disembodied observation but by our embodied—classed, raced, gendered, aged, and so on—responses to and a priori interpretations of the phenomenon.[70] Drucker's imagined map of embodied panic, distributed across lived realities, is thus an attempt to visualize a human response to a phenomenon without first "parameterizing" it with an equation (a mathematical move that would, again, conceal the interpreted character of the data with an artificial objectivity). The conversion of embodied panic into quantitative form would be an anti-humanistic distortion, regardless of whether or not the resulting numbers are visualized "accurately." Drucker's panic map brings to mind other imaginings of direct "immersion" into life's "networked flows" (in Chun's words) or immersion into the "body of real numbers originally known as chaos" (in Kittler's). These are Platonic dreams of interfacing with the world in a way that does not reduce phenomena through motivated parameterizations or encodings. Drucker, too, seems to have set as her goal a graphic but nevertheless *as-direct-as-possible* immersion into the subjectivity of embodied experience.

My iconophilic response remains the same as when I discussed Nagel's essay on bats: we are all already interfaces (isn't that what "constructed subjectivity" means?). Our natural memories are already encoded or parameterized one way or the other, so I see little reason to prefer as a general principle the embodied over the mathematical one, the natural over the artificial. And, of course, a truly unmediated immersion into the *entire* phenomenal flow of existence would be difficult for a human mind to survive. Our embodied interface—our instinct to interface with information in a way that visualizes it and thereby makes it comprehensible—has evolved for good reason. As provocative as I find the idea of visualizing an unmediated, nonparameterized human experience, this humanistic approach to data visualization leads me to wonder what rhetorical purpose such a visualization would serve that isn't served better by other genres—poetry, music, and all the arts of nonparameterized expression. Drucker acknowledges, for example, that Snow's reduction of the cholera epidemic into a legible image saved lives. Such was the exigency of *that* parameterization. Why, then, would we want to make the image less succinct, less "crucial to analysis," and more ambiguous and unclear, as would be a representation of the uncertainty and panic embodied in the human response to cholera? If our goal is emotional expression, that is a different matter, but if our goal is constructing knowledge to inform exigent decision-making, ambiguity at some point becomes a liability. (Presumably, a young child far from the pump would have panicked more than an elderly man near the pump, so a subjective panic map would have hindered rather than helped Snow's goal of discovering the source of the outbreak.) I have said it before: when it comes to constructing knowledge, there is value in artifice and distortion. We can all be grateful that Snow had the ingenuity to reduce the noise to find the signal, to deflect the socially influenced responses on the ground in order to produce a legible image of the epidemic that generated knowledge and saved lives.

All data are capta. The point is well taken. As Drucker notes, our visual models—of everything from a cholera epidemic to things like race, nation, and borders—reduce phenomenal complexity and interpretive bias into a single image whose graphical force conceals its own artifice and affirms its own supposed truth-value. It is important that a rhetoric of data visualization emphasizes how visualization techniques mask complexity and veil the already-interpreted nature of underlying data. I earlier posed a question in the same spirit: How might a network graph visualize its own centrality measurement? Nevertheless, there is a limit to the utility of building such critiques into visual models. "Ce qui est simple est toujours faux. Ce qui ne l'est pas est inutilisable," wrote Paul Valéry.[71] The vertigo-inducing spiral of epistemological criticism—highlighting the already-interpreted, pre-encoded nature of "capta"—might spawn the creation of superb art, but it would by necessity work against most goals of data visualization. It would turn Snow's interpretable map into a Salvador Dalí painting. More nuanced, yes, more truthful about capta, but far less useful. Such is the deal we make when we convert information into imagery; and such is the nature of the human qua interface (in both the natural and artificial construals of that metaphor). By interfacing with existence, by re-mediating phenomena into legible models, we lose ambiguity, complexity, and uncertainty, but we gain enough understanding to produce knowledge and to coordinate activity. Human models of the world mask a fluid and uncertain reality, but they are *good enough* in contexts where a more ambiguous model might hinder informed action. The species model, for example, is an obvious simplification of the volatility—the nearly irreducible complexity—of allele distribution. (It also conceals a deeply religious assumption regarding the unity of animalistic kinds.) However, by making the complexity of the animal world legible, by re-mediating the fluidity of allele distribution into a lucid image of speciation and descent, we lay the groundwork for the important work of species preservation.

The ethics of an imagistic model should not rise and fall on how much complexity it reduces, how much ambiguity it "distorts" into comprehensibility, or how much a priori motivation it fails to recognize. These are the muddy epistemological waters we knowingly wade into when we compress and visualize phenomena. Rather, the ethics of an image should rise and fall on the purposes for which it is created, the knowledge it makes discoverable, and the activity it facilitates. Drucker makes a similar point when she states that "all metrics are metrics about something for some purpose."[72] The *about something* and *for some purpose* should draw our critical attention, not the eminently human impulse to convert phenomena into our peculiar semiotic modes—this we do naturally, and this we will continue to do artificially. A digital art of memory would absolutely make room for deception detection, the critique of data visualization's obfuscating and normalizing tendencies; it would also explore new forms of visualization that display ambiguity, observer dependence, and the always-biased "capturedness" of data. However, a digital art of memory would also—by definition—include the ancient and cutting-edge arts of transforming the world of randomness and complexity into lucid imagery. It certainly would not deep-six the practice on ideological grounds or find ways to render our imagistic models so overinterpreted as to become incomprehensible all over again. Rather, it would ensure that our discourse about data visualization foregrounds ethical activity and the creative nature of the imagery. I said earlier that no one in antiquity confused *Ad Herennium*'s grotesque simulacra for the "reality" of a court case, no one confused mnemonic imagery for transparent reproductions of underlying information, and no one had any doubt that the forms of the mnemonic images were influenced by the lived, embodied idiosyncrasies of the individual rhetor. The work of a digital fourth canon might be summarized therefore as persuading the culture to understand the cyberscape's info displays in the same way that ancient and medieval rhetors understood the imagery within their memory palaces.

✳ CHAPTER 6 ✳

The Social Memory Palace

The previous chapter described data visualization as a digital analogue of the ancient canon of memoria. It focused, more specifically, on the fourth canon's precept regarding memory's relationship with creative invention and how that precept should inform the humanistic use of data visualizations today. This chapter examines the other essential precept found in the classical memory treatises: that the memory palace's loci and imagines take shape through the affective, idiosyncratic phantasms of the natural memoryscape. "Everyone," states the author of *Ad Herennium*, "should in equipping himself with images suit his own convenience."[1] (He notes, however, that "incidents of our childhood we often remember best," because such memories appear striking and affective before the mind's eye.)[2] Shifting emphasis from data visualization in its technical sense, I look in this chapter at the *personal* mnemonic imagery circulating on digital screens, from file folder names to hashtags to status updates to social media picture albums and all the digital externalizations of memory found online—all of which remain relevant to a digital canon of memory as well as to memory's relationship with inventio.

Earlier in the book, I argued that rhetoric's revival of memoria encompasses the ways humans recall or represent the past with external objects, from war memorials to family cookbooks. Here, I explore externalized memories as well, but I do so from the standpoint of mnemonic history, treating the social mediascape as an array of mnemonic cues. I ask in essence what happens to the memory palace when we transport it from the private mind to the networked screen. The memory palace, after all, was an interior construction. It was, to be sure, an *artificial construction*, a form of secondary knowledge. However, it remained locked in the interior psyche, accessible only to the individual rhetor who had built it. In the historical chapters, I did not spend much time considering differences between the interior memory palace and the mnemonic externalizations drawn or printed in late medieval and early modern treatises—Willis's repositories, Roselli's celestial spheres, Bruno's wheels of images, and so on—because in many cases these mnemonic forms were examples to be adapted by the user and thus tucked away once more into psychic interiority. Other printed mnemonics were diagrammatic structures to be used unaltered by all users (such as a Ramist diagram), and this static nature of the mnemonic cue made it uninteresting to discuss. What is interesting about an externalized representation of the past—what is interesting about it for this chapter, at any rate—is not its externalization per se but its presence as a social focal point, a mnemonic form accessible to multiple people for multiple purposes. To be sure, many external mnemonic cues are constructed, like Ramist diagrams, to foreclose on all but a single interpretation or form of interaction. Civil-rights and Native American memorials have been critiqued for forcing a consensus interpretation of the past that minimizes conflict.[3] However, other physical manifestations of the past, such as the Vietnam Veterans Memorial, are controversial precisely because they invite multiple interpretations and forms of interaction. Through its austere and bewildering appearance, the Vietnam Veterans Memorial does not seek a unified meaning, resolution, or closure but rather "embraces even contradictory interpretations. The Memorial both comforts and refuses comfort. It both provides closure and denies it. It does not offer a unitary message but multiple and conflicting ones."[4] The burden of meaning is placed on the viewers, who navigate meaning's creation in a shared social space.

The political meaning making that occurs (or fails to occur) in sanctioned memory spaces may or may not always be comparable to the nebulous process by which we make personal meanings online—the daily progression of creating and recreating, visualizing and reenvisioning ourselves and one another in the social mediascape. However, social media users do indeed create their identities and beliefs in a way that "does not offer a unitary message but multiple and conflicting ones."[5] They fashion themselves out of sensory remnants captured and shared in an endless stream of becoming that fails by design to reach a conclusion—an endless stream that "both provides closure and denies it" at every turn.[6] The imagistic shards of digital memory, like the imagistic shards of memory, are what we build meaning with, and as long as we continue to breathe, we will build without end. Once upon a time, this nebulous and never resolved process of identity formation was all but inscrutable, lost at death and locked in life within the individual phantasms of a million incommensurable memoryscapes. To be sure, glimpses of the process surfaced in diaries, scrapbooks, poems, and similar intimate spaces. Today, the process has been externalized in a much more radical way. With iPhones and Android phones at the ready, every phantasm impressed on the memoryscape is also impressed on silicon, not only made visual but also tagged, curated, shared, and circulated. The private interiority of the memoryscape is given external mnemonic form and thereby made known to the world (or at least to our followers). Indeed, the phantasms of the memoryscape are what provide the content of the mediascape. We have all become our own audience—and the movie we are watching reveals, as a secondary effect, the process by which we make ourselves and one another. We watch ourselves become ourselves, via a limitless stream of curated (and often not so curated) externalized memories.

Once we frame not only data visualizations but also the sights and sounds of social media as an array of mnemonic cues—as a digital memory palace—then the whole internet ecology at once falls under the fourth canon's purview, from issues of privacy and state surveillance to the ways corporate actors harness our externalized idiosyncrasies for targeted marketing (what Jeff Pruchnic and Kim Lacey call the "implication" of external memories in "the manipulation of our affective dispositions"[7]). Exploring the consequences of memory's externalization in the form of an open, networked memory palace should be an ongoing project within a digital canon of memory, pursued alongside the development of rhetorical visualization strategies, as discussed in the previous chapter.

In what follows, I hint at one possible direction that we might take an analysis of social media qua mnemonic artifact, examining not so much the externalization but, again, the socialization of the memory palace and how it relates to the "invention" not only of knowledge but also of ourselves and one another.

Digital Bricolage: Idiosyncratic Associations and Social Taxonomies

While Aristotle, faculty psychologists, and Victorian mnemonists theorized chains of reminiscence constructed from "logical" or culturally conditioned associations (from milk to white; hemlock recalls Socrates; thunder suggests lightning), the rhetorical treatises imagined a very different type of associational chain, one constructed from the sensory-emotional links that constitute the private memoryscape. Giordano Bruno understood the idea: "they are those things that make the heart pound, having the power of something wondrous, frightening, pleasant, sad; a friend, an enemy . . . ; things hoped for or which we are suspicious of, and all things that encroach powerfully on the inner emotions. . . . It is the power of the senses and imagination, and not only the cognitive faculty, that are able to make the imprint on memory."[8] However, one of the fundamental misunderstandings about these sensory links, inherited from Yates and Rossi, is the idea that loci et imagines are constructed from scratch, as though mnemonic imagery demands a talent for inner artistry. The classical treatises make it clear, however, that the rhetor must construct his memory palace according to his own proclivities and by means of the phantasms already existing within the natural memoryscape—"take what you hear" and connect it to "what you already know," the *Dissoi logoi* says.[9] *Ad Herennium*'s examples are just that: examples, not inflexible rules for constructing places and images. Peter of Ravenna's "maidens from youth" make the point well.[10] The affective, personalized creations inhabiting the memory palace are thus aptly compared to the social mediascape.

Insofar as the memory palace facilitated mnemonic recall, there is also a temptation to compare the ars memoria to Google or other search interfaces. However, as I discussed in previous chapters, search technology replicates the Aristotelian "hunt" for a particular piece of information via logical and necessary relationships. Given a query, a Google search returns information identified via pattern matching in vector space and via ranking algorithms that associate a given query with information returned in previous, related queries. Between search and recall lies a mathematically informed procedure connecting the user with the specific material requested. The memory palace, however, does not operate in this hyperparameterized way. It connects user with information via a more sensory, imaginative, and exploratory process. The rhetor moves through images of her own experience and design, whose links and associations are informed not by abstract logics but by her own penchants, experiences, and emotions. Indeed, the rhetor needn't search for any particular datum at all to find value in examining her memory palace. Through visual investigation, she hopes to alight on that one right piece of information for a current endeavor: a quote, a fact, an aphorism, a law, a line of verse, some desideratum unknown beforehand but recognizable upon discovery—a "Eureka!" moment. The classical memory palace, in short, is a bespoke collection of images, organized according to lived experience, emotional association, or some other custom scheme; its method of recall is exploratory and affective rather than logical and calculated. The memory palace finds its digital analogue not in the Google search bar but in the pictures, videos, GIF files, memes, filters, tags, and stream-of-consciousness updates that constitute the social media experience—a curated visual interface that enables personalized access to and management of accumulated experience. Like a multimodal and interactive scrapbook, social media allows users to represent selective bits of the past and to cobble them together into an artificial sinew of meaning and identity. Like the imagines of the memory palace, these secondary imagistic traces can be organized, manipulated, and inspected in digital space according to the user's own proclivities.

John McNair recognized two decades ago that even basic file folders and desktop icons reconstruct the precepts of the ars memoria, allowing a user to compress, organize, and visually customize her personal information for easier access and use.[11] Right-click to rename, select and drag: even a file-folder system presents myriad possibilities for structuring information in a customized, visual/spatial way. Of course, the hierarchical nature of folders has its pre-encoded limits. "Our electronic desktops are too faithful to the paper-based world," argue Eric Freeman and David Gelernter; "they force each document to be stored in exactly one folder."[12] The "desktop" metaphor itself, interface designers have long realized, does not effectively capture or reproduce how human minds and memories actually manage, categorize, integrate, and make sense of information. Freeman and Gelernter quote a user frustrated with the traditional desktop file system, the user providing several reasons why an alternative data-management/recall system would be preferable: "First, because I know that I naturally order and recall events in my life according to time cues, that 'memories' become less important to my daily activities the further in the past they recede (yet retain punch and applicability at discrete moments when recalled because of similarity to current events), and that I find it so incredibly annoying not to be able to recall something that might be applicable because the 'index' to that memory has been lost."[13] The mnemonic "index" refers to the fact that traditional file systems require each file to be given one and only one name and placed in one and only one named folder, despite the countering fact that "although names can be mnemonic devices, over time their value decays."[14] Most computer users are able to locate files on their machines not because they remember what they named a file—the names are always nondescript and forgettable, like "draft1.docx"—but because they remember where they *placed* the file: upper right-hand corner of the desktop, third folder under Documents, and so on. The point is, traditional desktop folder systems require files to be given one name and stored in one location; this works against how minds actually want to handle information. Freeman and Gelernter again remark, "Categorizing information might be the hardest information-management task people encounter, [but] information does not fall into neat categorizations that can be implemented on a system using basic labels."[15] Just as importantly from the mnemonic point of view, they state, traditional operating systems make it difficult for users to deploy the "tacit knowledge"—

the personalized, idiosyncratic, often sensory associations—that actually assist memory. "The lack of flexibility" of file-folder systems, Freeman and Gelernter observe,

> makes it very difficult for the user to leave his or her marks of acquired and tacit knowledge that will serve to allow for tracking down specific pieces of information in the future. . . . [For example,] notes about a meeting to discuss an application called Zowie for the Mac, where Smith, Piffel, and Schwartz were present, might be stored—in a conventional system—in the folder called "Zowie" or maybe one called "Mac applications." In retrospect you might need to consult your records of all meetings that Piffel attended. But suppose you didn't know that at the time. For this obvious reason, the brain categorizes memories dynamically and not statically. I can ask you to recall "all meetings that took place in room 300" even if you never consciously classified meetings by room numbers.[16]

The point they are making is that our minds do not actively "name" or "index" or "categorize" information every time new sensory data enters them. Information is categorized dynamically, not statically—recalling information from a meeting can probably be better facilitated, per their example, not by digging through old and poorly labeled files but by thinking about the room the meeting occurred in. Any number of particular visual or affective cues could aid memory. I can recall many of the questions asked during my first academic-conference presentation, not because my brain in that moment created a file called "FirstPresentation.docx" but because certain sensory and affective things about that day allow the entire experience to rush suddenly before my imagination—the general emptiness and chilliness of the room, for example, are forever imprinted in my memory palace.

An early study of office work and its implications for information-system designers, conducted in 1983 by T. W. Moran, discovered that "users prefer spatial over logical association," that "information can rarely be classified unambiguously into a single category," and that "access to information occurs normally by several attributes," including situational factors and contexts attendant to the information's initial creation.[17] Ironically, none of Moran's points seem to have influenced the primacy of the file folder and the desktop metaphor in digital information design. Traditional data-management systems do not facilitate situational or dynamic categorization and only barely facilitate spatial association over logical association. Only in the past decade have database and interface designers begun to reimagine what information management and recall might look like on the digital screen, envisaging systems that work more like and thus enhance our natural memories—systems that, for example, allow a person to "recollect some aspect of the past and use it as a cue for searching," "to remember richer aspects of otherwise forgotten experiences, or to view the experiences from a radically different perspective," and "to promote reminiscing or re-experiencing the past for purely social reasons." In this scenario, "Reminiscing can be a rewarding experience and an end in itself, supporting the feeling of reliving a shared experience as well as providing a basis for storytelling. Sometimes a user might even prefer to let the system choose the memories to be viewed, either because they do not have a specific experience in mind, or because serendipitous reminiscence is often quite pleasurable. When done with others, such activities could allow people to relate their memories to others and could help to socially and emotionally connect people."[18]Although the language above could fit neatly into the memory sections of *Ad Herennium* or the *Institutio oratoria*, it is in fact from an article describing a prototype operating system called MyLifeBits. The article and the prototype are from 2007, at the cusp of the social media age, so it is interesting to consider how the app-centric phone and tablet interfaces have or have not realized their prototype system, which promoted the sort of affective information management and serendipitous recall that, like the ars memoria, used memory itself as the basis for the mnemonic cue (using the past as a "cue for searching," as the researchers put it above). I don't think we're there yet, and hierarchical folder systems are still in widespread use, but the social mediascape nevertheless provides an opportunity to look at how personal memory and digital memory are beginning to converge.

Compared to file-folder systems, for example, hashtags offer a more sophisticated and mnemonically interesting alternative for structuring and managing information. Based on a networked rather than hierarchical database design, hashtags allow users to situate information and objects within multiple classes at once, thereby enhancing the potential for customized info association. For example, when it was announced in July 2018 that Yosemite Valley was being evacuated due to fire and smoke danger, the hashtags #Yosemite and #FergusonFire began trending on the social media app Twitter. Clicking on these hashtags, a user would be linked to a page where she could scroll through all the hashtagged tweets and view real-time updates, pictures, videos, and articles about the fire and the evacuation. As do all trending hashtags, #Yosemite and #FergusonFire functioned as digital Schelling points, locations across social media platforms where users know to assemble when looking for information as an event unfolds. However, if, during the evacuation, a user viewed these particu-

FIGURE 6.1. Tweet with #fergusonfire hashtag

FIGURE 6.2. Tweet with #fergusonfire hashtag

lar hashtag collections, she would have also discovered on any given tweet more personalized hashtags—more bespoke categorizations—appearing alongside #Yosemite or #FergusonFire. Some users, for instance, added the hashtags #climate and #drought to their tweets, linking the local disaster with global concerns about climate change (figure 6.1). Other users hashtagged personal trips taken to other locations due to the fire (figure 6.2). Still others used the hashtags to tell private jokes about living in the Yosemite area (figure 6.3) or to campaign for local politicians (the Ferguson fire occurred just before the 2018 midterm elections) (figure 6.4).

As natural phenomena, these added hashtags represent the idiosyncrasy of personal association: upon hearing news of a fire in Yosemite

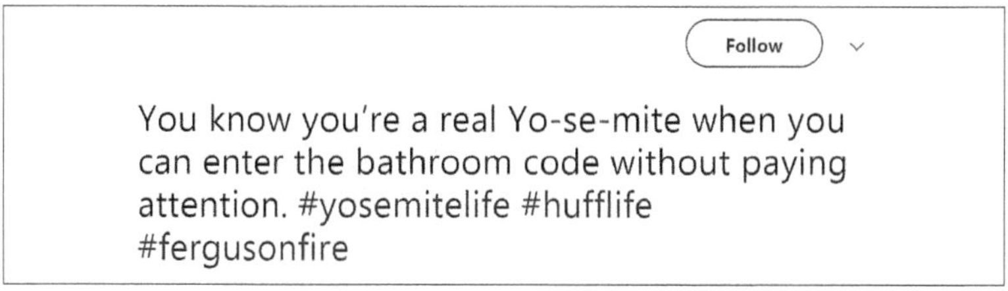

Follow ⌄

You know you're a real Yo-se-mite when you can enter the bathroom code without paying attention. #yosemitelife #hufflife #fergusonfire

FIGURE 6.3. Tweet with #fergusonfire hashtag (Yo-se-mite rhymes with right)

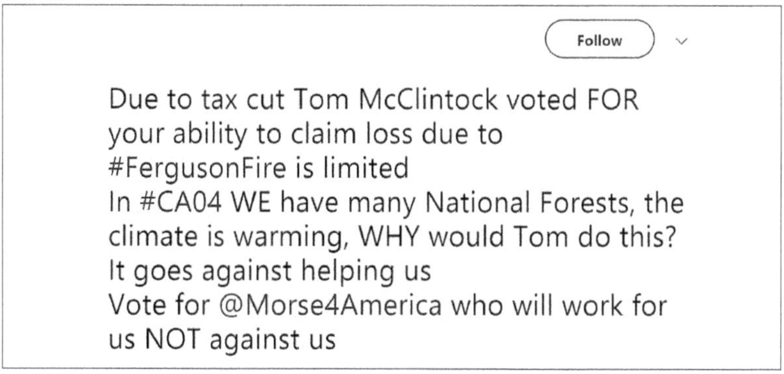

Follow ⌄

Due to tax cut Tom McClintock voted FOR your ability to claim loss due to #FergusonFire is limited
In #CA04 WE have many National Forests, the climate is warming, WHY would Tom do this?
It goes against helping us
Vote for @Morse4America who will work for us NOT against us

FIGURE 6.4. Tweet with #fergusonfire hashtag

Valley, one user's mind recalled a private joke, while another's went immediately to local elections. From a mnemonic point of view, these Twitter users were drawing on their personal associations to classify and manage digital information related to the fire (articles, pictures, or the tweets themselves). As artificial mnemonic devices, these hashtags characterize the sort of creative, bespoke info association that once informed the construction of the classical memory palace. Look again at the associations on display in figures 6.1 through 6.4: funny ways to pronounce *Yosemite*, upcoming elections in California's Fourth District, and private outings during the time of the fire. These are not the logical associations or necessary successions Aristotle had in mind, nor are they the sort of regular patterns Google discovers when a user queries a search. They are, however, examples of the personal mnemonic associations the author of *Ad Herennium* had in mind when describing the loci et imagines of the memory palace. If your imagination moves automatically from a Yosemite Valley fire to a trip you took somewhere else, that is a pre-embedded (visual) association in the psyche ready-made for embedding and recalling *new* information.

Nearly all social media platforms enable this sort of curated, networked classification through personal mnemonic association. To reiterate, hashtags emerge from natural associations in people's memory banks, but the hashtags themselves are secondary forms of knowledge and thus are mnemonic devices, beneficial like all mnemonic devices for managing, recalling, integrating, and applying information. But now we return to the more exigent point: the bespoke associations manifested in the hashtag are not only a mnemonic device but also a *social* mnemonic device. Unlike the loci et imagines of the interior memory palace, hashtags are shared with hundreds, thousands, and even millions of other users. They are open to others' scrutiny and use. Whenever a user scrolls through the #FergusonFire hashtags on Twitter, she will discover not only information related "logically" to the fire—for example, articles on acreage burned—but also the idiosyncratically linked information shown above. These sorts of links lay the groundwork for social inventio online.

Some apps, like the bookmarking site Delicious, allow multiple users to tag the same information or object, increasing by design the social character of this digital mnemonic. Other apps, like Twitter, do not allow multiple users to tag the same object directly (only the user who posted the content can do so), but even these platforms allow social tagging via other features: on Twitter, I can add my own tag by quote-tweeting the original tweet; on Facebook, I can share an already tagged object and add my own tags in the process. Collin Gifford Brooke and Thomas Rickert's inquiry into social tagging focuses in particular on the (now defunct) website Delicious, but much of what they say applies to tagging in general and, indeed, to all bespoke info association and categorization enabled by social media.[19]

Delicious allowed a user to view URLs displaying myriad tags with which other users had labeled the URLs (a user could of course add his own tags). For example, a link to the technologist David Weinberger's website was tagged with labels like **web2.0**, **book culture**, **Internet**, and **metadata**. Brooke and Rickert invoke Weinberger's book *Everything Is Miscellaneous* to explain how the ostensibly basic act of tagging on an app like Delicious generates an information ecosystem grounded in social rather than logical classification. In his book, Weinberger defines three types of information organization: the ordering of physical things (books on a library shelf), the ordering of information (card catalogs), and the ordering of information about information—that is, the ordering of metadata (tags on a Delicious link). Weinberger's argument, as Brooke and Rickert explain, is that the ability to organize/classify information according to metadata has unleashed a surplus of bespoke *info-classification schemes* to match the surplus of information itself in the digital age. Metadata have thus made obsolete the pursuit of a "best" or "perfect" or "universally valid" taxonomic system for any given information set—a fool's errand to begin with—and ushered in instead an era of multiple, networked, fuzzy, overlapping classification schemes that more accurately mimic how the mind itself makes sense of information. The mind does not utilize "objective" taxonomy and does not deploy one-to-one labeling; rather, as described a moment ago, it makes information accessible and readily deployable through multiple, exploratory, bespoke, context-dependent categorizations. (When you close your eyes, there is always more than one route to a memory.) In the digital ecosystem, as in the classical memory palace, information management is only valuable insofar as it aids data integration to generate something new and useful. If the messiness of networked tagging works better than the logic of hierarchical folders to meet that goal, so much the worse for the folders.

The creation of these fuzzy, interacting classification schemes relies on multiple users. The proliferation of unique hashtags during a Twitter event is a fundamentally public, collective process that "captures how information itself [becomes] social" in digital spaces.[20] Private associations are shared, and these shares accumulate into an open-ended array of associations and taxonomies. Novel connections abound. If a user scrolls through the #FergusonFire hashtag on Twitter, she will discover information about local pronunciations and California's Fourth Congressional District because other users externalized and shared those otherwise private associations. Similarly, if a Delicious user searches for Weinberger's website thinking about metadata, the tag **book culture** might compel him to think about Weinberger's work in a new way and rediscover certain strands within it that previously went overlooked. Like any social act, Brooke and Rickert argue, sharing a tag has the power to convey fresh meaning about or add nuance to information. The simple act of tagging may thus shape the perceptions and even the activities of others.[21] (Looking through information on the Yosemite fire, for example, I did end up cruising over to Wikipedia to learn about Tom McClintock and California's Fourth District. The tweet piqued my curiosity, and that is precisely the rhetorical value of the external mnemonic cues we call hashtags.)

If the social mediascape invalidates the idea of a perfect tag or set of tags for information (tweets, links, any digital objects), it trades comprehensive authority for generative interactivity. To put it in less pedantic terms, working to construct a perfect taxonomic system inevitably diverts one's energy away from doing something with the information being classified. It turns one into the father in the film *Amélie*—he loves to clean and arrange the tools in his toolbox but never seems to actually build any-thing. The open, semantically fuzzy, possibly messy, often idiosyncratic classification schemes unleashed through tagging and other social media capabilities compel users to abandon anal-retentive taxonomy and to generate insight instead, to consider novel connections. These schemes compel them to view information in interaction with multiple classifica-tions and associations—meaning, often, that they view information by the light of new ideologies. The viewing of information tagged and taxon-omized in multiple ways by multiple users ignites (or should ignite) the creative mind. It is an act of mnemonic bricolage. Assembling before the eye, within a single interface, the many ways information might be classi-fied, the many ways it might be associated with other information, should bring new lines of thought and inquiry before the imagination.

The sociality of tagging thus invokes once more that ancient link be-tween idiosyncratic info management and creativity. Like all ideas related to rhetorical memory, the ideas I'm exploring here do not stray far from memoria's central role as an aid to inventio. Like the curated arrangement of imagines within their loci, the personalized links and associations of the curated mediascape enable what Collin Gifford Brooke calls a *proairetics* of invention.[22]

Inventio in the Social Memory Palace

To understand Brooke's concept of proairetics and its applicability to the creation of our feeds and ourselves on social media, we must return briefly to the Middle Ages.

I have used the word "bricolage" throughout the book to describe the assemblage of information that mnemonic techniques have enabled throughout history. Stored information is useless, after all, until it is re-called, linked together, and put to use for making decisions or coordinat-ing action in a rhetorical context. This was a core assumption of mnemonic practice in the ancient and monastic worlds. However, for all its emphasis on a monk's ability to assemble biblical material—to move here and there through the scriptural "places" in his mnemonic eye—the medieval dis-course on artificial memory did not endorse quick or rootless wandering. Assembling strands of scripture into a prayer or a sermon was to be a delib-erate process, focused and slowly considered. It was an art of meditation as much as an art of invention; "firm concentration," the Roman theologian John Cassian states, was necessary to "give stability to the soul."[23] Indeed, the failure to concentrate on scripture in a proper meditative spirit was de-scribed by the monastics as a mnemonic "vice." Carruthers explains: "The great vice of *memoria* is not forgetting but disorder. This came to be called by some monastic writers *curiositas*. . . . In terms of mnemotechnic, curiosity constitutes both image 'crowding'—a mnemotechnical vice because crowding images together blurs them, blocks them, and thus dissipates their effectiveness for orienting and cueing—and randomness, or making backgrounds that have no pattern to them."[24] Carruthers quotes Cassian and the Egyptian Moses the Black, who further describe this mnemonic vice as "wantonness," as "aimless, fruitless, and shifting," and as a lack of aim or direction: the mind hooked on *curiositas*, states Abba Moses, "veers hither and yon by the hour, and by the minute is prey to outside influences and is endlessly the prisoner of what strikes first."[25] Speaking more explicitly of mnemonic bricolage, Cassian describes it further:

> Our minds think of some passage of a psalm. But it is taken away from us without our noticing it, and, stupidly, unknowingly, the spirit slips on to some other text of Scripture. It begins to think about it, but before it has been fully considered, another text slides into the memory and drives out the previous one. Meanwhile another one arrives and our mind turns to another meditation. . . . Ever on the move, forever wandering, [the spirit] is tossed along through all the body of Scripture, unable to settle on anything or hold on to anything, powerless to arrive at any full and judicious study, a dilettante and a nibbler on spiritual interpretation.[26]

Learning to focus the mind's eye on particular places of scripture requires serious effort, or *should* require it, and the student who failed to exert this effort signaled his disinterest in attaining spiritual insight. Ultimately, then, mnemonic *curiositas* revealed the more sinful vice of sloth.

Careful meditation on a mnemonic vision of scripture, as described by the monastics, is the polar opposite of the digital practice of surfing the internet. The hyperlinks, pingbacks, Instagram stories that disappear in an hour, six-second Vines, TikTok snippets, real-time updates, and swipes left or right that populate the social mediascape are the inverse of the slow meditation demanded by the monastic life. Cassian's choice of words to describe *curiositas* could apply to the average night on social media: we "slip" and "slide" and are "tossed along," "forever wandering" and "unable to settle on anything" presented to our senses. It is de rigueur, of course, to bemoan the traipsing and hasty digressions facilitated by social media. A hundred think pieces each year give the hyperlinked internet the same critique Plato gave writing: it makes us forgetful and stupid and ruins our attention spans. Professional techno-downer Nicholas Carr voices the opinion that "what the Net seems to be doing is chipping away my capacity for concentration and contemplation." He states, "My mind now expects to take in information the way the Net distributes it: in a swiftly moving stream of particles. Once I was a scuba diver in the sea of words. Now I zip along the surface like a guy on a Jet Ski."[27]

Without denying that a "full and judicious study," as Cassian describes it, of a given text or subject is often a desirable goal, Collin Gifford Brooke has nonetheless recognized that quick, peripatetic link tripping is in many respects a precondition of the deeper analysis venerated by Cassian (and Carr). Even if it weren't such a precondition, perhaps there is value in zipping across the web's sea of pictures, videos, links, and sites without a set goal in mind. If not "deep," such a practice might be mentally exhilarating nonetheless.

Many genres and contexts demand a concentrated effort to create coherent narrative strands that culminate in a satisfying resolution. Brooke recognizes, however, that the internet is that rare space in which resolution is not always an expectation. Why not embrace the rhetorical potential of that open-ended technological space? Working from Roland Barthes's description of "hermeneutic" and "proairetic" narrative strategies, Brooke posits what he calls a proairesis of invention that the internet enables. In literary contexts, proairesis and hermeneutics work in concert to produce a unified whole: they are, respectively, "the push of action and the pull of meaning,"[28] or, in other words, the empirical facts as they unfold and the treatment of those facts in a way that generates an expectation for and leads toward a tidy conclusion. In a murder mystery, for example, the discovery of a dead body by a maid in the hotel basement is a proairetic detail; the arrival of the detective tells us that the dead body is part of some larger "story" that will have a satisfying "conclusion." The dead body is a fact; that the dead body *means something* and will eventually give rise to an *explanation* is the hermeneutic code at work. The scriptural mnemonics of John Cassian and Moses the Black operated on a thoroughly hermeneutic code: the mind should not wander hither and yon, from point to point or fact to fact, but must come to rest on a particular line of thought that resolves in insight.

Although it is "difficult to isolate the push of proairesis from the pull of hermeneutics [or] the temptation of meaning,"[29] Brooke remarks, he suggests that a theory of inventio that permanently resists closure could be a valuable alternative to the demands for planned clarity and resolution that inform most rhetorical pursuits. The internet, again, is in many respects the perfect apparatus for enacting proairetic invention. Unlike when we sit down to a novel, an essay, or a film, we rarely sit down to the internet (to social media in particular) expecting a satisfying, meaningful resolution. We are simply looking for things that strike our interest, things we will bookmark for later consideration, and things we are content to experience for a moment before letting them slip back into the random noise of the web. We are simply seeking to post spur-of-the-moment thoughts, memes, stream-of-consciousness rants, and random pictures from earlier in the day. We do not sit down expecting each digital object discovered or shared to point to and move us toward a meaningful connective whole. Rather, the social web facilitates ongoing interaction and open-ended activity that never culminate in final meanings or conclusions. In the context of social media, this style of proairetic wandering resists hermeneutic closure by technological design. The Zuck wants you to keep clicking. However, most apps, platforms, and visualization tools are equally amenable to proairetic invention without the sinister undertones that the concept might exude in the context of Facebook. Brooke points to wikis, role-playing video games, and bookmarking sites such as Delicious as digital spaces that provide a model of invention "more concerned with practice than with product." Even the Google search bar can be treated as a proairetic rather than a hermeneutic technology: the key is to "resist the closure implied in search 'results,'" Brooke argues, "and to treat that page as a point of departure, even and especially when the results are mixed."[30]

Applied to social media, however, and in spite of the sinister connotation I just invoked, Brooke's idea of proairetic invention enriches the metaphor of social media as a memory palace. Proairesis within the social mediascape suggests that its users are constantly trapped between the *unfolding fact* and the *fulfilled story*, between *creating* and *having created* themselves (or at least the versions of themselves they invent online). The defunct app Storify lucidly illustrates this simultaneous push of proairesis and pull of hermeneutic meaning that occurs on the social web. Storify's motto was "Make the Web Tell a Story," and its app allowed users to literally construct a linear, narratively coherent timeline from social media posts—for example, Twitter reactions to the Oscars or Facebook posts during a hurricane. Of course, at the moment those posts were produced and shared, the users did not think of themselves as characters in a story; they did not think of their shared links, rants, images, or videos as plot devices or story elements leading toward an inevitable denouement. Those shared digital objects were proairetic—perhaps they were carefully designed, perhaps they were raw transferals of mind and memory to silicon substrate, but either way, they were *in the moment* and idiosyncratic, not yet imbued with larger significance. It was only after the fact that someone felt the pull of the hermeneutic code, "the temptation of meaning," and decided to piece together these proairetic facts into a unified whole—

molding separate externalized memories into a unified memory, turning many things into a single thing, and linking mnemonic cues gathered from the social memory palace, one by one, until collectively they told a story that achieved closure.

Fittingly, from the proairetic point of view, Storify went out of business and pulled its servers in May 2018, forcing all those stories assembled from separate mnemonic cues to dissolve back into the digital ether.

The classical art of memory operated within this tense middle space between the hermeneutic and the proairetic codes, between settling on a single possibility in pursuit of closure and the generation of other possibilities. All of the posting and link tripping within our digital memory palaces can also be understood as walking the proairetic/hermeneutic line. They are practices of constructing, deconstructing, and reconstructing patterns of identity against lived randomness.[31] Any image, video, status update, or idiosyncratic hashtag is a pulse with a valence—a single integer that may indeed unfold toward this pattern . . . or, indeed, this other one. What follows it? What follows that one? Another image, another hashtag, or another click might generate one pattern, one version of ourselves, or it might end up generating some different vision of self (and other). Every time a user clicks—every time she posts—she creates one data point that moves toward closure qua one particular version of herself. (Indeed, what else are marketing algorithms but attempts to determine the nature of "you" through all the digital traces you leave behind, all those clicks and posts?) However, to the chagrin of the market analysts, it is easy to collapse any given pattern, to start producing a new and unrelated one, and to create a pulse toward another version of one's self. Every share, every conversion of memory into a mnemonic cue within the digital memory palace, is an opportunity to inscribe meaning, to generate a pattern—or, conversely, to begin disassembling an old pattern, to efface meaning, like letters on a wax tablet, back into the noise and temporal flow of the mediascape's forgotten data. And then to pursue another pattern. . . . While our lives last, we are granted many avatars in online space-time.

Of course, our digital memory palaces do not represent the unmediated past any more than memories do. Rather, they allow humans to construct patterns from randomness, to find signals in our noise or the noise of others, and to reduce patterns back to randomness if they seem to be leading toward a closure we would rather not live out. Like data visualizations, the curated social mediascape reconnects memory and invention. Instead of inventing knowledge, however, social media qua mnemonic allows the user to invent herself proairetically, tag by tag, image by image, and post by post, without any preplanned plot or larger meaning for the whole empiric collection of tags, images, and Instagram stories that disappear in an hour. It allows her to invent others the same way, as she wanders *their* idiosyncratic mnemonic cues.

The value of the memory-palace metaphor is that it provides a conceptual touchstone, grounded in rhetorical history, for the otherwise nebulous spaces our minds inhabit when we enter digital space-time, whose physics deeply influence the visions we make of ourselves and others (even as those same physics hide behind the pixelated veil of familiarity). The remoteness of the memory palace technique from contemporary life is, in my view, what makes it a useful symbol for the cyberscape. Viewing the social web as a memory palace should produce a moment of minor disorientation—and, after that moment, we should be compelled to see on our screens what ancient rhetors saw within their memory palaces: not a place where information is stored and visualized in transparent form, but a place where we might create the images we hope to be most useful, beneficial, and salutary when at last we close the mind's eye and return to the agora that awaits us.

Acknowledgments

This book has my name on it, but it should have other names on it too. Invention is a social act.

Thanks to the Syracusans: to Collin Gifford Brooke, who inspired the idea in the first place and helped develop it; to Krista Kennedy, whose intellectual guidance and personal mentorship continue to be invaluable; to Lois Agnew, who motivated me to keep one foot in history while the other was playing online; to Derek Mueller, who was among the first to recognize that math and data visualizations are appropriate topics for rhetorical theory; and to Patrick Berry, who showed me how to build a web page from scratch and in the process reignited my teenage interest in computers.

Thanks to the University of Chicago Press: to the late Doug Mitchell, without whom this book would still be a scattered collection of Word documents; I owe Doug a debt (as do many younger scholars) and wish I'd gotten to know him better, but I am grateful for getting to know him at all. Thanks to Kyle Wagner and Dylan Joseph Montanari, who worked tirelessly to take the book from files on my desktop to this amazing object you have in your hand. Thanks to Serene Yang, who polished the prose and caught my citational errors (any lingering mistakes are, of course, mine alone). Thanks also to the anonymous reviewers who made the book better.

Thanks to the colleagues who have challenged my thinking and informed this book in a thousand direct and indirect ways: James J. Murphy, John Frederick Reynolds, Ken Fitch, Christopher Michael Brown, Ted Underwood, Scott Weingart, Jim Ridolfo, Bill Hart-Davidson, James Baker, Jana Rosinski, Alex Reid, Kevin Adonis Browne, Rebecca Moore Howard, Eileen Schell, and the many others whose names should be here. Thanks also to the helpful staff at the Calvin T. Ryan Library and to my colleagues in the English Department at the University of Nebraska at

Kearney—all of whom provided a friendly, enjoyable, and productive (and sometimes helpfully unproductive) environment to write in.

Finally, to the people whose love and support matter most and make my academic life possible at all: to my mother Rachel, my father Dave, my sister Rebekah, and my wife Christina. Thanks for all you've done and continue to do.

Notes

Introduction

1. Bolter, "Hypertext and the Rhetorical Canons," 109.
2. Crowley, "Modern Rhetoric and Memory," 39–41.
3. Young and Sullivan, "Why Write? A Reconsideration."
4. Vivian and Demo, "Introduction," 3.
5. Vivian and Demo, 2.
6. Vivian and Demo, 6.
7. Vivian, "On the Language of Forgetting," 90.
8. Confino, "Collective Memory," 1393.
9. Brooke, *Lingua Fracta*, 144; the emphasis is Brooke's.
10. Whittemore, *Rhetorical Memory*, 39–41.
11. Cicero, *De oratore*, II.357.
12. The thought-to-sight framework here is taken from Weingart, "From Trees to Webs."

Chapter 1

1. Cicero, *De oratore*, book II.357.
2. Wise et al., "Visualizing the Non-Visual," 51.
3. The scene reproduced here occurs in *Blade Runner*, 15:03–20:00.
4. *Blade Runner*, 29:01–30:02.
5. Harris, *Hannibal*, 270–71.
6. Whittemore, *Rhetorical Memory*, 38.
7. Whittemore, 204.
8. "Dissoi logoi or dialexeis," 166.
9. Ravennas, *Art of Memory*, 6–7.
10. Bruno, *De umbris idearum*, 85–86.
11. John A. Bargh and Tanya L. Chartrand's "The Unbearable Automaticity of Being" offers a representative example of the psychological sciences' construal of memory's essential (though possibly beneficial) fallibility. Also see Jeff Pruchnic and Kim Lacey's "The Future of Forgetting" for an example of the humanities' mistrust of memory.
12. Whittemore, *Rhetorical Memory*, 204.
13. *Blade Runner*, 30:05–30:09.
14. Carruthers, *Craft of Thought*, 13; the emphasis is Carruthers's.

15. Vivian, "On the Language of Forgetting," 90.

16. Eves, "Recipe for Remembrance," 280–97.

17. Confino, "Collective Memory," 1393.

18. Carruthers, *Book of Memory*, 17.

19. Pruchnic and Lacey, "Future of Forgetting," 477.

20. Tan et al., "Save Everything," 90.

21. Wright, "Rhetorical Spaces in Memorial Places," 72.

22. Reynolds, "Memory Issues," 7–9.

23. Allen, "Faculty of Memory," 45–46.

24. Gronbeck, "Spoken and the Seen," 129.

25. Welch, "Platonic Paradox," 7.

26. Ryan, "Memory, Literacy, and Invention," 37.

27. Van Ittersum, "Data-Palace."

28. Prior et al., "Re-situating and Re-mediating the Canons."

29. Vivian, "On the Language of Forgetting," 90.

30. Term frequency–inverse document frequency (tf-idf) is a common metric for a word's significance within a corpus. A simple example: consider a text containing one hundred words, and in this text, the word *memory* occurs three times. The term frequency (tf) for *memory* in this text is computed as $(3 \, / \, 100) = 0.03$. Now, assume this text under analysis is just one in a corpus of ten million texts. Across the entire corpus, *memory* occurs in one thousand of these ten million discrete texts. The inverse document frequency (idf) of memory is then calculated as $\log(10,000,000 \, / \, 1,000) = 4$. Finally, tf-idf is calculated by multiplying tf and idf. The tf-idf score for *memory* in this case is therefore $0.03(4) = 0.12$. Naturally, the "weight" or significance of a tf-idf score changes depending on the size of the corpus.

31. For a simple explanation of topic modeling, see Scott Weinberg's blog post "Topic Modelling and Network Analysis," http://www.scottbot.net/HIAL/index.html@p=221.html.

32. Latour, *Reassembling the Social*, 124.

33. Latour, "Visualization and Cognition," 7.

34. Latour, 4.

35. Latour, 4.

36. Latour, 5.

37. Latour, 13.

38. "Dissoi logoi or dialexeis," 156.

39. "Dissoi logoi or dialexeis," 166–67.

40. I will not make much of the distinction between representational/pictorial images and icons. On this distinction, see Galloway, *Interface Effect*, 42–45, 85.

41. Yates, *Art of Memory*, 43.

42. Cicero, *De oratore*, book II.354.

43. Scrolls were not an ideal medium for managing, compressing, or assembling information. Papyrus rolls were awkward objects, less than a foot wide but anywhere from 15 to 150 feet long, 150 feet being equal to the length required for Homer's epic poetry (see Diringer, *Hand-Produced Book*, 130). Especially long texts would be transcribed on multiple scrolls. Twelve were needed, for example, for the *Aeneid* (see Whitley, *Gilded Page*, 29). A common item in the ancient Mediterranean was a *capsa*, a "book box" with handles, used to transport multiple scrolls. Notwithstanding the word's digital meaning, a Greek could not *scroll* on a scroll. It was not possible to skip

from section to section on a papyrus roll, nor was it possible to flip back and forth, as one might do with a book. It was not easy to search through papyrus rolls in any manner. They were unwieldy things. In addition to their physical awkwardness, most Greek and later Roman papyrus rolls contained little in the way of identifiable markings. At most, they had the title, author, and perhaps total number of lines in the scroll (Diringer, *Hand-Produced Book*, 139) marked on either the inside of the scroll itself or on a small (and easily dislodged) title slip, called in Greek a *sillybos* and in Latin a *titulus*.

44. Pfeiffer, *Callimachus*, vol. 1, *Fragmenta*, 465. Callimachus seems to have been critiquing long poetry as much as the bulky scrolls it required.

45. Plato, "Phaedrus," 276a.

46. Drucker, *Graphesis*, 128.

47. Plato, "Phaedrus," 274d–275b.

48. Plato, 275d–e.

49. Lauer, "What's in a Name?"

50. Plato, "Phaedrus," 276a.

51. Plato, 277d–e.

52. Plato, 275a.

53. Plato, "Lesser Hippias," 368d; Plato, "Greater Hippias," 285d–286a.

54. Plato, "Meno," 82a–85e.

55. Plato, 85c.

56. Plato, 86b.

57. Coleman, *Ancient and Medieval Memories*, 11.

58. Coleman, 9.

59. Coleman, 9.

60. Yates, *Art of Memory*, 51.

61. Yates, 51.

62. Kittler, "There Is No Software," 155.

63. Aristotle, *On Memory*, 451a14.

64. See Sorabji, "Introduction," xv, for a further distinction in Aristotle between *phantasma* and *phantasia*, which treats the knowledge of seemingly nonexistent things.

65. Sorabji, "Introduction," xix.

66. Aristotle, *On Memory*, 453a4.

67. Aristotle, 451b18–451b29.

68. Aristotle, 452a12.

69. Aristotle, 452a17. Aristotle of course uses capital letters from the Koine Greek alphabet.

70. Ravasio and Tscherter, "Users' Theories of the Desktop Metaphor," 274–75.

71. Loisette, *Assimilative Memory*, 4.

72. *Rhetorica ad Herennium*, III.28.

73. *Rhetorica ad Herennium*, III.29.

74. The description of *loci* occurs in *Rhetorica ad Herennium*, III.29–32.

75. *Rhetorica ad Herennium*, III.30.

76. The description of imagines occurs in *Rhetorica ad Herennium*, III.33–40.

77. Yates, *Art of Memory*, 26.

78. Cicero, *De oratore*, II.357.

79. Quintilian, *Institutio oratoria*. The memory section described here can be found in book 11, chapter 2.

80. Quintilian, *Institutio oratoria*, 11.2.4–7.

81. Quintilian, 11.2.3.
82. Quintilian, 11.2.17.
83. Quintilian, 11.2.25–6.
84. Quintilian, *Institutio oratoria*, book 11.2.1.
85. Brooke, *Lingua Fracta*, 82–86.
86. Carruthers and Ziolkowski, *Medieval Craft of Memory*, 1–2.
87. *Rhetorica ad Herennium*, III.31.

Chapter 2

1. Yates, *Art of Memory*, 65.
2. A treasure trove of primary source material on feudal law can be found online at Fordham University's Internet Medieval Sourcebook, https://sourcebooks.fordham.edu/sbook-law.asp.
3. See, for example, Paul Marchegay, "Duel judiciaire entre des communautes religieuses, 1098," 552–64, which contains a Latin account of a dual between not individuals but two monasteries over some land: "And when the champions came together to do combat, the injustice [done by the monks of Holy Cross] did not remain in doubt for very long, but was quickly revealed by the Lord." An English translation is available at Fordham University's Internet Medieval Sourcebook, https://sourcebooks.fordham.edu/source/12Cduels.asp.
4. Johnson, *Nineteenth-Century Rhetoric*, 12–13.
5. Yates, *Art of Memory*, 55.
6. Hajdu, *Das mnemotechnische Schrifttum*, 134.
7. Guibert de Nogent, "Book about the Way," 172–73.
8. Acrostics will be familiar to anyone who has learned the notes of treble clef by recalling the line Every Good Boy Does Fine or learned biological taxonomies by remembering Do Kings Play Chess On Fine Greek Silk.
9. Assis, "Alphabetic Acrostic."
10. Brogan and Colon, "Acrostics," 6.
11. Sweet, "Pair of Double Acrostics."
12. See Kneale and Kneale, *Development of Logic*, 231–33.
13. Carruthers, *Book of Memory*, 109.
14. Carruthers, 114.
15. See Middleton, *Memory Systems*, 12–13, for an overview of Publicius's system.
16. Hanson, "Hand Mnemonics in Classical Chinese Medicine."
17. Hand mnemonics are still in use today: for example, associating the "peaks" and "valleys" of one's knuckles with different months, so that the peaks correspond to months with thirty-one days, and the valleys to months with thirty or twenty-eight days.
18. Bolzoni, *Web of Images*, 180–81.
19. Bolzoni, *Gallery of Memory*, 11.
20. For the full poem, see Lerner, *Story of Libraries*, 43.
21. Carruthers, *Book of Memory*, 80; also see Murphy, *Rhetoric in the Middle Ages*, 146.
22. In *Institutio oratoria* (11.2.25), Quintilian is very confused about the memory palace technique. While discussing mnemonic imagery, he seems to think one must create an image for every word in a speech. This misunderstanding leads him to com-

pare imagines to shorthand writing, which does indeed have a symbol for, for example, conjunctions. Quintilian then compares his own notae to his bowdlerized version of the imagines of the art of memory, which, again, he has just compared to shorthand. Ergo, the roundabout comparison of notae to shorthand.

23. Cappelli, *Elements of Abbreviation*, 1. Scribes employed shorthand in ancient Rome to take down the proceedings of court cases, among other uses.

24. Quintilian, *Institutio oratoria*, 11.2.22.

25. Yates, *Art of Memory*, 57.

26. Yates, 56.

27. Carruthers, *Book of Memory*, 113.

28. Carruthers, 129.

29. Ravennas, *Art of Memory*, 6–7.

30. Quintilian, *Institutio oratoria*, 11.2.27.

31. Carruthers, *Book of Memory*, 96–97.

32. Hugh of St. Victor, "Three Best Memory Aids," 32–40.

33. Yates, *Art of Memory*, 67.

34. Carruthers, *Craft of Thought*, 60.

35. Carruthers, 55.

36. Bede, for example, uses 122 examples from the Bible and only 3 from poetic or nonscriptural sources in his treatise on rhetorical tropes. An interesting counterexample is Alberic of Monte Cassino. In his "Flowers of Rhetoric" (131–62), written in the mid-1100s, Alberic pulls most of his examples from pagan sources: Cicero, Sallust, Ovid, Lucan, Terence, and Virgil. However, this foretaste of Renaissance learning is an exception to the general rule that the Bible served as the prime exemplar of rhetoric and indeed all learning in the Middle Ages.

37. Maurus, "On the Training of the Clergy," 125–26.

38. Alan of the Isles, "Compendium," 230–33.

39. Thomas of Citeaux, "Commentary on the Song of Songs," 241–42.

40. Guibert de Nogent, "Book about the Way," 164.

41. Honorius of Autun, "Exile of the Soul," 204.

42. Carruthers, *Book of Memory*, 32. In places, Carruthers actually wavers on this point. It is not always clear if she believes that when the monastics talk about their mnemonic visions of scripture, they mean visions of the literal words of scripture or of the imagined worlds conjured by their reading of scripture. Whenever we read, after all, two memories form: a memory of reading these printed words on these particular pages at this particular time and place, and also a memory of the imagined phantasms—the characters, the scenery, the sounds—conjured by the words themselves. I can recall certain torn pages from my childhood copy of *A Wrinkle in Time*; but I can more vividly recall my inner (and no doubt idiosyncratic) visualizations of Meg, Mrs. Whatsit, and the antiseptic halls of CENTRAL Central Intelligence. I for one find it difficult to construe the medieval sources to mean this latter sort of "textual memory," which is not text memory at all but part and parcel with the visual phantasms of the memoryscape. The relationship between remembering a book and remembering the imaginary visions conjured by the book is a fascinating topic, and I wish I could do more than nod at it in an endnote.

43. Carruthers, *Book of Memory*, 176.

44. Carruthers, 87.

45. Geoffrey of Vinsauf, "The New Poetics," 105.

46. Carruthers, 117.

47. Carruthers, 87.

48. Carruthers, 190, emphasis mine.

49. Hugh of St. Victor, "Three Best Memory Aids," 39.

50. Cassian, *Conferences*, X.10.

51. Bruno, *De umbris idearum*, 85.

52. Carruthers, *Craft of Thought*, 132.

53. Cassian, *Conferences*, X.8.

54. Cassian, *Conferences*, X.10.

55. Carruthers, *Craft of Thought*, 121.

56. Julius Victor, "On Memory," 298.

57. Fortunatianus, "On Memory," 296.

58. Dilts and Kennedy, introduction to *Two Greek Rhetorical Treatises*, ix–xi.

59. Conley, *Rhetoric in the European Tradition*, 53–65.

60. Martianus Capella, *Martianus Capella and the Seven Liberal Arts*, 204.

61. Yates, *Art of Memory*, 64

62. Diringer, *Hand-Produced Book*, 203.

63. Diringer, 162.

64. It is possible that the papyrus roll would have suggested its own mnemonic metaphor to anyone whose memory worked better with *text as such* than with the phantasms of the mind's eye. Papyrus rolls were divided into margins, columns, and lines by those who wrote them. However, per chapter 1's argument regarding the difficulty of navigating scrolls, these divisions were not standardized in Greek and Latin texts (Diringer, *Hand-Produced Book*, 137). It was the practice for writers to structure pages according to their own needs rather than to a fixed standard. Quintilian's advice to segment an oration on the page, with plenty of space between the subdivisions, would have thus been congruent with contemporary Roman writing practices. In addition, his advice to mark segments with symbolic notae finds a parallel in earlier Greek papyri, whereupon major section divisions are sometimes indicated with a fanciful shape or drawing, called a *coronis* (Diringer, 159).

65. Diringer, *Hand-Produced Book*, 210.

66. Watson, *Illuminated Manuscripts*, 62.

67. Alexander, *Medieval Illuminators*, 35–72.

68. Diringer, *Hand-Produced Book*, 206–7. The quote is from a twelfth-century sermon and can be found in Durham Cathedral Manuscripts, MS B.IV.12.

69. Scattered medieval exegesis demonstrates that the bestiary, a pictorial inventory of didactic material presented with *animalia*, possessed a secondary mnemonic purpose. See Carruthers, *Book of Memory*, 137–38 and 159–60. Related to the bestiary is the *ysopet*, a collection of didactic fables (usually Aesop's) in medieval French literature, and here one finds more evidence that illumination possessed mnemonic intent. See Whalen, "Visualizing Morality," 299.

70. Diringer, *Illuminated Book*, 23–24.

71. Alexander, *Medieval Illuminators*, 92. See Diringer on medieval art in general: "until the thirteenth century, the individual form of expression used by the artist played very little part in comparison with conventional forms, which were nearly always symbolic" (*Illuminated Book*, 24).

72. Murphy, *Rhetoric in the Middle Ages*, 299.

73. Guibert de Nogent, "Book about the Way," 169.

74. Guibert de Nogent, 164. Guibert does recommend pastors read some of the church fathers, such as John Cassian.

75. Damian, *De sancta simplicitate*, praef., PL 145.697.

76. Humbert of Romans, "Treatise on Preaching," 250.

77. Murphy, *Rhetoric in the Middle Ages*, 299.

78. Guibert de Nogent, "Book about the Way," 169. Ironically, Guibert's treatise—like many homiletic treatises—contains inaccurate bible citations and paraphrases due to his failing, sluggish memory. The inaccuracies, however, are not major. It was common in antiquity and the Middle Ages to find material quoted from memory rather than from documented reference; minor inaccuracies abound.

79. Cicero, *De oratore*, I.18.

80. Quintilian, *Institutio oratoria*, 11.2.

81. The time between 1100 and 1375 is generally designated as Catholicism's "classical" period, during which time Roman legal treatises were rediscovered, the jurist Gratian produced the first collection of canon law, and the University of Bologna began to educate doctors of canon law.

82. Carruthers, *Book of Memory*, 196–97.

83. See Carruthers and Ziolkowski, *Medieval Craft of Memory*, for translations of and commentary on these and other late medieval mnemonic treatises.

84. Bradwardine, "On Acquiring a Trained Memory," 207.

85. Yates, *Art of Memory*, 104. The vivid codex illuminations, stained-glass windows, and painted frescoes associated in the modern mind with the word *medieval* likewise tend to hail from the 1200s and afterward.

86. John of Salisbury, *Metalogicon*, 217.

87. Carruthers, *Book of Memory*, 145.

88. Alcuin of York, *The Rhetoric of Alcuin*, 137.

89. Dales, *Alcuin*, 214.

90. Dales, 175.

91. Hugh of St. Victor, "Little Book," 57.

92. Hugh of St. Victor, 45.

93. Much later, the Jesuit memory artist Athanasius Kircher (d. 1680) would also use the ark as a giant memory palace and an "organizer of a grand encyclopedic museum" (Bolzoni, *Gallery of Memory*, 258).

94. Guibert de Nogent, "Book about the Way," 175.

95. Medieval authors write about God's forgiveness as a solvent for one's memory of past sin. Forgiveness cleanses the memoryscape, converting it to a space of joy in the knowledge of divine mercy. "In what way will my [past] life be displaced from my memory?" asks Bernard of Clairvaux. "To leave my memory intact and yet wash away its blotches, what penknife can I use? Only that living and effective word sharper than a two-edged sword: 'Your sins are forgiven you'" (Bernard of Clairvaux, *Sermons on Conversion*, 64). God's forgiveness blots out sin, according to Bernard, not by causing it to be lost from his memory but by converting sin into a memory that no longer stains his mind but rather allows him to trust in the knowledge of his own salvation.

96. Honorius of Autun, "Exile of the Soul," 206.

97. Carruthers, *Craft of Thought*, 68–69.

98. Boncompagno da Signa, "On Memory," 112. Even though Boncompagno's use of idiosyncratic mnemonic imagery hearkens back to the classical memory palace technique, his distaste for using corporeal imagery for "ineffable" things (112) leads him

to ignore the general principle in this section of his rhetorical treatise, *Rhetorica novissima*. He attempts to describe a "memory chamber," but it is overly geometrical and not at all like the classical loci. He mentions the use of mnemonic alphabets, but otherwise, the memoria section in his treatise is devoted to a pseudopsychological treatment of memory and to mundane tricks for rote memorization of names, dates, and places.

99. Guibert de Nogent, "Book about the Way," 175.

100. Plato, *Theaetetus*, 191d.

101. Aristotle, *On the Soul*, 424a18ff.

102. Carruthers, *Book of Memory*, 21.

103. Carruthers, 17.

104. Carruthers, 292.

105. Cicero, *De partitione oratoria*, vii.26.

106. Carruthers, *Book of Memory*, 21.

107. Against appearances, I do not want to overemphasize my disagreement with Carruthers on this issue. Overall, her emphasis on the creative aspects of medieval mnemonics is crucial to my argument in later chapters, where I imagine what the digital ecology might look like if we treated our data visualizations the way medieval monks treated their own mnemonic cues—as creative tools rather than reified representations.

108. Delagrange, *Technologies of Wonder*.

109. Delagrange, "Wunderkammer."

110. Stafford, *Visual Analogy*, quoted in Delagrange, "Wunderkammer."

111. See *Rhetorica ad Herennium* 3.17.31.

112. Bradwardine, "On Acquiring a Trained Memory," 214.

113. Bradwardine, 214.

114. Haines, "Introduction," in *Notory Art of Shorthand*, 15–39. Haines's intriguing discussion of rational versus irrational writing in the Middle Ages has informed much of this section.

115. *Ars notoria*, 11–12.

116. *Ars notoria*, 26.

117. Lawrence-Mathers and Escobar-Vargas, *Magic and Medieval Society*, 38.

118. For an overview of astral and image magic, see Lawrence-Mathers and Escobar-Vargas, *Magic and Medieval Society*, 27–43.

119. *Ars notoria*, 8.

120. *Ars notoria*, 18.

121. A related art—which escaped condemnation due to its "practical" veneer as a simple shorthand system—was the *ars notoria notarie*, detailed in *The Notary Art of Shorthand*. However, in his introduction to that text, John Haines has persuasively argued that the system itself doesn't actually work and provides only a salacious foretaste of an actual "notorious" art for perfect memory. The anonymous author provides subtle and not-so-subtle hints that his text is a magical one: for example, he claims to have received knowledge of the art from the martyr Saint Thomas Becket while in an opium-fueled trance.

Chapter 3

1. Cicero, *De oratore*, I.18.

2. Quintilian, *Institutio oratoria*, 11.2.1.

3. Fons, *Improving Web Visibility*, 16.

4. Bolzoni, *Web of Images*, 6.

5. See Bolzoni, *Il teatro della memoria*. It has also been argued that early modern Wunderkammern—cabinets of curiosity—were likewise influenced by the idea of a physical memory palace to contain newly discovered knowledge (Bolzoni, *Gallery of Memory*, 255; Westerhoff, "World of Signs").

6. Hutchins, *Cognition in the Wild*, 96.

7. Yates, *Art of Memory*, 114.

8. The argument occurs in chapters 10 and 12 of *Art of Memory* (231–43, 266–87).

9. Culianu, *Eros and Magic*, 62–63.

10. West, "Memory," 490.

11. Sharon Crowley's *Methodical Memory* remains one of the strongest articulations of the "modernist reformers" argument.

12. Green and Murphy, *Renaissance Rhetoric*; Plett, *English Renaissance Rhetoric*; Middleton, *Memory Systems*; British Library, Incunabula Short Title Catalogue. Green and Murphy was the primary source.

13. Buringh and Van Zanden, "Charting the 'Rise of the West,'" 418.

14. Wilson, *Arte of Rhetorique*, 257–58.

15. Ong, *Rhetoric, Romance, and Technology*, 85–86.

16. Conley, *Rhetoric in the European Tradition*, 143.

17. Bolzoni, *Gallery of Memory*, 71.

18. Ravennas, *Art of Memory*, 6–7.

19. On the specifics of these techniques, see Middleton, *Memory Systems*, 10–20, and Von Feinaigle, *New Art of Memory*, 222–319. There is a serious tendency in these systems, however, to become so "schematic" or "geometrical" that they become too dry to be mnemonically useful. Also see Kuwakino below.

20. Kuwakino, "From *domus sapientiae*," 58–79.

21. Jardine, "Humanistic Logic," 186.

22. Ong, *Ramus, Method*, 245.

23. Ong, 245–46.

24. Naturally, Ramus was not the first to organize material in page space in this manner, but Ramist method was certainly influenced by the Gutenberg era's "preoccupation with space as a vehicle of intelligibility" (Ong, *Ramus, Method*, 76).

25. Ramus, *Arguments in Rhetoric*, 159.

26. Jardine, "Humanistic Logic," 189.

27. Crowley, *Methodical Memory*, 35.

28. Quintilian, *Institutio oratoria*, 11.2.27–32.

29. For a discussion of method's negative influence on classical invention, see Sloane, *Donne, Milton*, 137–42.

30. Arrangement/memory is nevertheless a part of dialectic, Ramus avers, because without it, knowledge cannot be effectively comprehended or communicated.

31. Ong, *Ramus, Method*, 76.

32. Rossi, *Logic and the Art of Memory*, 101, italics in original.

33. Ong, *Ramus, Method*, 280.

34. Bolter, "Hypertext and the Rhetorical Canons," 109.

35. Yates, *Art of Memory*, 231.

36. Sloane, *Donne, Milton*, 137.

37. Rossi, *Logic and the Art of Memory*, 119. However, see Rhodri Lewis, "A Kind of Sagacity," for a reappraisal of Bacon's use of visual mnemonics and the classical art of memory.

38. Natural philosophers and alchemists—Bacon included—worked not only by passive observation but also by active experiment. If one was to learn anything from experimentation—in which the truth was coaxed out of nature, so to speak—one needed "to follow a particular method of inquiry," as Bruce Moran states, in order to organize the facts one observed. Otherwise, it would be impossible to repeat the experiment and to develop theories from those recurring observations (*Distilling Knowledge*, 133). Experiment was thus grounded in "processes and procedures [that] acquired the status of artifacts" through their methodical and replicable regularity (*Distilling Knowledge*, 42). With the rise and dominance of natural experimentation, it was thus perhaps inevitable that artificial memory would lose its status as an inventive practice and be relegated to being an art of reconstructing ordered (scientific) activity and thought.

39. For example, Conley, *Rhetoric in the European Tradition*, 140–43.

40. Yates, *Art of Memory*, 271.

41. In fact, the notae of the ars notoria had always been associated with memory "seals."

42. Bruno, *De umbris idearum*, 72.

43. Bruno, 116.

44. Bruno, 85.

45. Bruno, 19.

46. Bruno, 66.

47. Gosnell, "Introduction," in *Thirty Seals*, 10.

48. Rossi, *Logic and the Art of Memory*, 82–84.

49. Bruno, *Thirty Seals*, 21.

50. Kircher used Noah's ark as his image of an encyclopedia. He also developed a combinatorial system that produced religious hymns.

51. Yates, *Art of Memory*, 266.

52. Yates, 267.

53. Yates, 270.

54. Yates, 266.

55. For extracts from contemporaneous accounts, including the account containing the slight about the accent, see McNulty, "Bruno at Oxford," 202–3.

56. Daniel, *The vvorthy tract of Paulus Iouius*. Daniel in fact describes imprese as superior to the arcane symbology of Bruno. Imprese was a badge system for families and militaries, much like heraldry, that used beasts and mottos that were not too ambiguous about their meanings. See also Weiner, "Expelling the Beast," for a thorough examination of Bruno's time in England.

57. For the more cautious take, see Bremmer, "Iconoclast, Iconoclastic, and Iconoclasm," and Budd, "Rethinking Iconoclasm."

58. Yates, *Art of Memory*, 234–35.

59. Yates, 237.

60. Bergin, *Making of the French Episcopate*, 340.

61. Yates, *Art of Memory*, 233.

62. For Luther's and Lutheran views on images, see Leroux, *Luther's Rhetoric*, 73–95, and Bremmer, "Iconoclast, Iconoclastic, and Iconoclasm," 15–16.

63. Mack, *History of Renaissance Rhetoric*, 121. For more on imagery and emotion in Melanchthon's rhetoric, see Mack, 116–21.

64. Rossi, *Logic and the Art of Memory*, 131.

65. Latour, "What Is Iconoclash?," 18.

66. Latour, 18.

67. Chun, *Programmed Visions*, 71.

68. Chun, "On Software," 44.

69. Galloway, *Interface Effect*, 56–61.

70. Jameson, "Cognitive Mapping," 353. Jameson of course states that the totality of social structures is ultimately unable to be represented. He also denies that a cognitive map would look anything like a map (*Postmodernism*, 409). However, it is difficult to imagine what a mapping of social structures (and of a subject's place within them) would entail without some recourse to visual, spatial mimesis.

71. This popular quote appears in the foreword to Kircher's *Ars magna Sciendi, sive Combinatoria*, which translates to *The Great Art of Knowledge, or the Combinatorial Art*.

72. Chun, *Programmed Visions*, 75.

73. Chun, 75.

74. Kittler, "There Is No Software," 151.

75. Kittler, 155.

76. Marino, "Critical Code Studies."

77. Latour, "What Is Iconoclash?," 16.

78. Lewis, *A Grief Observed*, 66.

79. Barfield, *Saving the Appearances*, 172–86, but see especially his comment on icons/idols as necessary evils on 185–86.

80. Nagel, "What Is It Like to Be a Bat?"

81. Cicero, *De oratore*, I.18.

82. Doran, *Monarchy and Matrimony*, 59.

83. Fulwood, *Castel of Memorie*, 2.

84. Fulwood, 103.

85. Fulwood, 97.

86. Fulwood, 106.

87. Yates, *Art of Memory*, 325.

88. Rzepka, "Direct Ideas," 179.

89. Rzepka, 172.

90. Von Feinaigle, *New Art of Memory*, 257.

91. Von Feinaigle, 252.

92. For a complete printing of Herdson's system, see von Feinaigle, *New Art of Memory*, 297–318.

93. Fuller, *Holy State*, 165.

94. Hultzen's "Charles Butler on Memory" contains a full translation with commentary.

95. Wilson, *Arte of Rhetorique*, 254. Wilson goes on to recognize the important mnemonic principle of idiosyncratic association: "When we come to a place where we haue not bene many a day before, wee remember not onely the place it selfe, but by the place, wee call to remembraunce many thinges done there. . . . Sometimes a chimney telleth them of many late drinkinges and sitting up by the fire" (Wilson, 256).

96. Wilson, 255.

97. In Roman mythology, Cacus stole cattle from Hercules.

98. Wilson, *Arte of Rhetorique*, 254.

99. Wilson, 257.

100. Wilson, 257.

101. See Wilson, 252–58, for Wilson's complete treatment of the memory palace technique.

102. Hultzen, "Charles Butler on Memory," 52.

103. Hultzen, 53.

104. Hultzen, 54–55.

105. Hultzen, 54–55.

106. Connors, *Composition-Rhetoric*, 127.

Chapter 4

1. Buringh and Van Zanden, "Charting the 'Rise of the West,'" 418.

2. Middleton, *Memory Systems*, 107.

3. Middleton, 111.

4. Otake, "How Can Anyone Remember?"

5. Middleton, *Memory Systems*, 125.

6. D'Assigny, *Art of Memory*, xvi.

7. D'Assigny, 56.

8. Hugh of St. Victor, "Three Best Memory Aids," 39.

9. D'Assigny, *Art of Memory*, 55.

10. This system predates but was popularized in the nineteenth century by a printer and mnemonist named Major Beniowski, in his oddly titled *The Anti-Absurd or Phrenotypic English Pronouncing and Orthographical Dictionary*. Hence the name, major system.

11. Some early modern treatises include lists of images for numbers along with their visual alphabets. It is often unclear if these numbers were to be used as indexed loci, like the alphabets, or as actual forms for recalling numbers as such.

12. Sarma, "Katapayadi Notation."

13. Atkinson, *Memory Culture*, 88.

14. Middleton, *Memory Systems*, 27.

15. For an overview of these major systems, see Middleton, *Memory Systems*, 25–51.

16. Middleton, *Memory Systems*, 27.

17. Middleton, 28.

18. See Middleton, 25–61, for Middleton's overview of modern mnemonic systems.

19. Loisette, *Assimilative Memory*, 4.

20. Crowley, *Methodical Memory*, 17.

21. Locke, *Essay Concerning Human Understanding*, 1.25.1

22. Locke, 4.1.2.

23. Bain, *English Composition*, 3.

24. Aristotle, *On Memory*, 452a12.

25. Middleton, *Memory Systems*, 25–61.

26. Middleton, 39.

27. Middleton, 47.

28. Middleton, 60.

29. Middleton, 60.

30. Gardner, "*Ars Magna* of Ramon Lull," 24 and n14.

31. Bonner, "Llull's Thought," 55.

32. Bonner, 55.

33. For a full translation and lucid examination of Llull's art, see Llull, "Ars brevis," in *Doctor Illuminatus,* ed. Anthony Bonner, 292–361.

34. Llull, "Ars brevis," 298.

35. Llull, "Ars brevis," 298.

36. In *Tractatus novus de astronomia,* Llull himself uses combinatorial letters to represent planets and the elements to work out problems in astrology (Yates, "Art of Ramon Lull," 119–20).

37. Cramer, *Words Made Flesh,* 58.

38. Rossi, *Logic and the Art of Memory,* 105.

39. Rossi, 104.

40. Schuchard, *Restoring the Temple of Vision,* 73. Also see Pring-Mill, "Ramon Lull," 547–51.

41. Strickland, *Leibniz and the Two Sophies,* 355.

42. Leibniz, "On the Art of Combination," 10–11.

43. Leibniz, *Leibniz,* 656.

44. Cramer, *Words Made Flesh,* 36.

Chapter 5

1. Drucker, *Graphesis,* 194.

2. Cicero, *De oratore,* 2.357.

3. Drucker, *Graphesis,* 71.

4. Delagrange, *Technologies of Wonder,* 27.

5. Catarci et al., "Structure Everything," 110.

6. Wise et al., "Visualizing the Non-Visual," 51.

7. Marshall, "How People Manage Information," 73.

8. Freeman and Gelernter, "Beyond Lifestreams," 26.

9. Rachael Tatman, @rctatman, July 5, 2018, https://twitter.com/rctatman /status/1014915906508451840.

10. Auerbach, *Mimesis,* 27.

11. Nagel, "What Is It Like to Be a Bat?," 438.

12. Schutt and O'Neil, *Doing Data Science,* 19.

13. Tufte, *Visual Display,* 57.

14. Tufte, *Envisioning Information,* 9.

15. Drucker, *Graphesis,* 125.

16. Drucker, 128.

17. Schutt and O'Neil, *Doing Data Science,* 19, 25.

18. Schutt and O'Neil, 354.

19. The word is from Drucker, *Graphesis,* 129: "grotesquely distorts the complexity, but also the basic ambiguity, of the phenomenon under investigation."

20. McAlister, "Algorithms Are More Like Puppies."

21. *Rhetorica ad Herennium,* III.31.

22. Allington, Brouillette, and Golumbia, "Neoliberal Tools."

23. Quote appears in the foreword to Kircher's *Ars magna Sciendi, sive Combinatoria.*

24. See Nelson Cowan's "What Are the Differences between Long-Term, Short-Term, and Working Memory?" on the difference between short-term and working memory, a distinction that need not concern us here.

25. McCutchen, "From Novice to Expert," 57–58.

26. Young and Sullivan, "Why Write? A Reconsideration," 215–25.

27. Haas, *Writing Technology*, 117.

28. Haas, 118.

29. Qu, Luo, and Mo, "Dynamic Mental Representations," 933–48. Also see Glenberg, Meyer, and Lindem, "Mental Models," 69–83.

30. Reisberg, "Mental Images," 374–90.

31. Knauff, *Space to Reason*.

32. Rossi, *Logic and the Art of Memory*, 24.

33. Haas, *Writing Technology*, 120–21.

34. Haas, 120–21.

35. Drucker, "Humanities Approaches to Interface Theory," 1–19.

36. Ramsay, *Reading Machines*, 48.

37. Latour, "Tarde's Idea of Quantification," 160.

38. Schutt and O'Neil, *Doing Data Science*, 235, 251.

39. Harley, "Deconstructing the Map."

40. Borges, *Universal History*, 141.

41. Haraway, "Situated Knowledges," 584.

42. Haraway, 588–90.

43. Harley, "Deconstructing the Map," 12–13.

44. Haraway, "Situated Knowledges," 589.

45. Rice, *Digital Detroit*, 141–42.

46. Drucker, *Graphesis*, 71.

47. Sweet, "Vanished New Orleans."

48. Drucker, *Graphesis*, 82.

49. Bratton, *The Stack*, 234–35.

50. Latour, "What Is Iconoclash?," 16.

51. Chun, *Programmed Visions*, 1.

52. Chun, 71.

53. Bratton, *The Stack*, 235.

54. Chun, *Programmed Visions*, 75.

55. Drucker, *Graphesis*, 103.

56. Many references to the primacy of the first canon could be inserted here. For an overview, see Janice Lauer, *Invention in Rhetoric and Composition*.

57. Farrell, "Practicing the Arts of Rhetoric," 79–80.

58. Drucker, *Graphesis*, 125.

59. Drucker, 125.

60. Drucker, 126–27.

61. Tufte, *Visual Display*, 53.

62. Drucker, 103.

63. Box, "Robustness," 2–3.

64. Nester, "An Applied Statistician's Creed."

65. Drucker, *Graphesis*, 126–27.

66. Drucker, 136–37.

67. Drucker, 137.

68. Moretti, "Operationalizing."

69. Drucker, *Graphesis*, 128.

70. Drucker, 128.

71. "What is simple is always false; what is not is unusable." Valéry, *Collected Works*, 466.

72. Drucker, *Graphesis*, 133.

Chapter 6

1. *Rhetorica ad Herennium*, 223.

2. *Rhetorica ad Herennium*, 219.

3. Gallagher, "Memory and Reconciliation," 306.

4. Blaire, Jeppeson, and Pucci Jr., "Public Memorializing," 281.

5. Blaire, Jeppeson, and Pucci Jr., 281.

6. Blaire, Jeppeson, and Pucci Jr., 281.

7. Pruchnic and Lacey, "Future of Forgetting," 487.

8. Bruno, *De umbris idearum*, 85–86.

9. "Dissoi logoi or dialexeis," 166.

10. Ravennas, *Art of Memory*, 6–7.

11. McNair, "Computer Icons," 77–86.

12. Freeman and Gelernter, "Beyond Lifestreams," 24.

13. Freeman and Gelernter, 41.

14. Freeman and Gelernter, 21.

15. Freeman and Gelernter, 24–25.

16. Freeman and Gelernter, 24–25.

17. For an overview of Moran's study, see Ravasio and Tscherter, "Users' Theories of the Desktop Metaphor," 267–68.

18. Tan et al., "Save Everything," 92.

19. Brooke and Rickert, "Being Delicious," 163–79.

20. Brooke and Rickert, 175.

21. Brooke and Rickert, 173.

22. Brooke's detailed treatment of proairesis occurs in *Lingua Fracta*, 74–77, 81–86.

23. Cassian, *Conferences*, X.14.

24. Carruthers, *Craft of Thought*, 82.

25. Carruthers, 82.

26. Cassian, *Conferences*, X.13.

27. Carr, "Is Google Making Us Stupid?"

28. Brooke, *Lingua Fracta*, 77.

29. Brooke, 77.

30. Brooke, 82–83.

31. See Brooke, *Lingua Fracta*, 89–112. Brooke suggests that this pattern/randomness binary is more beneficial for understanding mnemonic practice than the traditional binary metaphor of presence/absence (that is, a thing is either stored or not stored in memory).

Bibliography

Alan of the Isles, "A Compendium on the Art of Preaching." In *Readings in Medieval Rhetoric*, edited and translated by Joseph Miller, Michael H. Prosser, and Thomas W. Benson, 228–40. Bloomington: Indiana University Press, 1973.

Alberic of Monte Cassino. "Flowers of Rhetoric." In *Readings in Medieval Rhetoric*, edited and translated by Joseph Miller, Michael H. Prosser, and Thomas W. Benson, 131–62. Bloomington: Indiana University Press, 1973.

Alcuin of York. *The Rhetoric of Alcuin and Charlemagne*. Translated by Wilbur Samuel Howell. New York: Russell & Russell, 1965.

Alexander, Jonathan J. G. *Medieval Illuminators and Their Methods of Work*. New Haven: Yale University Press, 1992.

Allen, Virginia. "The Faculty of Memory." In *Rhetorical Memory and Delivery*, edited by John Frederick Reynolds, 45–65. Mahwah, NJ: Lawrence Erlbaum Associates, 1993.

Allington, Daniel, Sarah Brouillette, and David Golumbia. "Neoliberal Tools (and Archives): A Political History of Digital Humanities." *Los Angeles Review of Books*, May 1, 2016. https://lareviewofbooks.org/article/neoliberal-tools-archives-political-history-digital-humanities/.

Aristotle. *Aristotle on Memory*. Translated by Richard Sorabji. London: Briston Classical Press, 2012.

———. *On Rhetoric*. Translated by George A. Kennedy. Oxford: Oxford University Press, 2007.

———. *On the Soul*. Translated by Fred D. Miller Jr. Oxford: Oxford University Press, 2018.

Ars notoria: The Notory Art of Solomon. Translated by Robert Turner. London, 1657. Transcribed by Benjamin Rowe, 1999. https://www.ancient-code.com/wp-content/uploads/2016/04/Ars_notoria.pdf.

Assis, Elie. "The Alphabetic Acrostic in the Book of Lamentations." *Catholic Biblical Quarterly* 69 (2007): 710–24.

Atkinson, William W. *Memory Culture*. Chicago: The Psychic Research Company, 1903.

Auerbach, Erich. *Mimesis: The Representation of Reality in Western Literature*. Princeton, NJ: Princeton University Press, 2003.

Bain, Alexander. *English Composition and Rhetoric: A Manual*. 2nd ed. London: Longmans, Green, 1869.

Barfield, Owen. *Saving the Appearances: A Study in Idolatry*. 2nd ed. Middletown, CT: Wesleyan University Press, 1988.

Bargh, John A., and Tanya L. Chartrand. "The Unbearable Automicity of Being." *American Psychologist* 54, no. 7 (1999): 462–79.

Bergin, Joseph. *The Making of the French Episcopate, 1589–1661*. New Haven: Yale University Press, 1996.

Bernard of Clairvaux. *Sermons on Conversion*. Translated by Marie Bernard Said. Collegeville, MN: Cistercian Publications, 1981.

Blair, Carole, Marsha S. Jeppeson, and Enrico Pucci Jr. "Public Memorializing in Postmodernity: The Vietnam Veterans Memorial as Prototype." *Quarterly Journal of Speech* 77, no. 3 (1991): 263–88.

Bloch, David. *Aristotle on Memory and Recollection: Text, Translation, Interpretation, and Reception in Western Scholasticism*. Leiden: Brill, 2007.

Bolter, Jay David. "Hypertext and the Rhetorical Canons." In *Rhetorical Memory and Delivery*, edited by John Frederick Reynolds, 97–113. Mahwah, NJ: Lawrence Erlbaum Associates, 1993.

Bolzoni, Lina. *Il teatro della memoria: Studi su Giulio Camillo*. Padova: Liviana, 1984.

———. *The Gallery of Memory: Literary and Iconographic Models in the Age of the Printing Press*. Toronto: University of Toronto Press, 2001.

———. *The Web of Images*. Burlington, VT: Ashgate, 2004.

Boncompagno da Signa. "On Memory." In *The Medieval Craft of Memory*, translated by Sean Gallagher and edited by Mary Carruthers and Jan M. Ziolkowski, 104–17. Philadelphia: University of Pennsylvania Press, 2002.

Bonner, Anthony. "Llull's Thought." In *Doctor Illuminatus: A Ramon Llull Reader*, edited by Anthony Bonner, 1–44. Princeton, NJ: Princeton University Press, 1993.

Borges, Jorge Luis. *A Universal History of Infamy*. Translated by Norman Thomas di Giovanni. New York: E. P. Dutton, 1972.

Bouchot, Henri. *The Book: Its Printers, Illustrators, and Binders*. London: H. Gevel and Co., 1890.

Box, George E. P. "Robustness in the Strategy of Scientific Model Building." *MRC Technical Summary Report #1954*. Mathematics Research Center, University of Wisconsin–Madison, May 1979.

Bradwardine, Thomas. "On Acquiring a Trained Memory." In *The Medieval Craft of Memory*, edited and translated by Mary Carruthers and Jan M. Ziolkowski, 205–15. Philadelphia: University of Pennsylvania Press, 2002.

Bratton, Benjamin H. *The Stack: On Software and Sovereignty*. Cambridge, MA: MIT Press, 2015.

Bremmer, Jan. "Iconoclast, Iconoclastic, and Iconoclasm: Notes towards a Genealogy." *Church History and Religious Culture* 88, no. 1 (2008): 1–17.

British Library. "Incunabula Short Title Catalogue." https://www.bl.uk/catalogues/istc/.

Brogan, T. V. F., and D. A. Colon. "Acrostics." In *The Princeton Encyclopedia of Poetry and Poetics*, 4th ed., edited by Roland Greene, 6. Princeton, NJ: Princeton University Press, 2012.

Brooke, Collin Gifford. *Lingua Fracta: Towards a Rhetoric of New Media*. New Jersey: Hampton Press, Inc., 2009.

Brooke, Collin Gifford, and Thomas Rickert. "Being Delicious." In *Beyond Postprocess*, edited by Sidney Dobrin, J. A. Rice, and Michael Vastola, 163–79. Logan: Utah State University Press, 2011.

Bruno, Giordano. *Thirty Seals & The Seal of Seals*. Translated by Scott Gosnell. Amazon CreateSpace, 2016.

———. *De umbris idearum: On the Shadow of Ideas and the Art of Memory*. Translated by Scott Gosnell. Amazon CreateSpace, 2013.

Budd, Joel. "Rethinking Iconoclasm in Early Modern England: The Case of Cheapside Cross." *Journal of Early Modern History* 4, no. 3–4 (2000): 379–404.

Buringh, Eltjo, and Jan Luiten Van Zanden. "Charting the 'Rise of the West': Manuscripts and Printed Books in Europe, A Long-Term Perspective from the Sixth through Eighteenth Centuries." *Journal of Economic History* 69, no. 2 (2009): 409–45.

Cappelli, Adriano. *The Elements of Abbreviation in Medieval Latin Paleography*. Translated by David Heimann and Richard Kay. Lawrence: University of Kansas Libraries, 1982.

Carr, Nicholas G. "Is Google Making Us Stupid?" *The Atlantic*, July 1, 2008. https://www.theatlantic.com/magazine/archive/2008/07/is-google-making-us-stupid/306868/.

Carruthers, Mary. *The Book of Memory: A Study of Memory in Medieval Culture*. Cambridge: Cambridge University Press, 1990.

———. *The Craft of Thought: Meditation, Rhetoric, and the Making of Images, 400–1200*. Cambridge: Cambridge University Press, 2000.

Carruthers, Mary, and Jan M. Ziolkowski, eds. *The Medieval Craft of Memory: An Anthology of Texts and Pictures*. Philadelphia: University of Pennsylvania Press, 2002.

Cassian, John. *Conferences*. Translated by Colm Luibheid. Mahwah, NJ: Paulist Press, 1985.

Catarci, Tiziana, Luna Dong, Alon Halevy, and Antonella Poggi. "Structure Everything." In *Personal Information Management*, edited by William Jones and Jaime Teevan, 108–26. Seattle: University of Washington Press, 2007.

Chun, Wendy Hui Kyong. "On Software, or the Persistence of Visual Knowledge." *Grey Room* 18, no. 4 (January 2005): 26–51.

———. *Programmed Visions: Software and Memory*. Cambridge, MA: MIT Press, 2011.

Cicero. *De oratore (On the Ideal Orator)*. Translated by James M. May and Jakob Wisse. Oxford: Oxford University Press, 2001.

———. *De partitione oratoria*. Translated by H. Rackham. Cambridge, MA: Harvard University Press, 1942.

Coleman, Janet. *Ancient and Medieval Memories*. Cambridge: Cambridge University Press, 1992.

Confino, Alon. "Collective Memory and Cultural History: Problems of Method." *American Historical Review* 102, no. 5 (1997): 1386–1403.

Conley, Thomas M. *Rhetoric in the European Tradition*. Chicago: University of Chicago Press, 1990.

Connors, Robert J. *Composition-Rhetoric: Backgrounds, Theory, and Pedagogy*. Pittsburgh: University of Pittsburgh Press, 1997.

Corbett, Edward P. J., and Robert J. Connors. *Classical Rhetoric for the Modern Student*. 4th ed. Oxford: Oxford University Press, 1999.

Cowan, Nelson. "What Are the Differences between Long-Term, Short-Term, and Working Memory?" *Progress in Brain Research* 169 (2008): 323–38.

Cramer, Florian. *Words Made Flesh: Code, Culture, Imagination.* Rotterdam: Piet Zwart Institute, 2005. https://www.netzliteratur.net/cramer/wordsmadeflesh-pdf.pdf.

Crowley, Sharon. *The Methodical Memory: Invention in Current-Traditional Rhetoric.* Carbondale: Southern Illinois University Press, 1990.

———. "Modern Rhetoric and Memory." In *Rhetorical Memory and Delivery*, edited by John Frederick Reynolds, 31–45. Mahwah, NJ: Lawrence Erlbaum Associates, 1993.

Cukier, Kenneth, and Viktor Mayer-Schönberger. "The Rise of Big Data: How It's Changing the Way We Think about the World." *Foreign Affairs* 92, no. 3 (2013): 28–40.

Culianu, Ioan. *Eros and Magic in the Renaissance.* Chicago: University of Chicago Press, 1987.

Dales, Douglas. *Alcuin: Theology and Thought.* Cambridge: James Clarke and Co., 2013.

Damian, Peter. "De sancta simplicitate." In *Patrologia Latina*, vol. 144–45, edited by J. P. Mingne, 696–701. Oxford: Oxford University Press, 1853.

Daniel, Samuel. *The vvorthy tract of Paulus Iouius, contayning a discourse of rare inuentions, both militarie and amorous called imprese.* Ann Arbor, MI: Text Creation Partnership. https://quod.lib.umich.edu/e/eebo/A01764.0001.001.

D'Assigny, Marius. *The Art of Memory.* London: J. Darby, 1706.

Delagrange, Susan H. "Wunderkammer, Cornell, and the Visual Canon of Arrangement." *Kairos* 13, no. 2 (Spring 2009). http://kairos.technorhetoric.net/13.2/topoi/delagrange/index.html.

———. *Technologies of Wonder: Rhetorical Practice in a Digital World.* Logan: Utah State University Press/Computers and Composition Digital Press. 2011. https://ccdigitalpress.org/book/wonder/.

Dilts, Mervin R., and George A. Kennedy. Introduction to *Two Greek Rhetorical Treatises from the Roman Empire*, edited by Mervin R. Dilts and George A. Kennedy, ix–xix. New York: Brill, 1997.

Diringer, David. *The Hand-Produced Book.* New York: The Philosophical Library, 1953.

———. *The Illuminated Book.* New York: The Philosophical Library, 1957.

"Dissoi logoi or dialexeis." Translated by Rosamond Kent Sprague. *Mind* 77, no. 306 (1968): 155–67.

Doran, Susan. *Monarchy and Matrimony: The Courtships of Elizabeth I.* London: Routledge, 2002.

Drucker, Johanna. *Graphesis: Visual Forms of Knowledge Production.* Cambridge, MA: Harvard University Press, 2014.

———. "Humanities Approaches to Interface Theory." *Culture Machine* 12 (2011): 1–20.

Eves, Rosalyn Collings. "A Recipe for Remembrance: Memory and Identity in African-American Women's Cookbooks." *Rhetoric Review* 24, no. 3 (2005): 280–97.

Farrell, Thomas. "Practicing the Arts of Rhetoric." In *Contemporary Rhetorical Theory: A Reader*, edited by John Louis Lucaites, Celeste Michelle Condit, and Sally Caudill, 79–100. New York: Guilford Press, 1999.

Farrington, Benjamin. *The Philosophy of Francis Bacon*. Liverpool: Liverpool University Press, 1964.

Fauvel-Gouraud, Francis. *Phreno-mnemotechny, or The Art of Memory*. New York: Wiley and Putnam, 1845.

Fons, Ted. *Improving Web Visibility: Into the Hands of Readers*. American Library Association, 2016.

Fortunatianus, Consultus. "On Memory." In *The Medieval Craft of Memory*, edited and translated by Mary Carruthers and Jan M. Ziolkowski, 295–97. Philadelphia: University of Pennsylvania Press, 2002.

Freeman, Eric, and David Gelernter. "Beyond Lifestreams: The Inevitable Demise of the Desktop Metaphor." In *Beyond the Desktop Metaphor*, edited by Victor Kaptelinin and Mary Czerwinski, 19–48. Cambridge, MA: MIT Press, 2007.

Fuller, Thomas. *The Holy State and the Profane State*. London: William Pickering, 1840.

Fulwood, William. *The Castel of Memorie*. Edited by Ian Delaney, Kate Danskin, and Erin Clinch. Amazon CreateSpace, 2018.

Gallagher, Victoria J. "Memory and Reconciliation in the Birmingham Civil Rights Institute." *Rhetoric & Public Affairs* 2, no. 2 (1999): 303–20.

Galloway, Alexander R. *The Interface Effect*. Malden: Polity, 2012.

Gardner, Martin. "The *Ars Magna* of Ramon Lull." In *Logic Machines and Diagrams*, edited by Martin Gardner, 1–27. Chicago: University of Chicago Press, 1982.

Geoffrey of Vinsauf. "The New Poetics." Translated by Jane Baltzell Kopp. In *Three Medieval Rhetorical Arts*, edited by James J. Murphy, 27–108. Berkeley: University of California Press, 1971.

Glenberg, Arthur M., Marion Meyer, and Karen Lindem. "Mental Models Contribute to Foregrounding during Text Comprehension." *Journal of Memory and Language* 26, no. 1 (1987): 69–83.

Gosnell, Scott. "Introduction." In *Thirty Seals & the Seal of Seals*. Translated by Scott Gosnell. Amazon CreateSpace, 2016.

Green, Lawrence D., and James J. Murphy. *Renaissance Rhetoric Short-Title Catalogue 1460–1700*. 2nd ed. Burlington, VT: Ashgate, 2006.

Gronbeck, Bruce E. "The Spoken and the Seen: The Phonocentric and Ocularcentric Dimensions of Rhetorical Discourse." In *Rhetorical Memory and Delivery*, edited by John Frederick Reynolds, 139–57. Mahwah, NJ: Lawrence Erlbaum Associates, 1993.

Guibert de Nogent. "A Book about the Way a Sermon Ought to Be Given." In *Readings in Medieval Rhetoric*, edited and translated by Joseph Miller, Michael H. Prosser, and Thomas W. Benson, 172–73. Bloomington: Indiana University Press, 1973.

Haas, Christina. *Writing Technology: Studies on the Materiality of Literacy*. Mahwah, NJ: Lawrence Erlbaum Associates, 1996.

Haines, John. "Introduction." In *The Notory Art of Shorthand (Ars notoria notarie): A Curious Chapter in the History of Writing in the West*, translated by John Haines, 1–86. Paris: Peeters, 2014.

Hajdu, Helga. *Das mnemotechnische Schrifttum des Mittelalters*. Amsterdam: E. J. Bonset, 1967.

Hanson, Marta E. "Hand Mnemonics in Classical Chinese Medicine: Texts, Earliest Images, and Arts of Memory." *Asia Major* 21, no. 1 (2008): 325–47.

Haraway, Donna. "Situated Knowledges: The Science Question in Feminism and the Privilege of Partial Perspective." *Feminist Studies* 14, no. 3 (1988): 575–99.

Harley, J. B. "Deconstructing the Map." *Cartographica* 26, no. 2 (Summer 1989): 1–20.

Harris, Thomas. *Hannibal.* New York: Delta Trade Paperbacks, 2005.

Honorius of Autun, "Concerning the Exile of the Soul and Its Fatherland." In *Readings in Medieval Rhetoric*, edited and translated by Joseph Miller, Michael H. Prosser, and Thomas W. Benson, 198–207. Bloomington: Indiana University Press, 1973.

Hugh of St. Victor. "A Little Book about Constructing Noah's Ark." In *The Medieval Craft of Memory*, translated by Jessica Weiss and edited by Mary Carruthers and Jan M. Ziolkowski, 41–71. Philadelphia: University of Pennsylvania Press, 2002.

———. "The Three Best Memory Aids for Learning History." In *The Medieval Craft of Memory*, edited and translated by Mary Carruthers and Jan M. Ziolkowski, 1–32. Philadelphia: University of Pennsylvania Press, 2002.

Hultzen, L. S. "Charles Butler on Memory." *Speech Monographs* 6 (1939): 44–65.

Humbert of Romans. "Treatise on Preaching, II.8–9." In *Readings in Medieval Rhetoric*, edited and translated by Joseph Miller, Michael H. Prosser, and Thomas W. Benson, 245–50. Bloomington: Indiana University Press, 1973.

Hutchins, Edwin. *Cognition in the Wild.* Cambridge, MA: MIT Press, 1996.

Jameson, Fredric. "Cognitive Mapping." In *Marxism and the Interpretation of Culture*, edited

by Cary Nelson and Lawrence Grossberg, 347–57. London: Macmillan Education, 1988.

———. *Postmodernism, or, The Cultural Logic of Late Capitalism.* Durham, NC: Duke University Press, 1991.

Jardine, Lisa. "Humanistic Logic." In *The Cambridge History of Renaissance Philosophy*, edited by Charles B. Schmitt and Quentin Skinner, 173–99. Cambridge: Cambridge University Press, 1988.

John of Salisbury. *The Metalogicon of John of Salisbury.* Translated by Daniel D. McGarry. Berkeley: University of California Press, 1955.

Johnson, Nan. *Nineteenth-Century Rhetoric in North America.* Carbondale: Southern Illinois University Press, 1991.

Kircher, Athanasius. *Ars magna Sciendi, sive Combinatoria.* Weijerstraet, 1669.

Kittler, Friedrich. "There Is No Software," *C-Theory: Theory, Technology, Culture* 32 (1995). http://www.ctheory.com/article/a032.html.

Knauff, Markus. *Space to Reason: A Spatial Theory of Human Thought.* Cambridge, MA: MIT Press, 2013.

Kneale, William Calvert, and Martha Kneale. *The Development of Logic.* Oxford: Clarendon Press, 1962.

Kuwakino, Koji. "From *domus sapientiae* to *artes excerpendi*: Lambert Schenkel's *De memoria* (1593) and the Transformation of the Art of Memory." In *Forgetting Machines: Knowledge Management Evolution in Early Modern Europe*, edited by Alberto Cevolini, 58–78. Leiden: Brill, 2016.

Latour, Bruno. *Reassembling the Social: An Introduction to Actor-Network Theory.* Oxford: Oxford University Press, 2005.

———. "Tarde's Idea of Quantification." In *The Social After Gabriel Tarde: Debates and Assessments*, edited by Mattei Candea, 145–62. London: Routledge, 2010.

———. "Visualization and Cognition: Drawing Things Together." *Knowledge and Society Studies in the Sociology of Culture, Past and Present* 6 (1986): 1–40.

———. "What Is Iconoclash? or Is There a World beyond the Image Wars?" In *Iconoclash: Beyond the Image-Wars in Science, Religion and Art*, edited by Peter Weibel and Bruno Latour), 14–37. Cambridge, MA: ZKM and MIT Press, 2002.

Lauer, Janice M. *Invention in Rhetoric and Composition*. West Lafayette: Parlor Press, 2004.

Lauer, Claire. "What's in a Name?" *Kairos* 17, no. 1 (Fall 2012). http://kairos.technorhetoric.net/17.1/inventio/lauer/inventio.html.

Lawrence-Mathers, Anne, and Carolina Escobar-Vargas. *Magic and Medieval Society*. New York: Routledge, 2014.

Leibniz, Gottfried Wilhelm.. *Leibniz: Philosophical Papers and Letters*. Edited and translated by Leroy Loemaker. Dordrecht: D. Reidel Publishing, 1969.

———. "On the Art of Combination." In *Leibniz: Logical Papers*, edited and translated by G. H. R. Parkinson. Oxford: Oxford University Press, 1966.

Lerner, Fred. *Story of Libraries: From the Invention of Writing to the Computer Age*. New York: Continuum, 2001.

Leroux, Neil. *Luther's Rhetoric: Strategies and Style from the Invocavit Sermons*. St. Louis, MO: Concordia Academic Press, 2002.

Lewis, C. S. *A Grief Observed*. New York: Harper Collins, 1991.

Lewis, Rhodri. "A Kind of Sagacity: Francis Bacon, the Ars Memoriae and the Pursuit of Natural Knowledge." *Intellectual History Review* 19, no. 2 (2009): 155–75.

Llull, Ramon. "Ars brevis." In *Doctor Illuminatus: A Ramon Llull Reader*, edited and translated by Anthony Bonner, 292–361. Princeton, NJ: Princeton University Press, 1993.

Locke, John. *An Essay Concerning Human Understanding*. Edited by Peter H. Nidditch. Oxford: Clarendon Press, 1975.

Loisette, Alphonse. *Assimilative Memory, Or, How to Attend and Never Forget*. New York: Funk & Wagnalls Company, 1896.

Mack, Peter. *A History of Renaissance Rhetoric, 1380–1620*. Oxford: Oxford University Press, 2011.

Marchegay, Paul. "Duel judiciaire entre des communautes religieuses, 1098." *Bibliotheque de l'Ecole des Chartes* 1 (1839–1840): 552–64.

Marino, Mark C. "Critical Code Studies." *Electronic Book Review*, December 4, 2006. http://electronicbookreview.com/essay/critical-code-studies/.

Marshall, Catherine C. "How People Manage Information Over a Lifetime. " In *Personal Information Management*, edited by William Jones and Jaime Teevan, 57–75. Seattle: University of Washington Press, 2007.

Martianus Capella. *Martianus Capella and the Seven Liberal Arts*. Vol. 2, *The Marriage of Philology and Mercury*. Translated by William Harris Stahl and Richard Johnson. New York: Columbia University Press, 1977.

Maurus, Rabanus. "On the Training of the Clergy." In *Readings in Medieval Rhetoric*, edited and translated by Joseph Miller, Michael H. Prosser, and Thomas W. Benson, 125–28. Bloomington: Indiana University Press, 1973.

McAlister, Matt. "Algorithms Are More like Puppies than Monsters, They Want to Please You." *The Guardian*, June 6, 2016. https://www.theguardian.com/media-network/2016/jun/06/algorithms-more-puppies-than-monsters-please-you-natural-language-processing.

McCutchen, Deborah. "From Novice to Expert: Implications of Language Skills and Writing Relevant Knowledge for Memory during the Development of Writing Skill." *Journal of Writing Research* 3, no. 11 (2011): 51–68.

McNair, John R. "Computer Icons and the Art of Memory." *Technical Communication Quarterly* 5, no. 1 (1996): 77–86.

McNulty, Robert. "Bruno at Oxford." *Renaissance News* 13 (1960): 300–305.

Mebane, John S. *Renaissance Magic and the Return of the Golden Age*. Lincoln: University of Nebraska Press, 1992.

Middleton, A. E. *Memory Systems New and Old*. New York: G. S. Fellows and Co., 1888.

Middleton, Joyce Irene. "Oral Memory and the Teaching of Literacy: Some Implications from Toni Morrison's *Song of Solomon*." In *Rhetorical Memory and Delivery*, edited by John Frederick Reynolds, 113–25. Mahwah, NJ: Lawrence Erlbaum Associates, 1993.

Moran, Bruce T. *Distilling Knowledge: Alchemy, Chemistry, and the Scientific Revolution*. Cambridge, MA: Harvard University Press, 2005.

Moretti, Franco. "Operationalizing, or, the Function of Measurement in Modern Literary Theory." *Literary Lab* 6 (December 2013): 2–13.

Murphy, James J. *Rhetoric in the Middle Ages*. Berkeley: University of California Press, 1974.

Nagel, Thomas. "What Is It Like to Be a Bat?" *Philosophical Review* 83, no. 4 (1974): 435–50.

Nester, Marks R. "An Applied Statistician's Creed." *Journal of the Royal Statistical Society. Series C (Applied Statistics)* 45, no. 4 (1996): 401–10.

Ong, Walter. *Ramus, Method, and the Decay of Dialogue*. New York: Octagon Books, 1974.

———. *Rhetoric, Romance, and Technology: Studies in the Interaction of Expression and Culture*. Ithaca, NY: Cornell University Press, 1971.

Otake, Tomoko. "How Can Anyone Remember 100,000 Numbers?" *Japan Times*, December 17, 2006. https://www.japantimes.co.jp/life/2006/12/17/to-be-sorted/how-can-anyone-remember-100000-numbers/.

Pfeiffer, Rudolf. *Callimachus*. Vol. 1, *Fragmenta*. Oxford: Clarendon Press, 1949.

Plato. "Greater Hippias." Translated by Paul Woodruff. In *Plato: Complete Works*, edited by John M. Cooper, 898–922. Indianapolis: Hackett Publishing Company, 1997.

———. "Lesser Hippias." Translated by Nicholas D. Smith. In *Plato: Complete Works*, edited by John M. Cooper, 922–37. Indianapolis: Hackett Publishing Company, 1997.

———. "Meno." Translated by G. M. A. Grube. In *Plato: Complete Words*, edited by John M. Cooper, 870–98. Indianapolis: Hackett Publishing Company, 1997.

———. "Phaedrus." Translated by Alexander Nehemas and Paul Woodruff. In *Plato: Complete Works*, edited by John M. Cooper, 506–77. Indianapolis: Hackett Publishing Company, 1997.

———. "Theaetetus." Translated by M. J. Levett. In *Plato: Complete Works*, edited by John M. Cooper, 157–235. Indianapolis: Hackett Publishing Company, 1997.

Plett, Heinrich F. *English Renaissance Rhetoric and Poetics: A Systematic Bibliography of Primary and Secondary Sources*. Leiden: Brill, 1995.

Pring-Mill, F. D. "Ramon Lull." In *Dictionary of Scientific Bibliography*, vol. 8, edited by Charles Gillespie, 547–51. New York: Charles Scribner, 1973.

Prior, Paul, Janine Solberg, Patrick Berry, Hannah Bellwoar, Bill Chewning, Karen J. Lunsford, Liz Rohan, Kevin Roozen, Mary P. Sheridan-Rabideau, Jody Shipka, Derek Van Ittersum, and Joyce R. Walker. "Re-situating and Re-mediating the Canons: A Cultural-Historical Remapping of Rhetorical Activity." *Kairos* 11, no. 3 (Summer 2007). http://kairos.technorhetoric.net/11.3/topoi/prior-et-al/core/core.pdf.

Pruchnic, Jeff, and Kim Lacey. "The Future of Forgetting: Rhetoric, Memory, Affect." *Rhetoric Society Quarterly* 41, no. 5 (2011): 472–94.

Qu, C., Y. J. Luo, and L. Mo. "Dynamic Mental Representations in Language Comprehension." *Perceptual and Motor Skills* 108, no. 3 (2009): 933–48.

Quintilian. *Institutio oratoria (The Orator's Education, Books 11–12)*. Translated by Donald A. Russell. Cambridge, MA: Harvard University Press, 2001.

Ramsay, Stephen. *Reading Machines: Toward an Algorithmic Criticism*. Urbana: University of Illinois Press, 2011.

Ramus, Petrus. *Arguments in Rhetoric against Quintilian*. Translated by Carole Newlands. Carbondale, IL: Southern Illinois University Press, 2010.

Ravasio, Pamela, and Vincent Tscherter. "Users' Theories of the Desktop Metaphor, or Why We Should Seek Metaphor-Free Interfaces." In *Beyond the Desktop Metaphor*, edited by Victor Kaptelinin and Mary Czerwinski, 265–95. Cambridge, MA: MIT Press, 2007.

Ravennas, Petrus. *The Art of Memory, That Otherwyse Is Called the Phenix*. Translated by Robert Copland. London: Edwards Brothers, 1548.

Reisberg, Daniel. "Mental Images." In *The Oxford Handbook of Cognitive Psychology*, edited by Daniel Reisberg, 374–90. Oxford: Oxford University Press, 2013.

Reynolds, John Frederick. "Memory Issues in Composition Studies." In *Rhetorical Memory and Delivery*, edited by John Frederick Reynolds, 1–17. Mahwah, NJ: Lawrence Erlbaum Associates, 1993.

Rhetorica ad Herennium. Translated by Harry Caplan. Cambridge, MA: Harvard University Press, 1954.

Rice, Jeff. *Digital Detroit: Rhetoric and Space in the Age of the Network*. Carbondale: Southern Illinois University Press, 2012.

Rossi, Paolo. *Logic and the Art of Memory*. Chicago: University of Chicago Press, 2000.

Ryan, Kathleen J. "Memory, Literacy, and Invention: Reimagining the Canon of Memory for the Writing Classroom." *Composition Studies* 32, no. 1 (2004): 35–47.

Rzepka, Adam. "'Direct Ideas': The Quotidian Imagination in John Willis's 1618 Memory Theater." In *Knowing Nature in Early Modern Europe*, edited by David Beck, 165–80. New York: Routledge, 2016.

Sarma, Sreeramula Rajeswara. "Katapayadi Notation on a Sanskrit Astrolabe." *Indian Journal of History Science* 34, no. 4 (1999): 273–87.

Schuchard, Marsha Keith. *Restoring the Temple of Vision: Cabalistic Freemasonry and Stuart Culture*. Leiden: Brill, 2002.

Schutt, Rachel, and Cathy O'Neil. *Doing Data Science*. Sebastopol, CA: O'Reilly Media, 2014.

Scott, Ridley, dir. *Blade Runner: The Final Cut*. Los Angeles: Warner Bros., 2007.

Sloane, Thomas O. *Donne, Milton, and the End of Humanistic Rhetoric*. Berkeley: University of California Press, 1985.

Sorabji, Richard. "Introduction to the Second Edition." In *Aristotle on Memory*, translated by Richard Sorabji. London: Bristol Classical Press, 2012.

Stafford, Barbara Maria. *Visual Analogy: Consciousness as the Art of Connecting*. Cambridge, MA: MIT Press, 1999.

Strickland, Lloyd, ed. *Leibniz and the Two Sophies: The Philosophical Correspondence*. Toronto: Centre for Reformation and Renaissance Studies, 2011.

Sweet, R. F. G. "A Pair of Double Acrostics in Akkadian." *Orientalia* 38 (1969): 459–60.

Sweet, Sam. "A Vanished New Orleans Captured on 'Straight from the Projects.'" *New Yorker*, September 13, 2015. https://www.newyorker.com/culture/culture-desk/a-vanished-new-orleans-captured-on-straight-from-the-projects.

Tan, Desney, Emma Berry, Mary Czerwinski, Gordon Bell, Jim Gemmell, Steve Hodges, Narinder Kapur, Brian Meyers, Nuria Oliver, George Robertson, and Ken Wood. "Save Everything: Supporting Human Memory with a Personal Digital Lifetime Store." In *Personal Information Management*, edited by William Jones and Jaime Tevan, 90–108. Seattle: University of Washington Press, 2007.

Thomas of Citeaux. "Commentary on the Song of Songs." In *Readings in Medieval Rhetoric*, edited and translated by Joseph Miller, Michael H. Prosser, and Thomas W. Benson, 240–44. Bloomington: Indiana University Press, 1973.

Tufte, Edward. *Envisioning Information*. Cheshire, CT: Graphics Press, 1998.

———. *The Visual Display of Quantitative Information*. 2nd ed. Cheshire, CT: Graphics Press, 2001.

Valéry, Paul. *Collected Works of Paul Valéry*. Vol. 14, *Analects*. Translated by Stuart Gilbert. Princeton, NJ: Princeton University Press, 1970.

Van Ittersum, Derek. "Data-Palace: Modern Memory Work in Digital Environments." *Kairos* 11, no. 3 (Summer 2007). http://kairos.technorhetoric.net/11.3/topoi/prior-et-al/about/abstract_vanittersum.html.

Victor, Julius. "On Memory." In *The Medieval Craft of Memory*, edited and translated by Mary Carruthers and Jan M. Ziolkowski, 297–98. Philadelphia: University of Pennsylvania Press, 2002.

Vivian, Bradford. "On the Language of Forgetting." *Quarterly Journal of Speech* 95, no. 1 (2009): 89–104.

Vivian, Bradford, and Ann Teresa Demo. "Introduction." In *Rhetoric, Remembrance, and Visual Form*, edited by Bradford Vivian and Ann Teresa Demo, 1–14. New York: Routledge, 2012.

Von Feinaigle, Gregor. *The New Art of Memory*. London: Sherwood, Neely, and Jones, 1813.

Watson, Rowan. *Illuminated Manuscripts and their Makers*. London: V&A Publications, 2003.

Welch, Kathleen E. "The Platonic Paradox: Plato's Rhetoric in Contemporary Rhetoric and Composition Studies." *Written Communication* 5 (1988): 3–21.

Weiner, Anthony D. "Expelling the Beast: Bruno's Adventures in England." *Modern Philology* 78 (1980): 1–13.

Weingart, Scott. "From Trees to Webs: Uprooting Knowledge through Visualization." Scottbot.net, August, 9, 2013. http://www.scottbot.net/HIAL/index.html@p=38807.html.

———. "Topic Modeling and Network Analysis." Scottbot.net, November 15, 2011. http://www.scottbot.net/HIAL/index.html@p=221.html.

West, William N. "Memory." In *Encyclopedia of Rhetoric*, edited by Thomas O. Sloane, 482–92. Oxford: Oxford University Press, 2001.

Westerhoff, Jan C. "A World of Signs: Baroque Pansemioticism, the Polyhistory and the Early Modern Wunderkammer." *Journal of the History of Ideas* 62, no. 4 (2001): 633–50.

Whalen, Logan E. "Visualizing Morality in the Manuscripts of Marie de France's Isopet." In *The Social Life of Illumination: Manuscripts, Images, and Communities in the Late Middle Ages*, edited by Joyce Coleman, Mark Cruse, and Kathryn A. Smith, 297–311. Turnhout, Belgium: Brepols, 2013.

Whitley, Kathleen P. *The Gilded Page: The History and Technique of Manuscript Gilding*. New Castle, DE: Oak Knoll Press, 2000.

Whittemore, Stewart. *Rhetorical Memory: A Study of Technical Communication*. Chicago: University of Chicago Press, 2015.

Wilson, Thomas. *The Arte of Rhetorique*. Hiidenkirja: CreateSpace Independent Publishing, 2012.

Wise, James, James J. Thomas, Kelly Pennock, David Lantrip, Marc Pottie, Anne Schur, and Vern Crow. "Visualizing the Non-Visual: Spatial Analysis and Inter-action with Information from Text Documents." In *Proceedings of the Conference on Information Visualization (IEEE)* (1995): 51–58.

Wright, Elizabethada. "Rhetorical Spaces in Memorial Places: The Cemetery as a Rhetorical Memory Place/Space." *Rhetoric Society Quarterly* 35, no. 4 (2005): 51–81.

Yates, Frances. *The Art of Memory*. London: Bodley Head/Penguin Random House, 2014.

———. "The Art of Ramon Lull: An Approach to It through Lull's Theory of the Elements." *Journal of the Warburg and Courtauld Institutes* 17, no. 1/2 (1954): 115–73.

———. *Giordano Bruno and the Hermetic Tradition*. Chicago: University of Chicago Press, 1964.

Young, Richard, and Patricia Sullivan. "Why Write? A Reconsideration." In *Essays on Classical Rhetoric and Modern Discourse*, edited by Robert J. Connors, Lisa S. Ede, and Andrea Lunsford, 215–25. Carbondale: Southern Illinois University Press, 1984.

Index

Lightning Source UK Ltd.
Milton Keynes UK
UKHW020703280121
377787UK00003B/193